Bil Zelman

AND HERE WE ARE

Stories from the Sixth Extinction

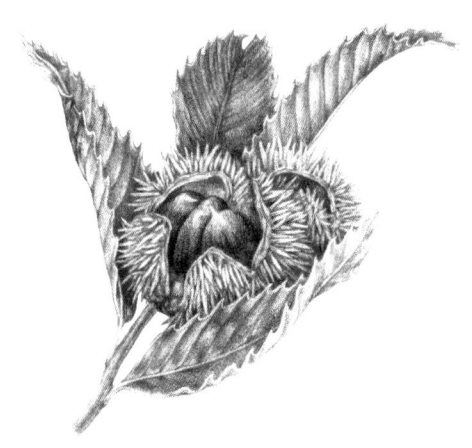

Daylight

Cofounders: Taj Forer and Michael Itkoff
Art Director: Ursula Damm
Copy Editor: Barbara Richard

© 2019 Daylight Community Arts Foundation

Photographs © 2018, 2019 by Bil Zelman

Illustrations © Zoe Keller
Text © 2019 by Bil Zelman

ISBN 978-1-942084-75-4

Printed by Artron, China

Daylight Books
E-mail: info@daylightbooks.org
Web: www.daylightbooks.org

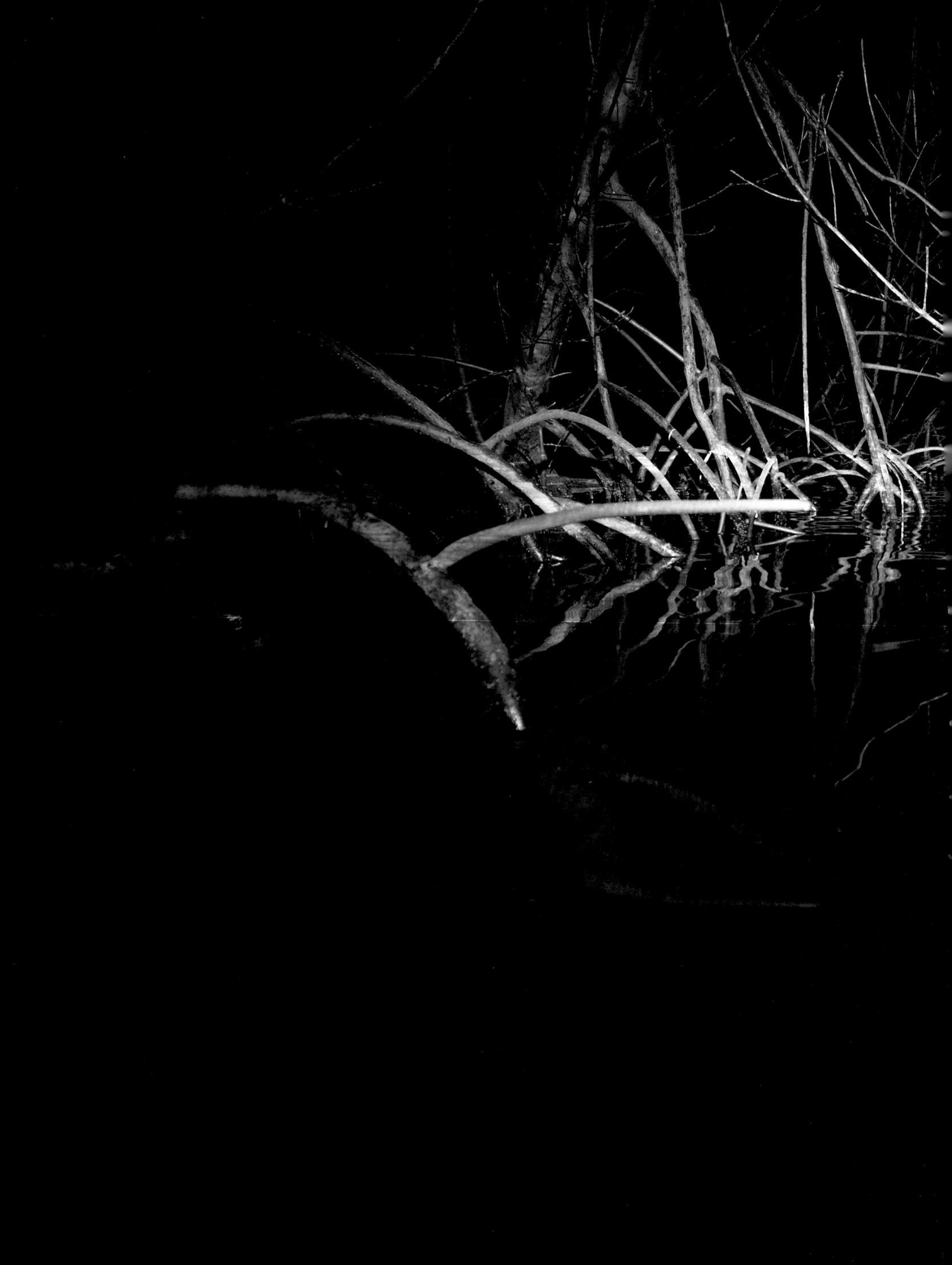

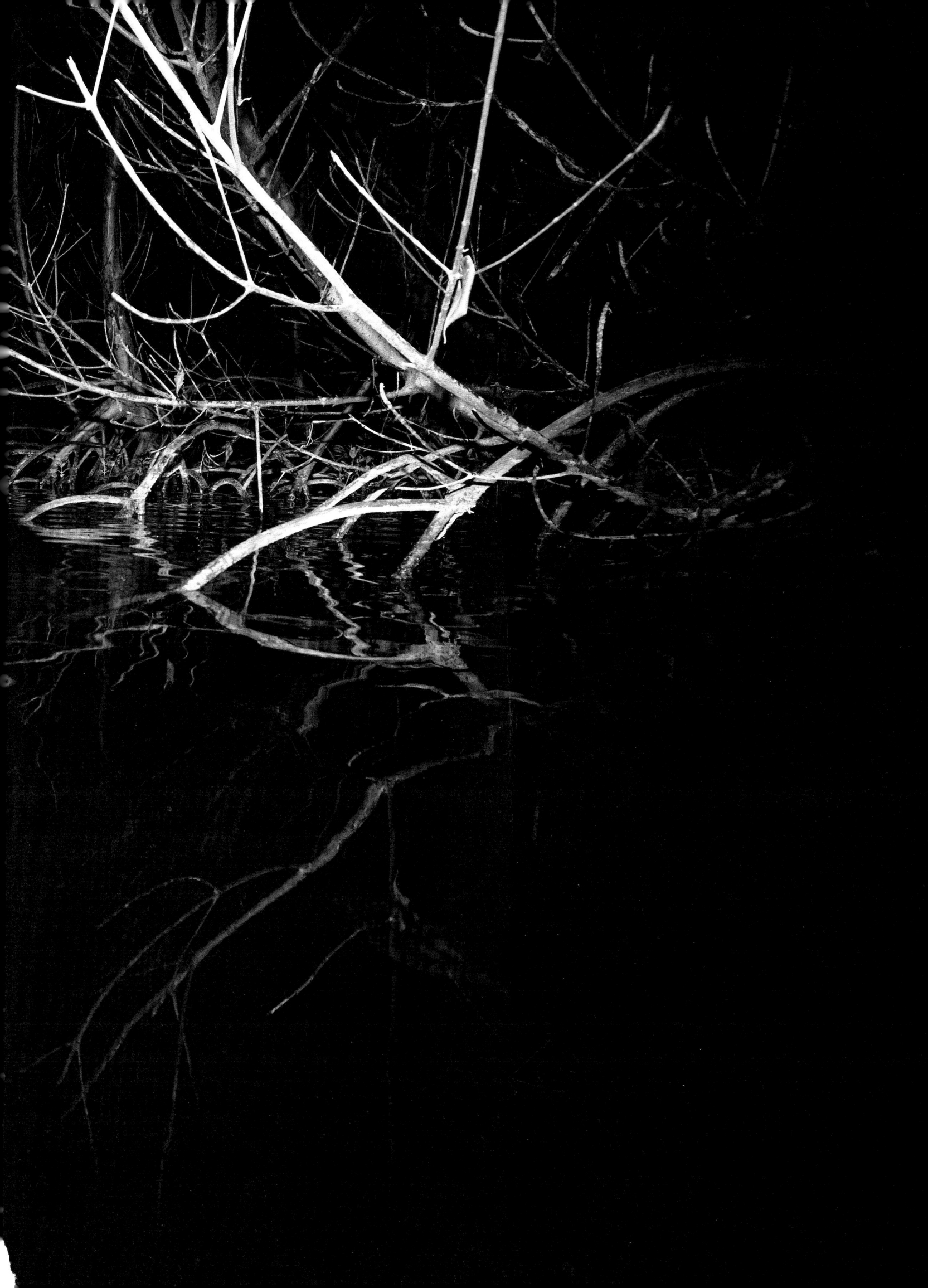

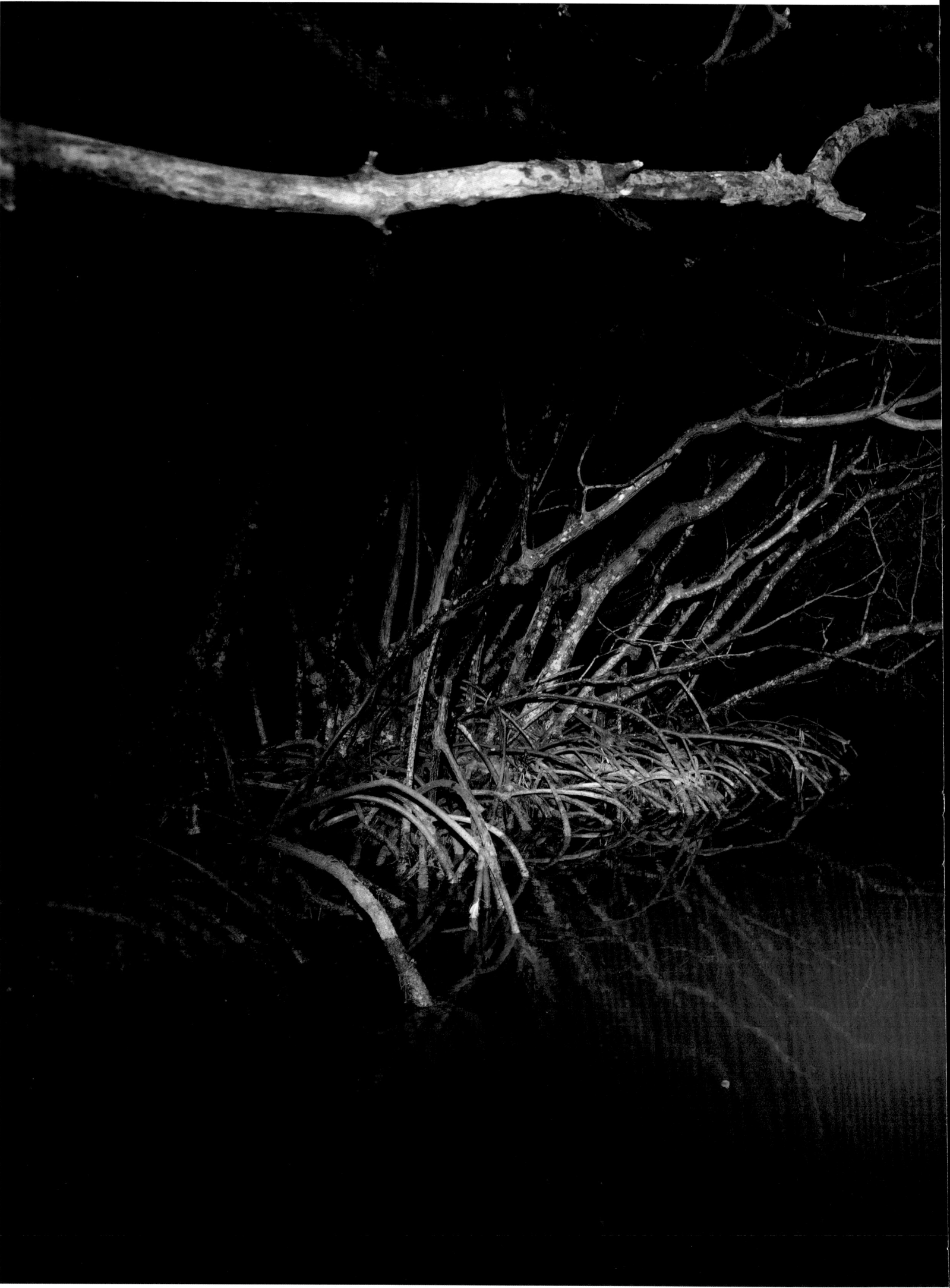

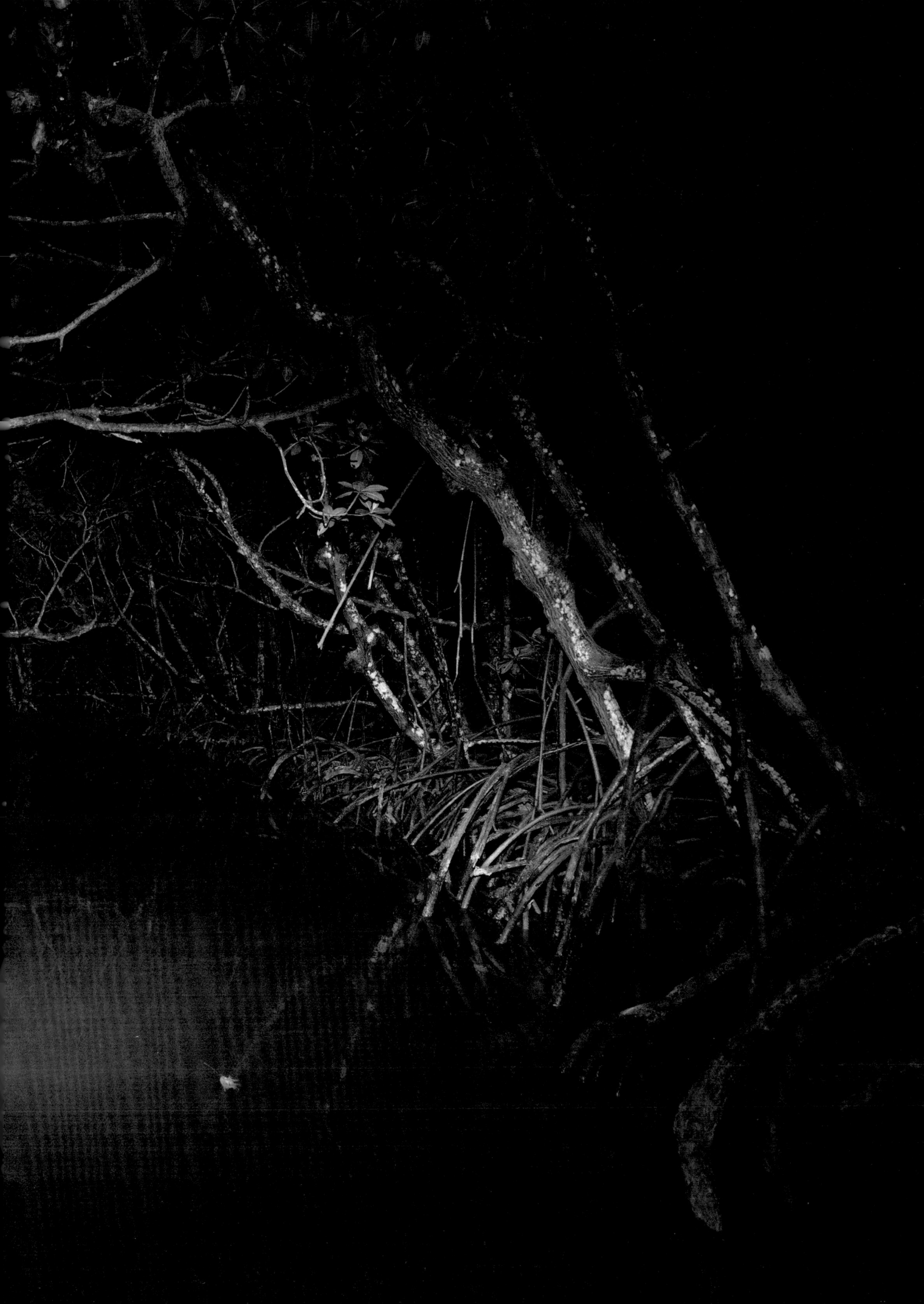

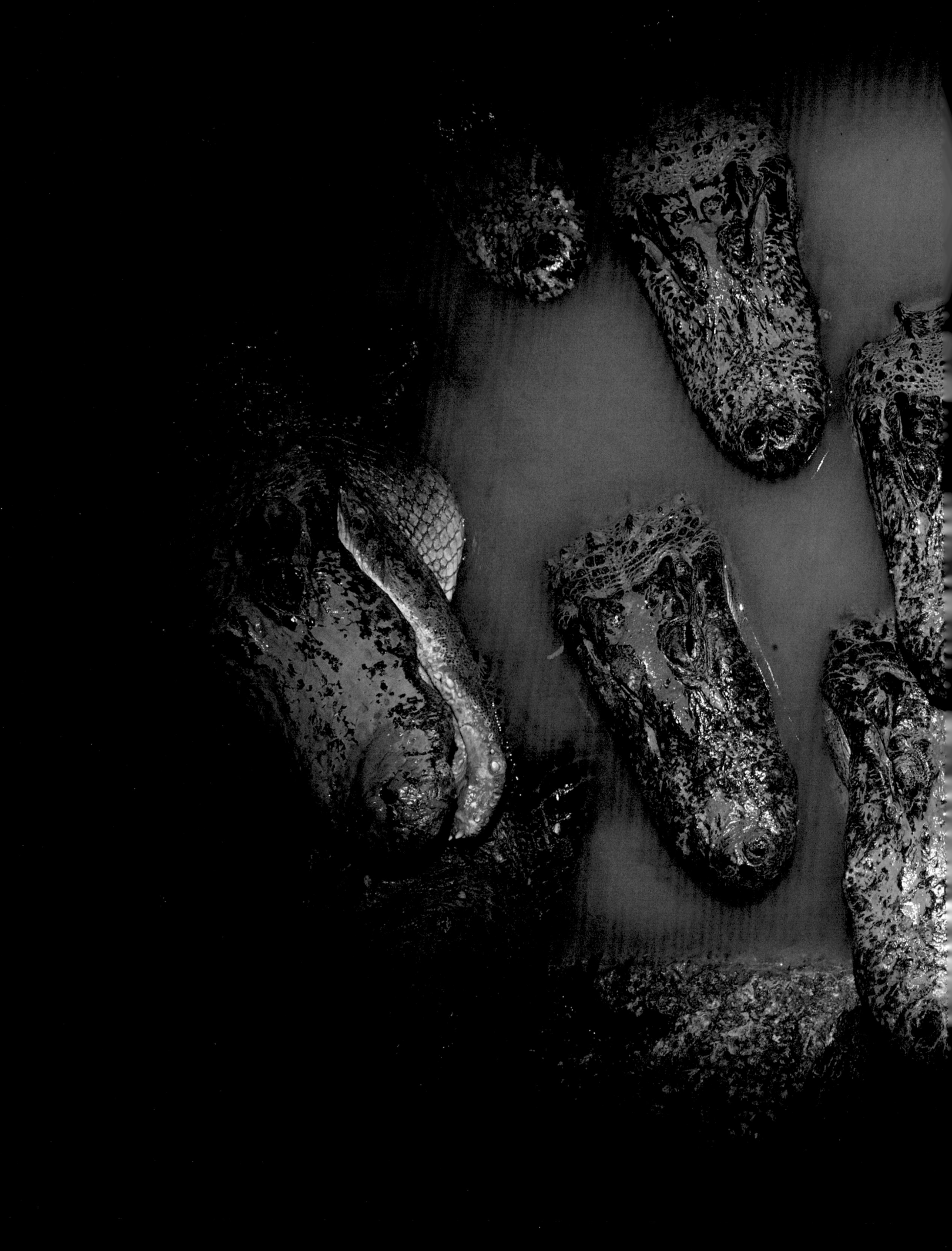

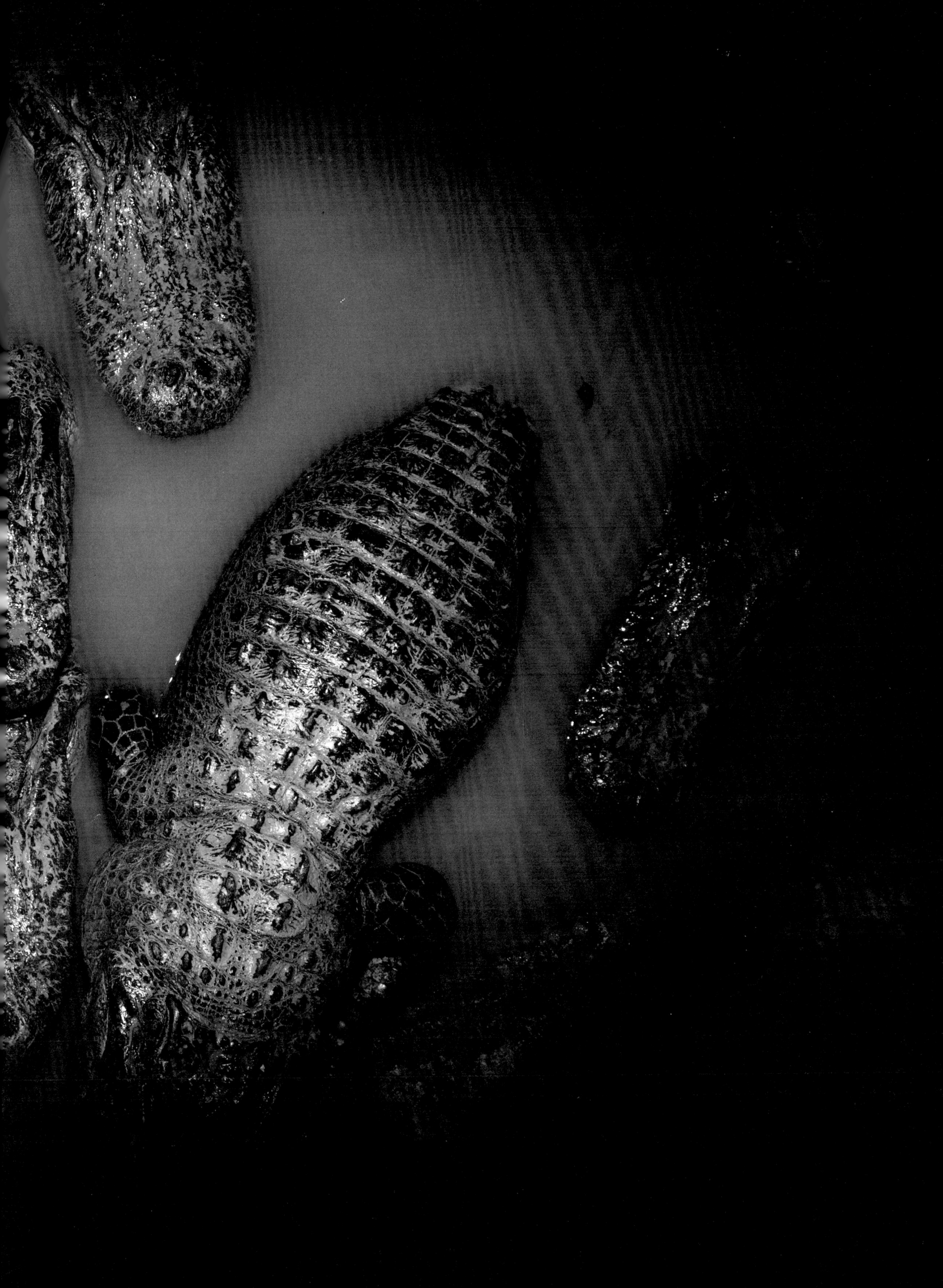

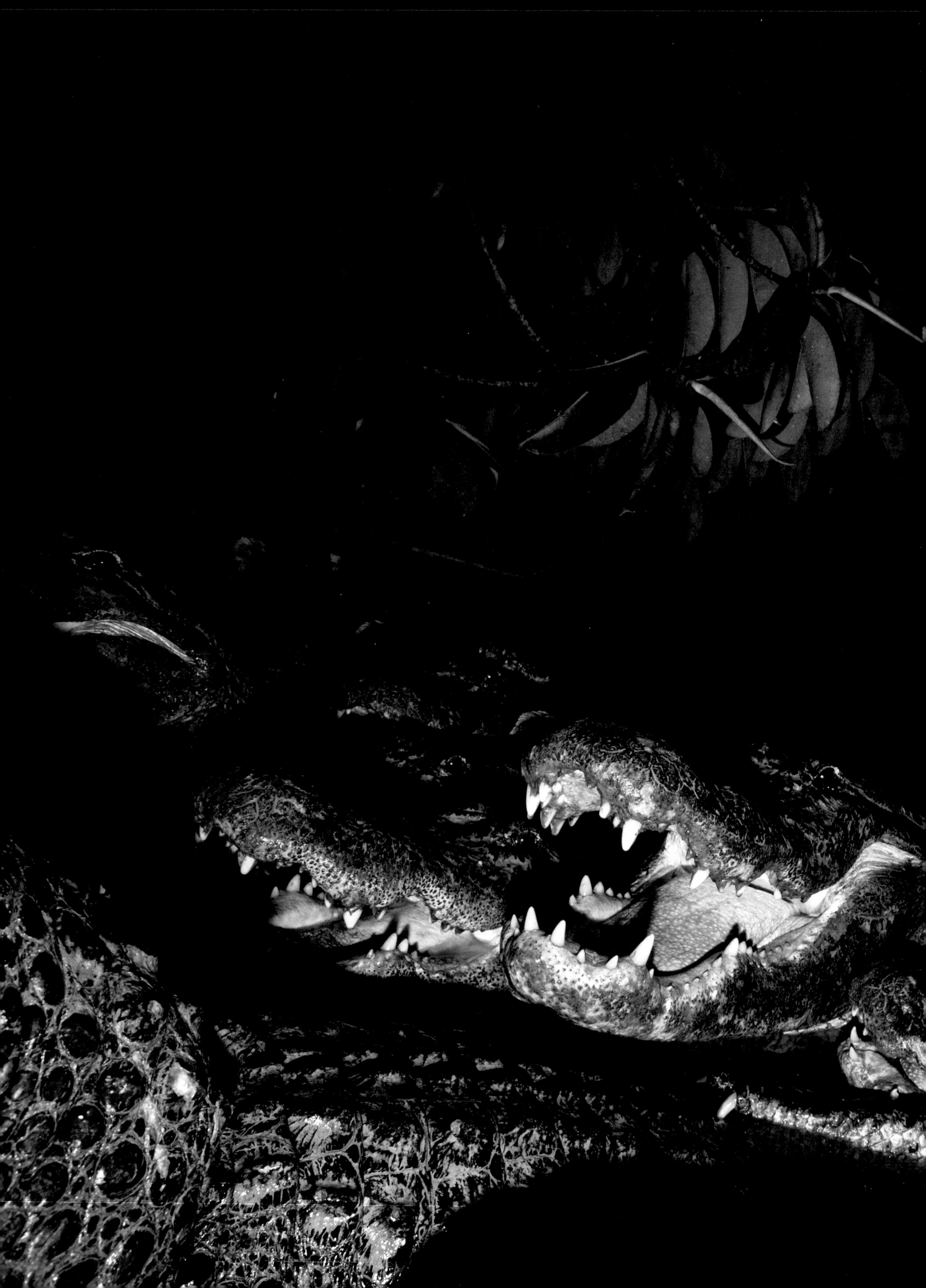

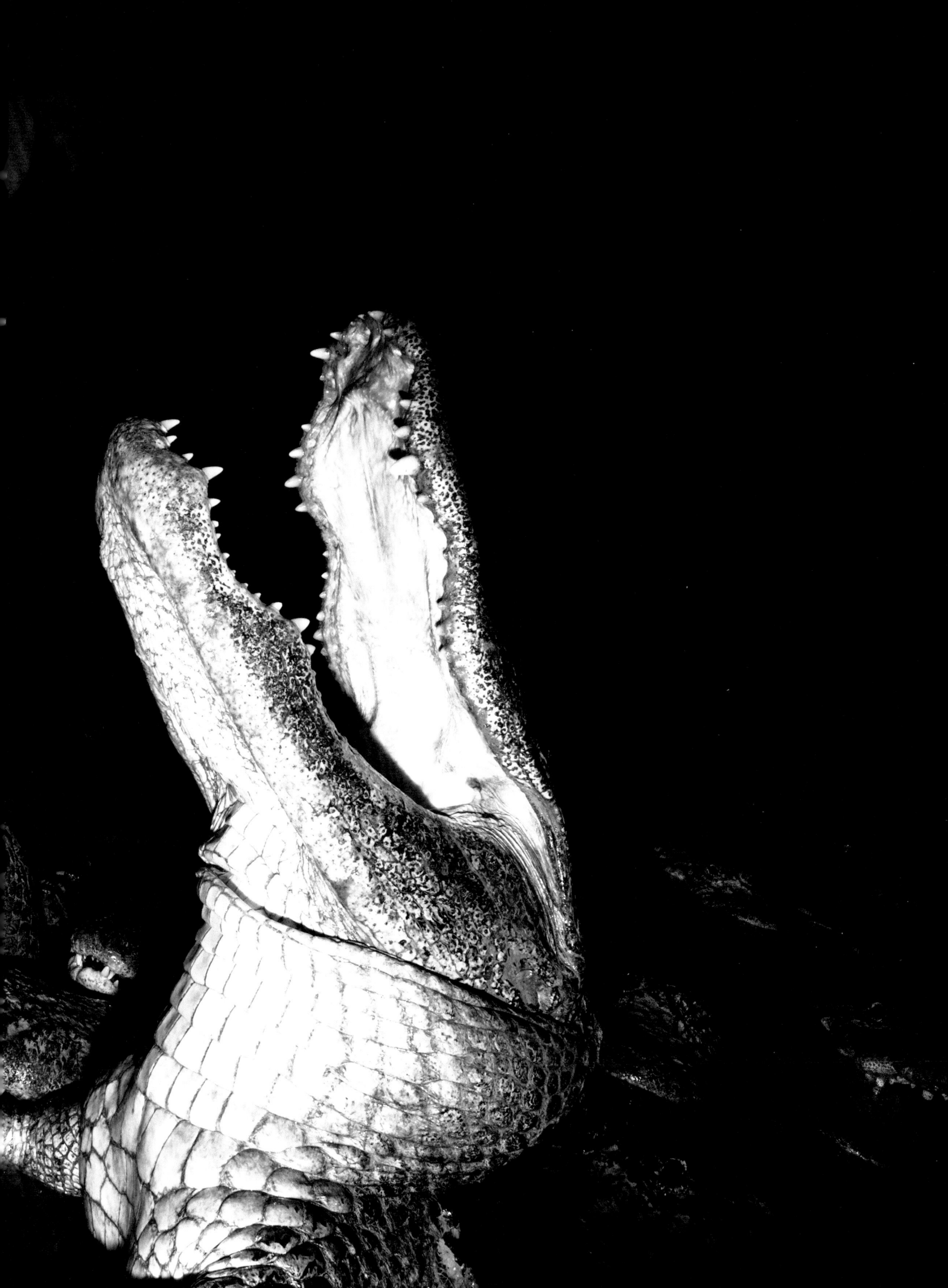

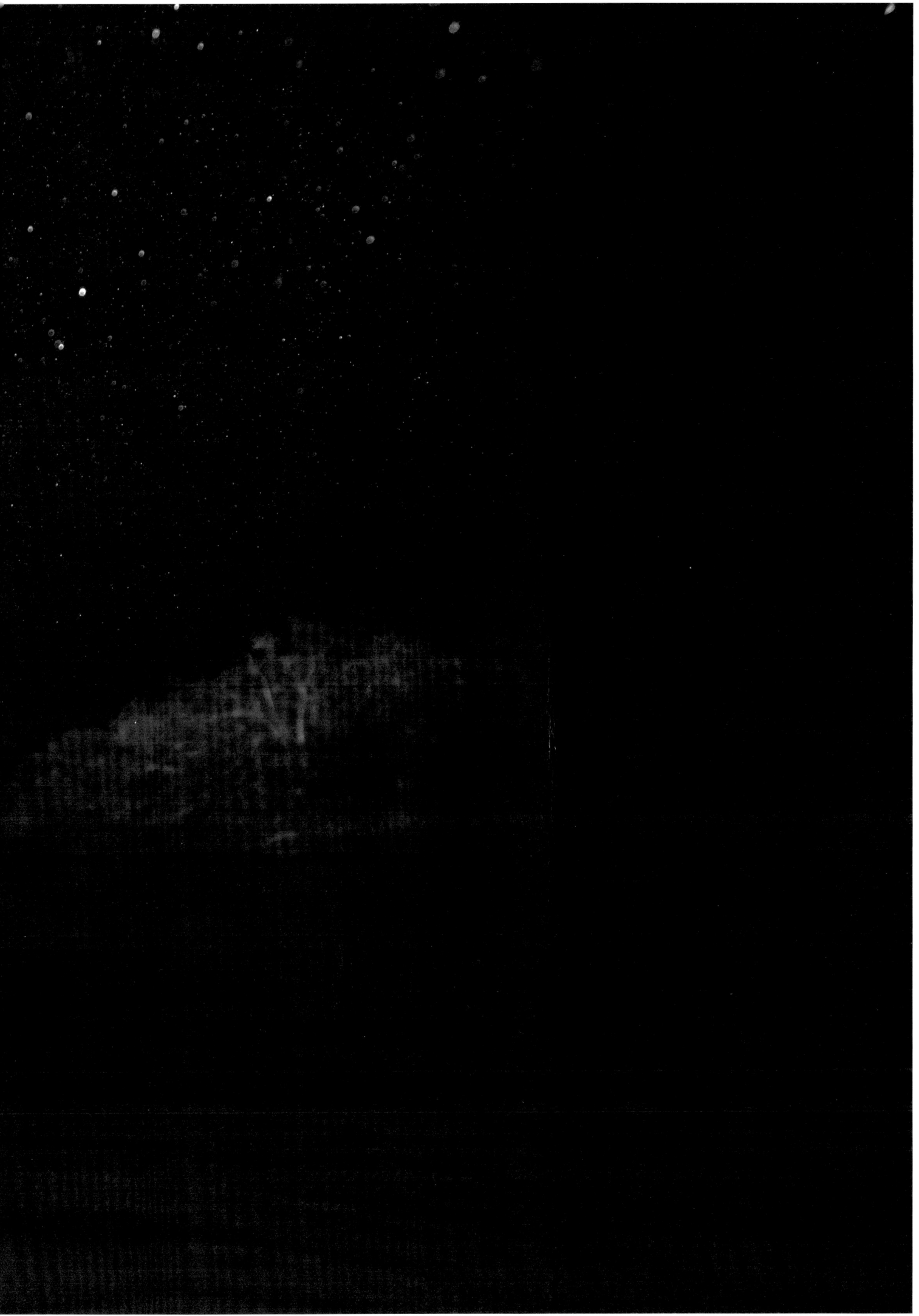

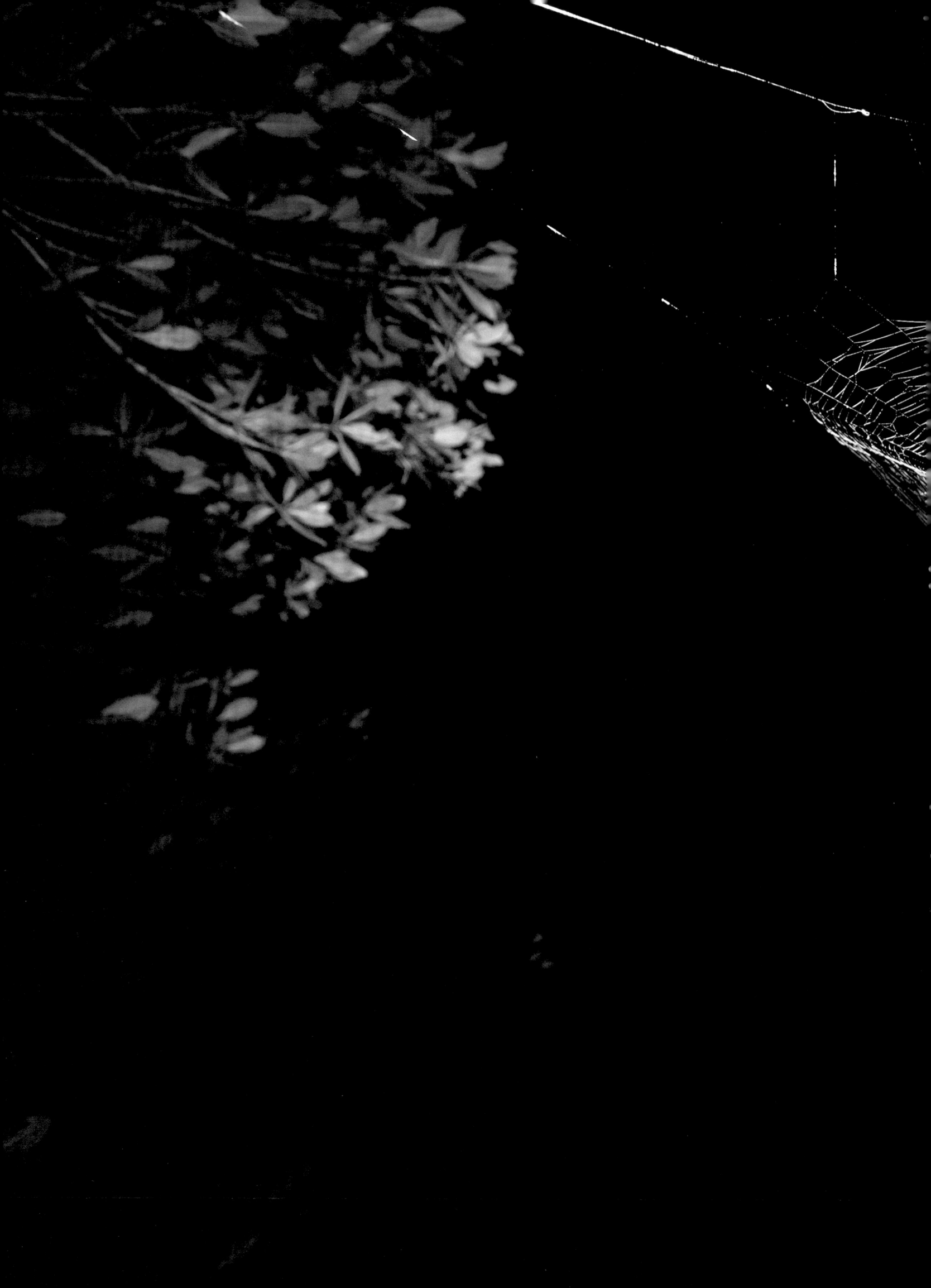

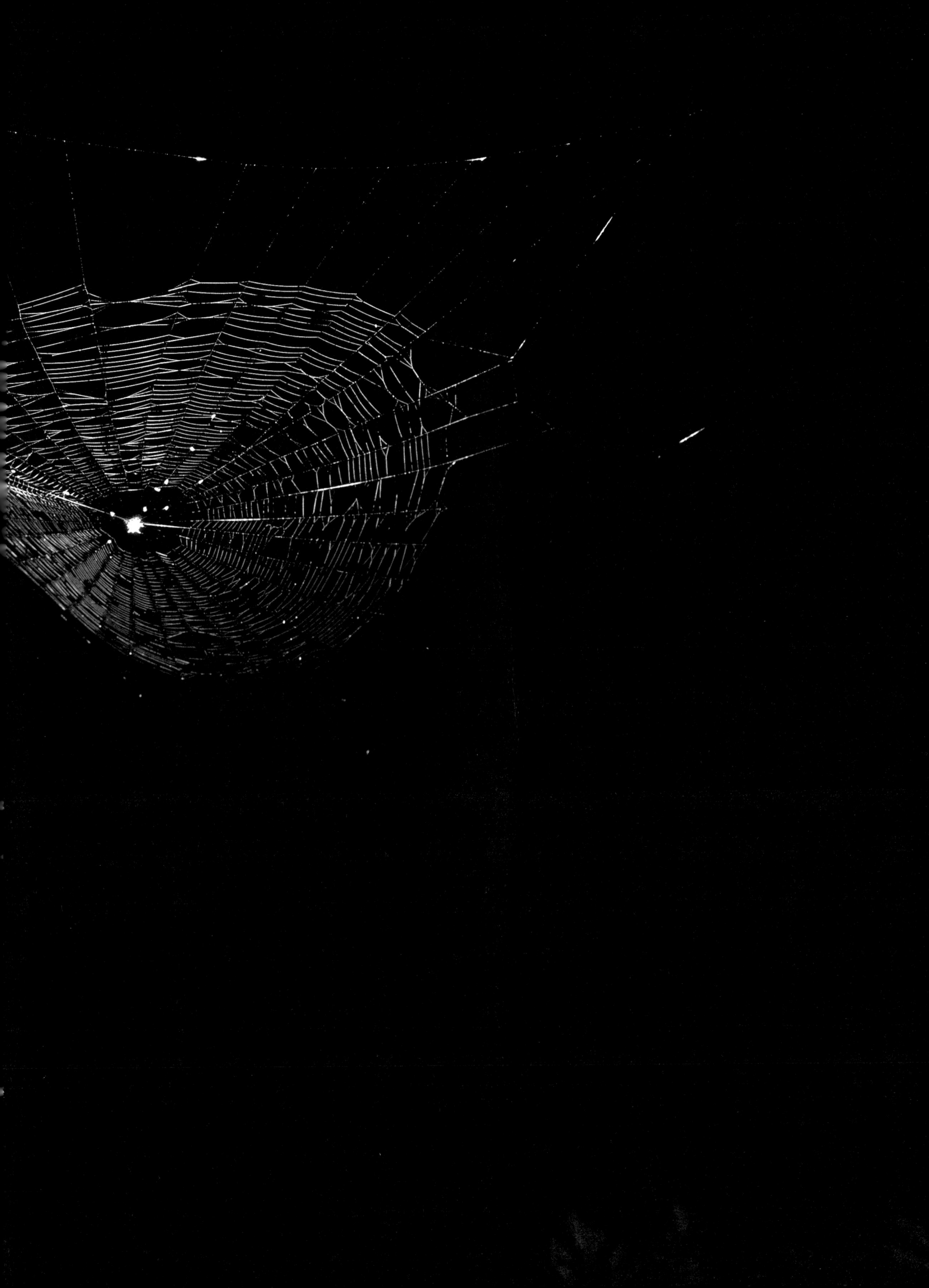

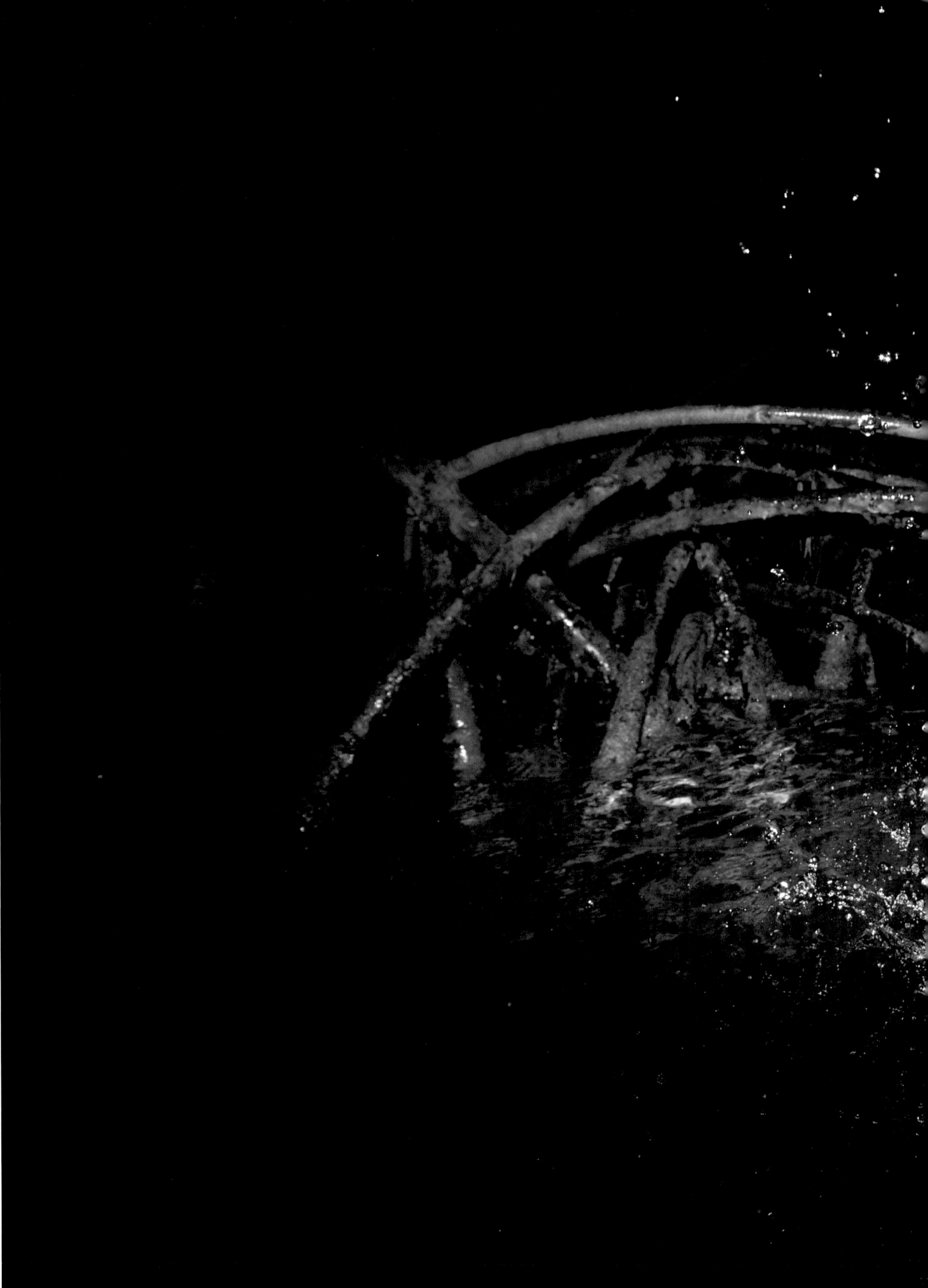

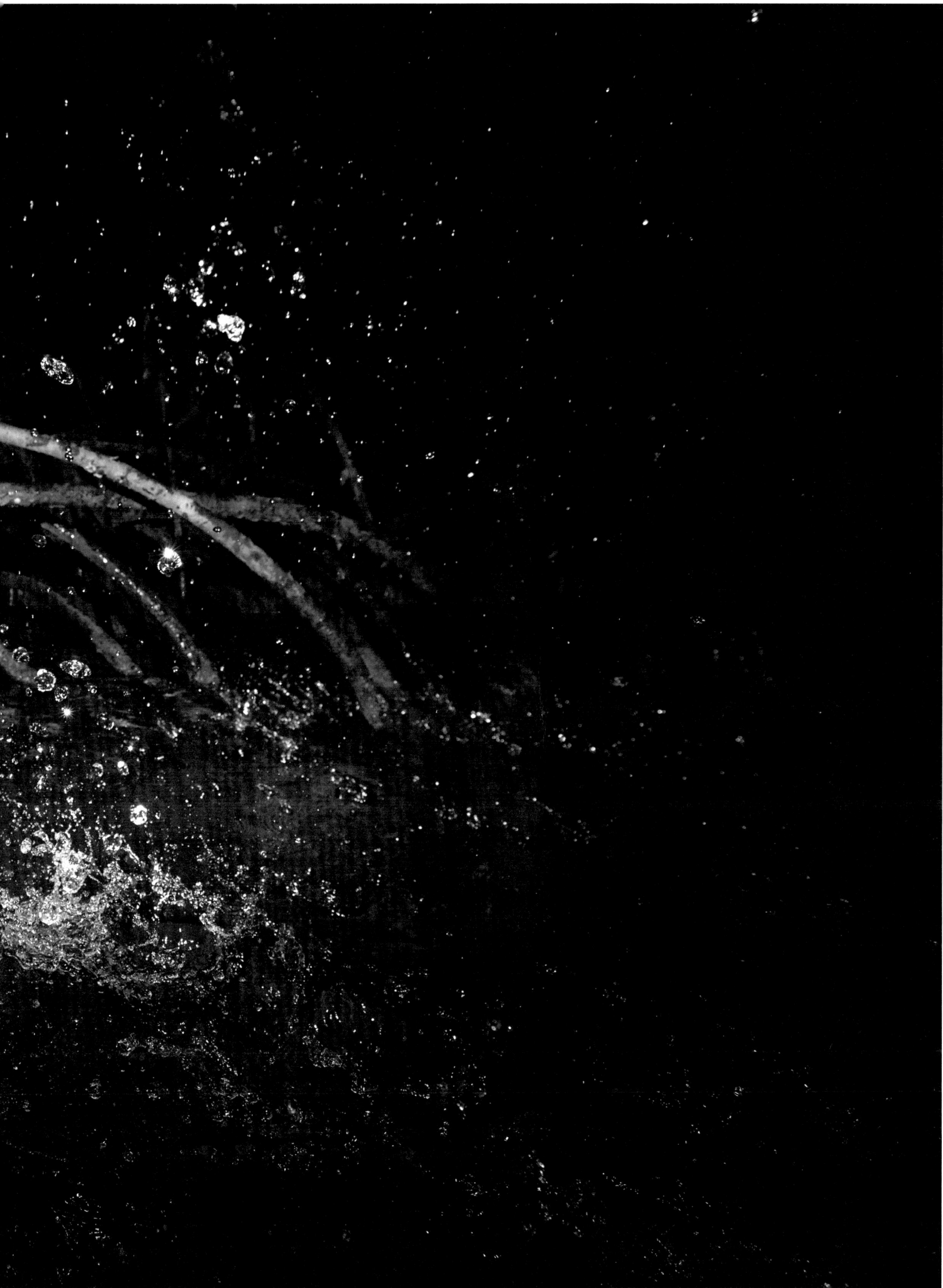

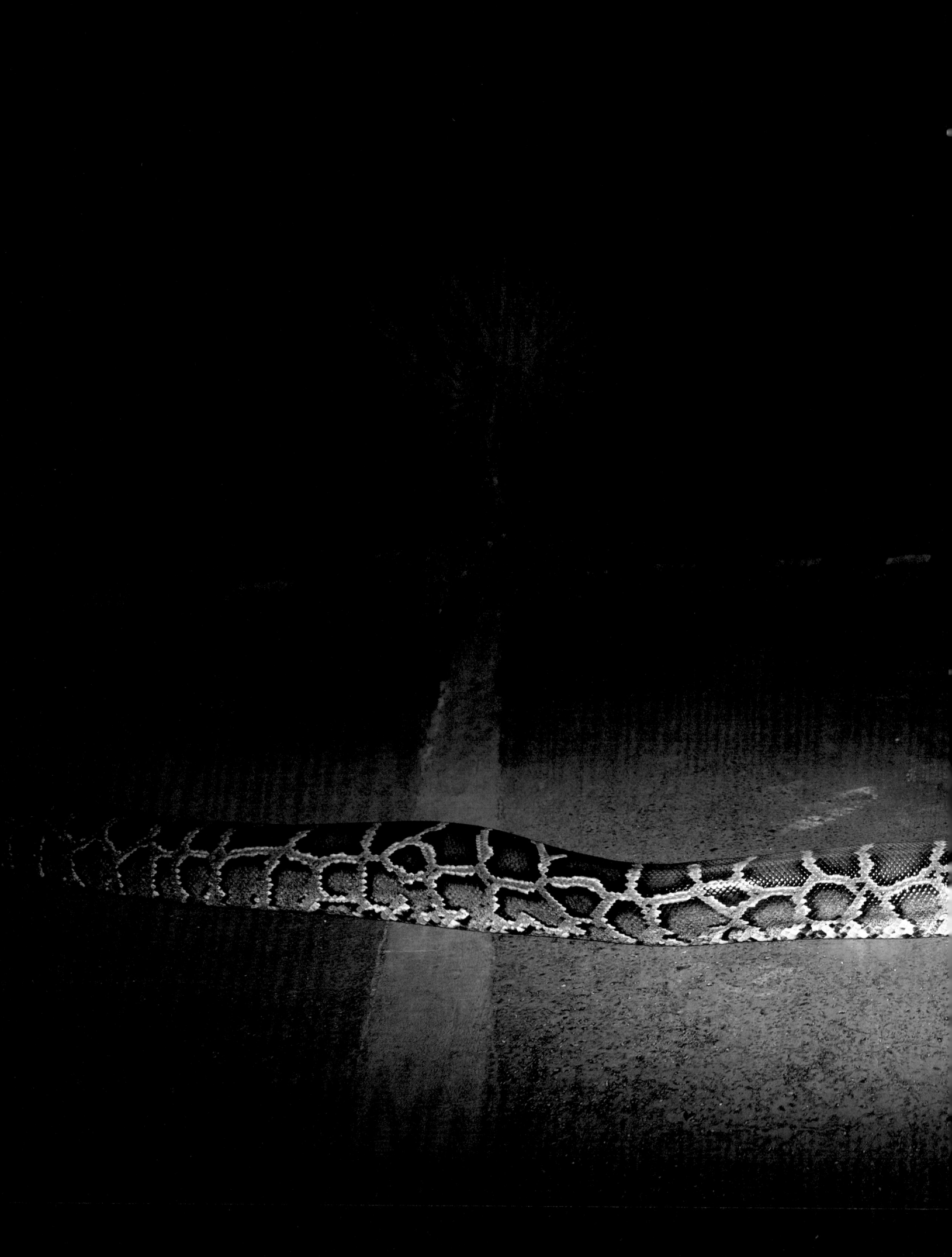

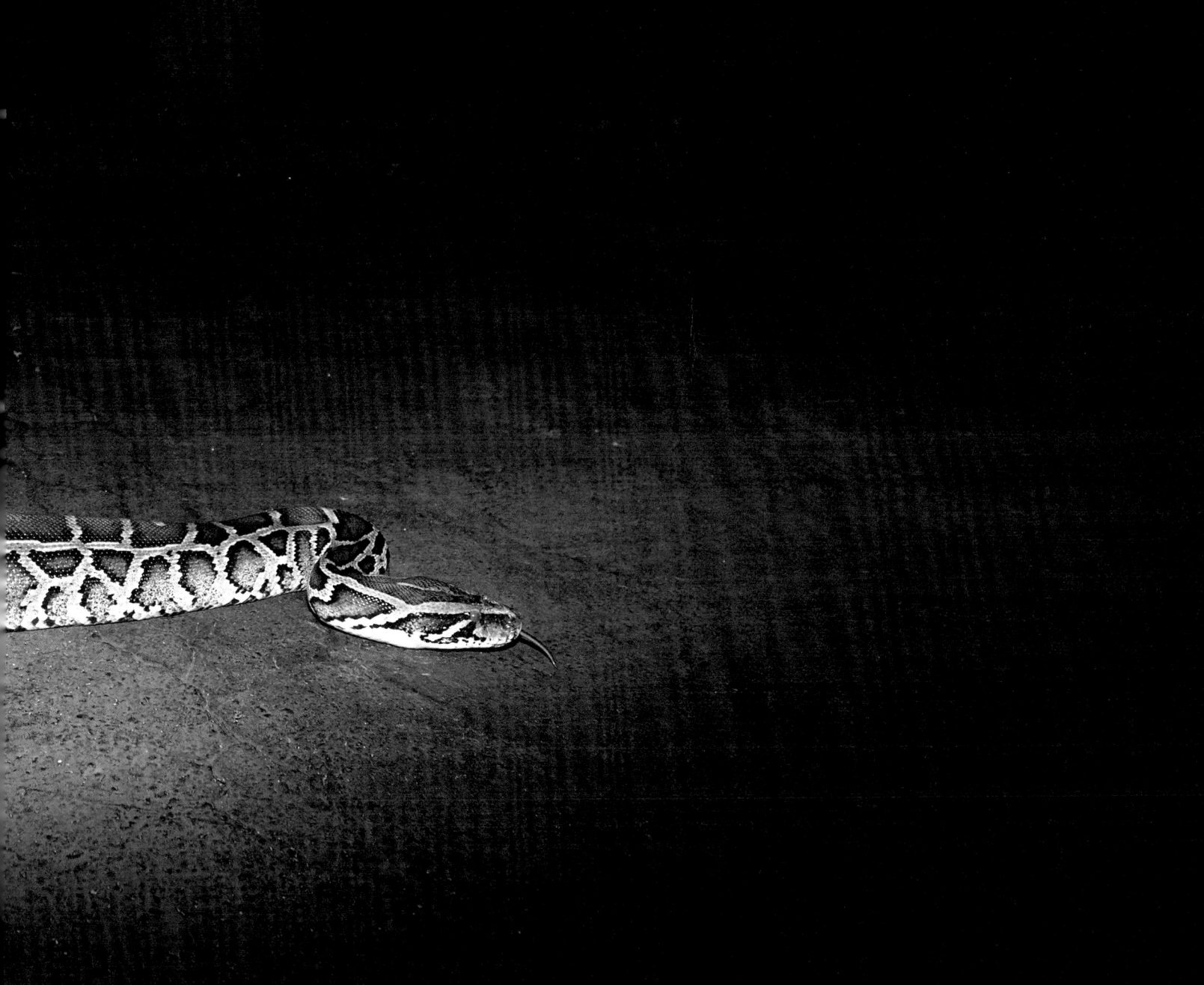

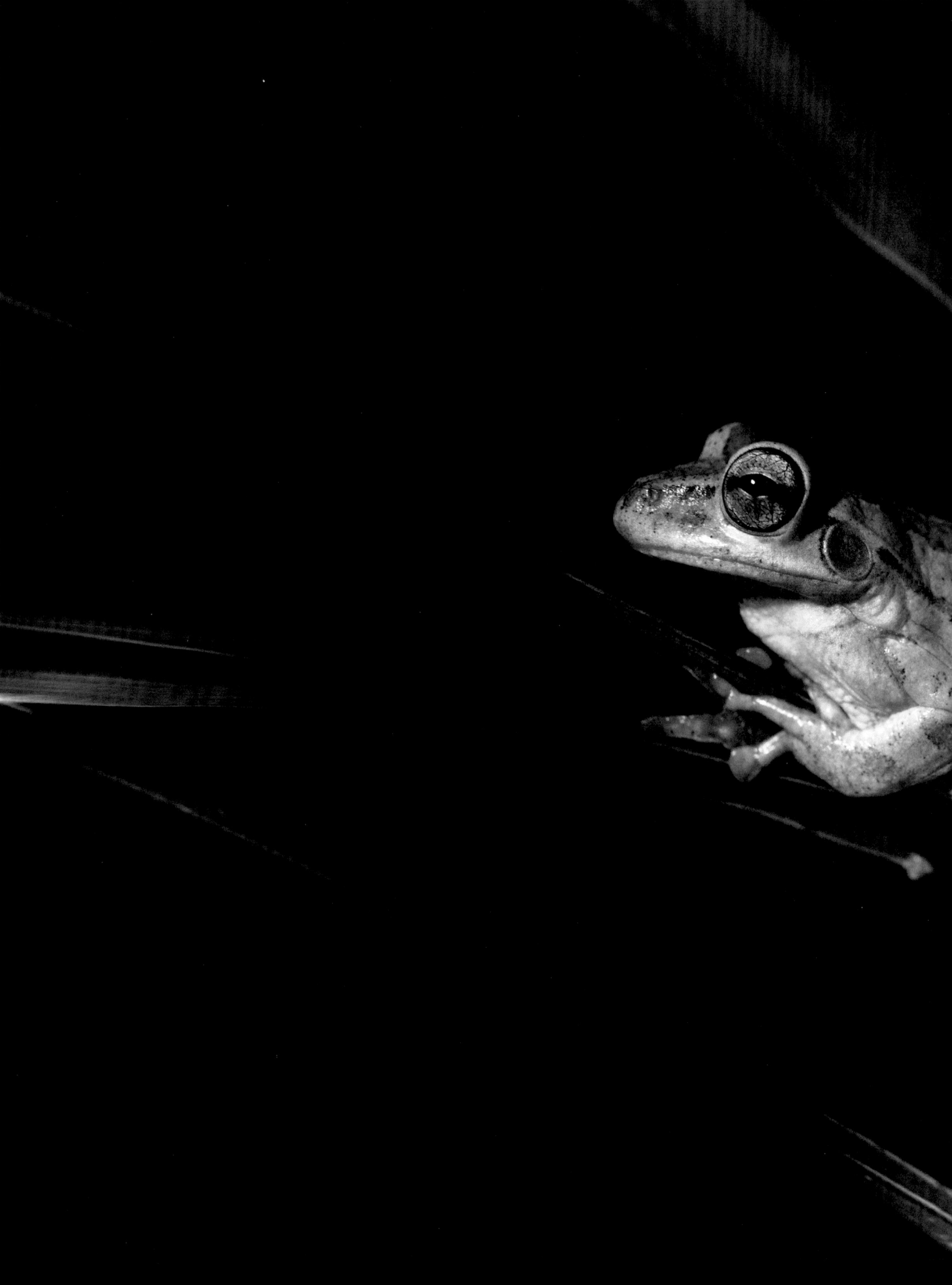

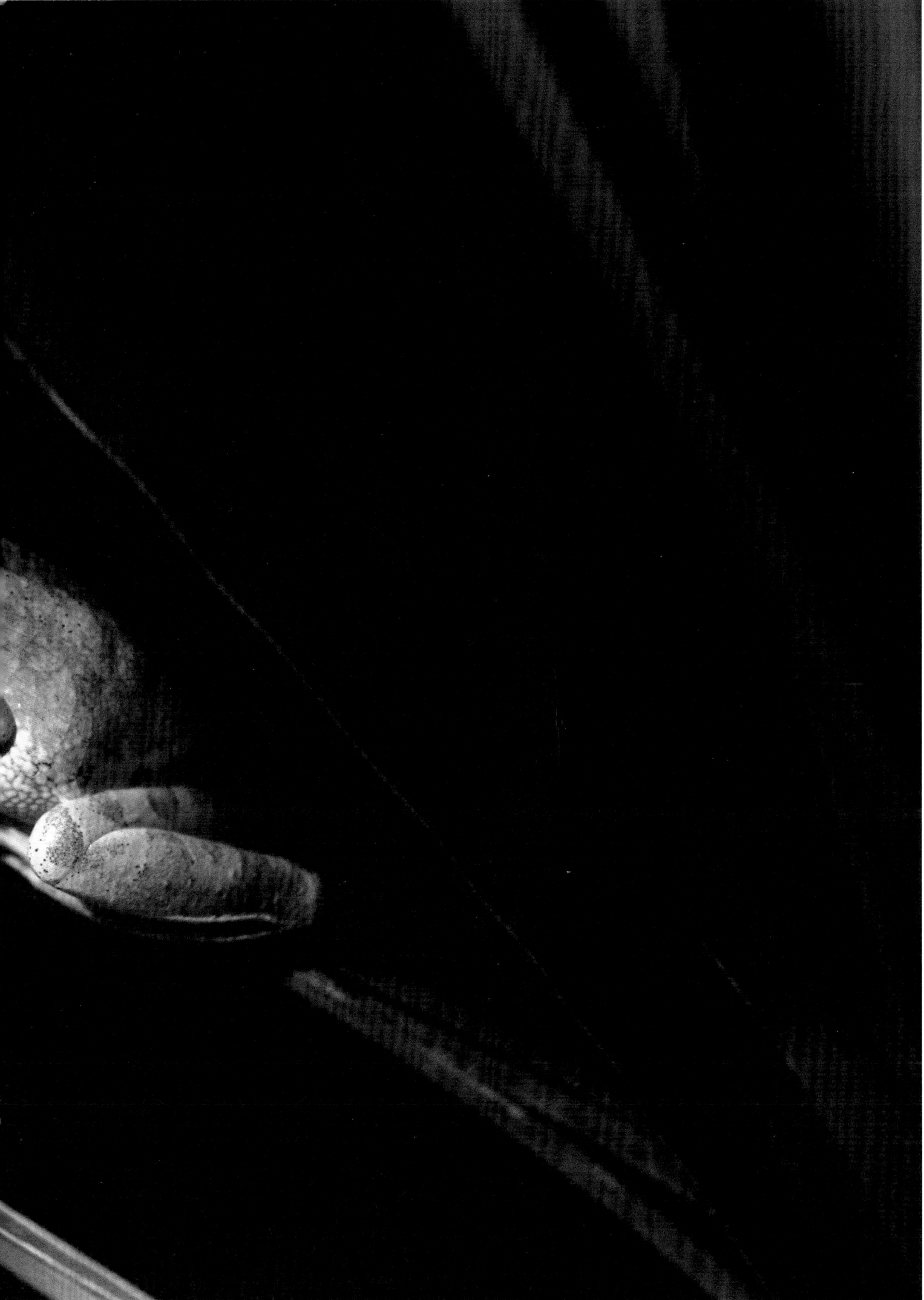

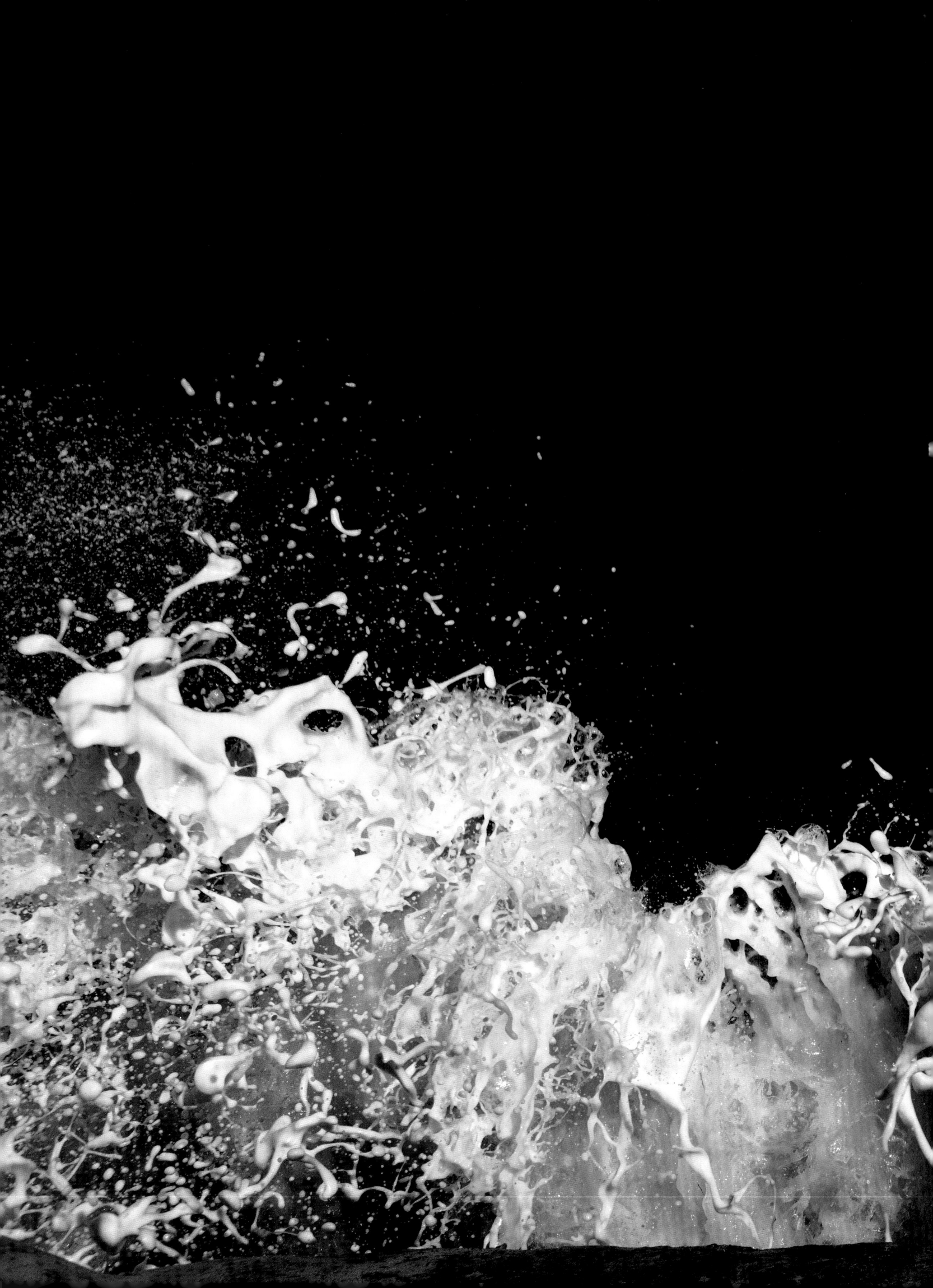

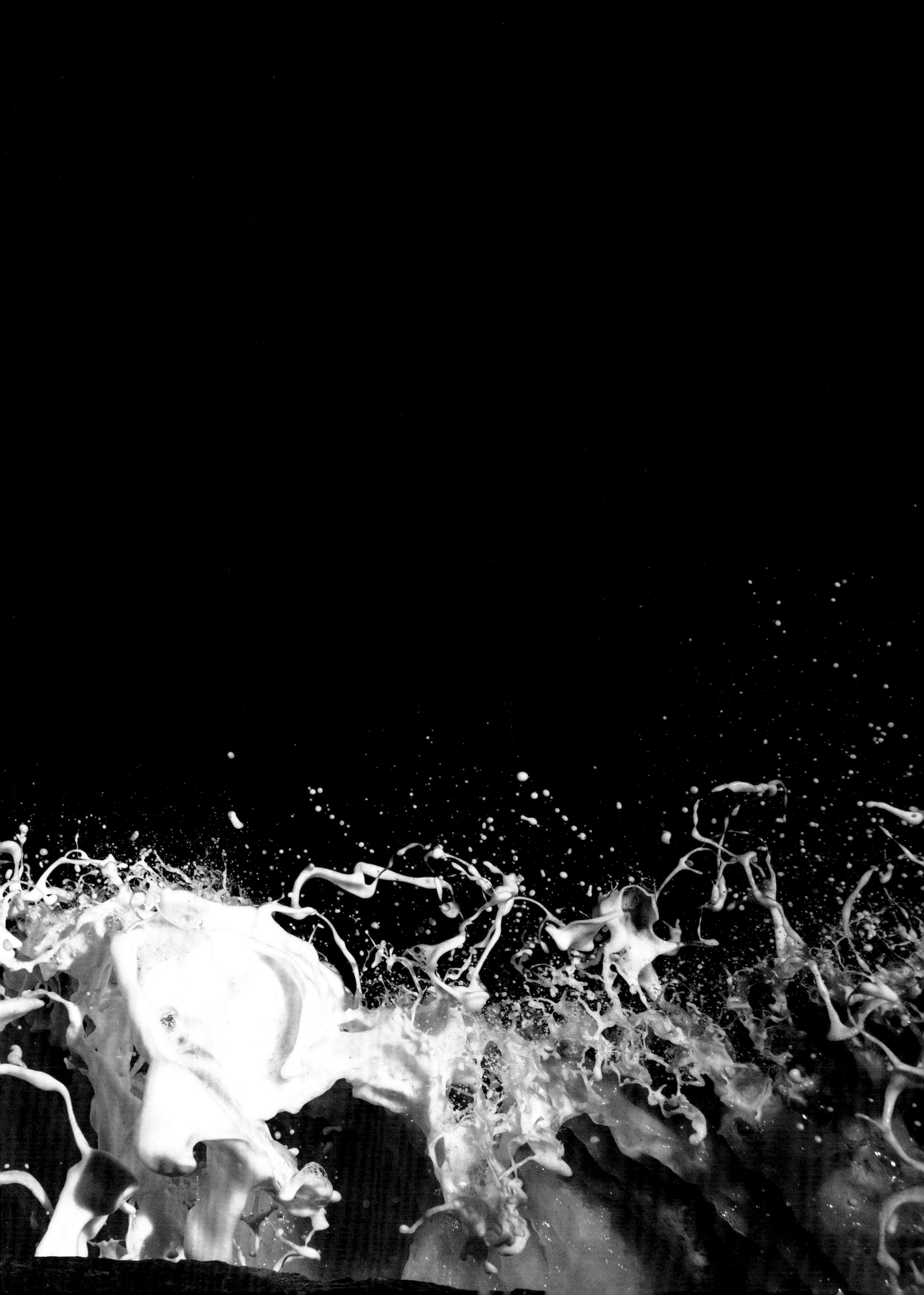

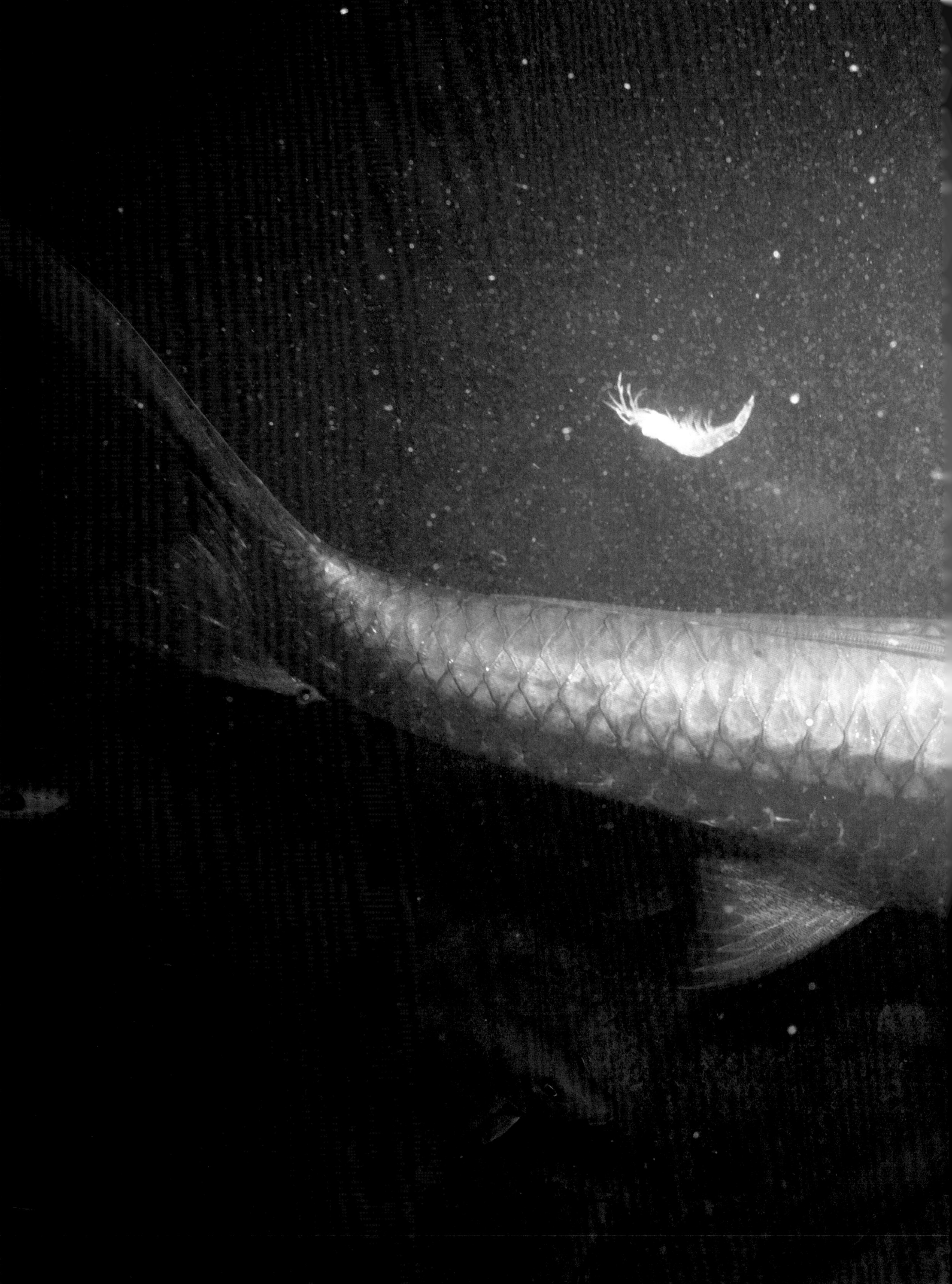

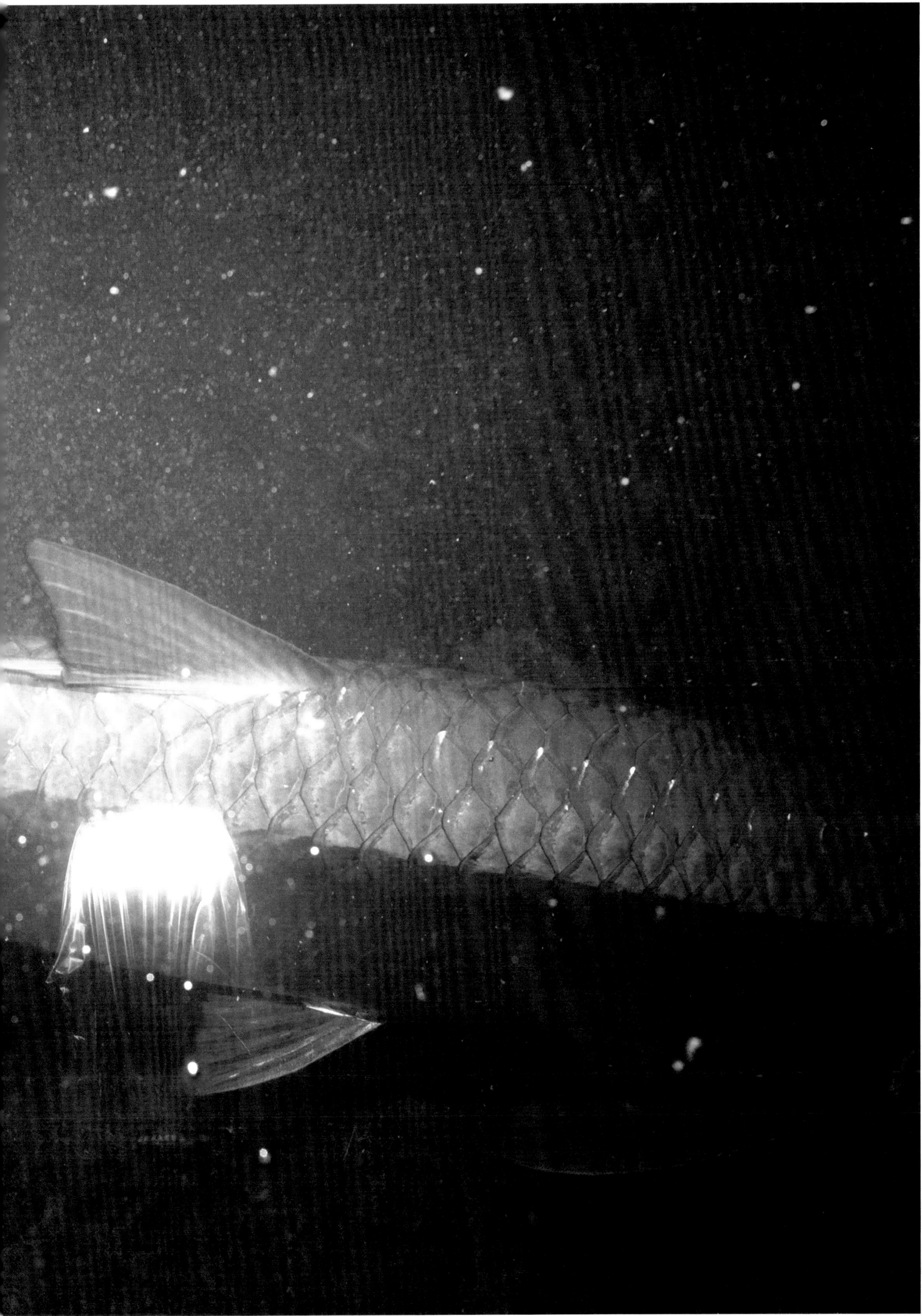

Mangroves, Everglades, Since Destroyed, 2017

Mangrove, Everglades, Since Destroyed (2), 2017

American Alligators, 2017

American Alligators (2), 2017

Coastal Fog, Everglades, 2017

Orb Weaver, Everglades, 2017

Unseen Animal Moving in Mangrove Forest, 2017

Invasive Burmese Python, Parking Lot, Everglades, 2017

Invasive Cuban Tree Frog, Everglades, 2018

El Niño Storm, West Coast, 2019

Tarpon, Frozen Shrimp, South Florida, 2017

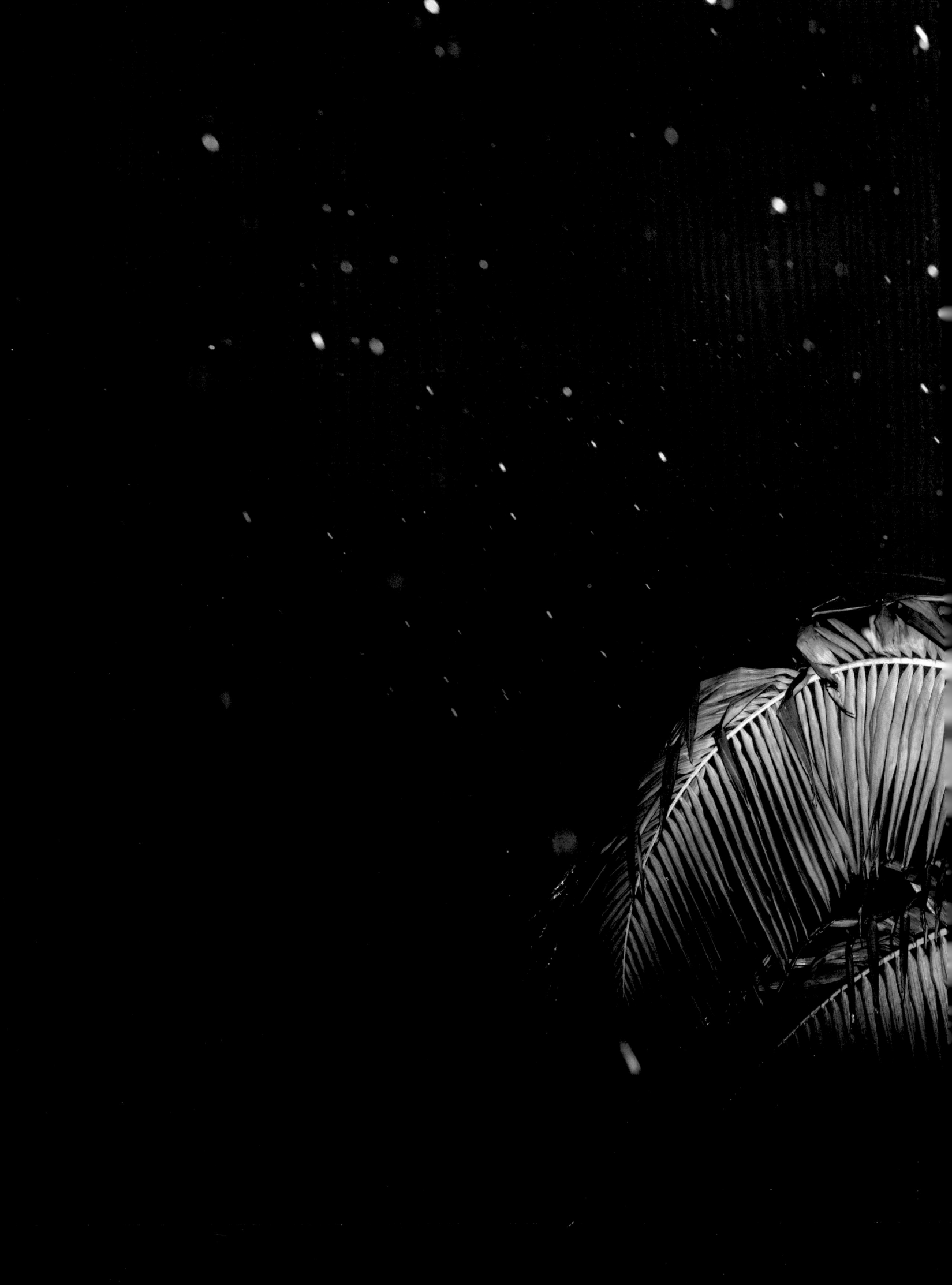

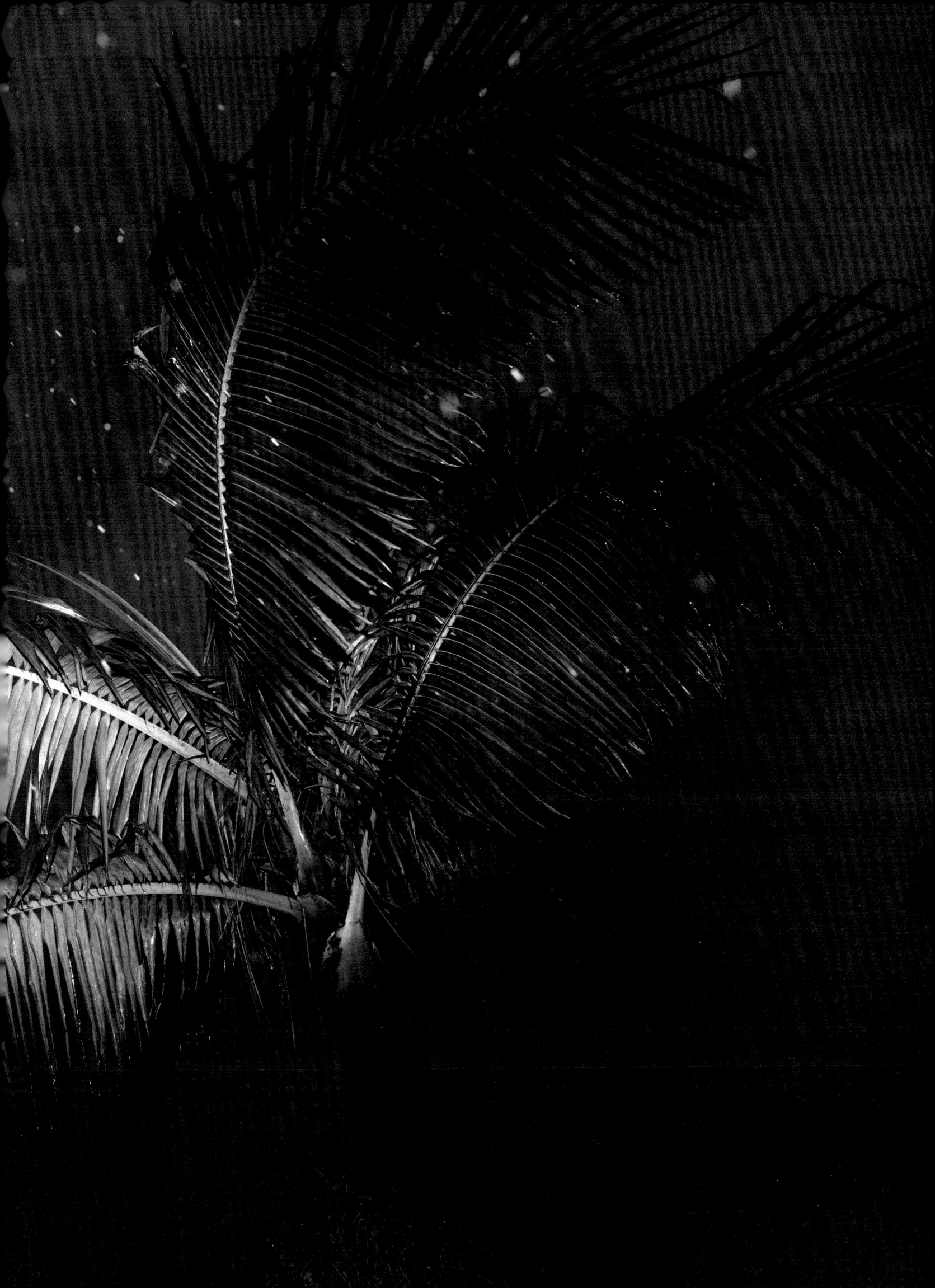

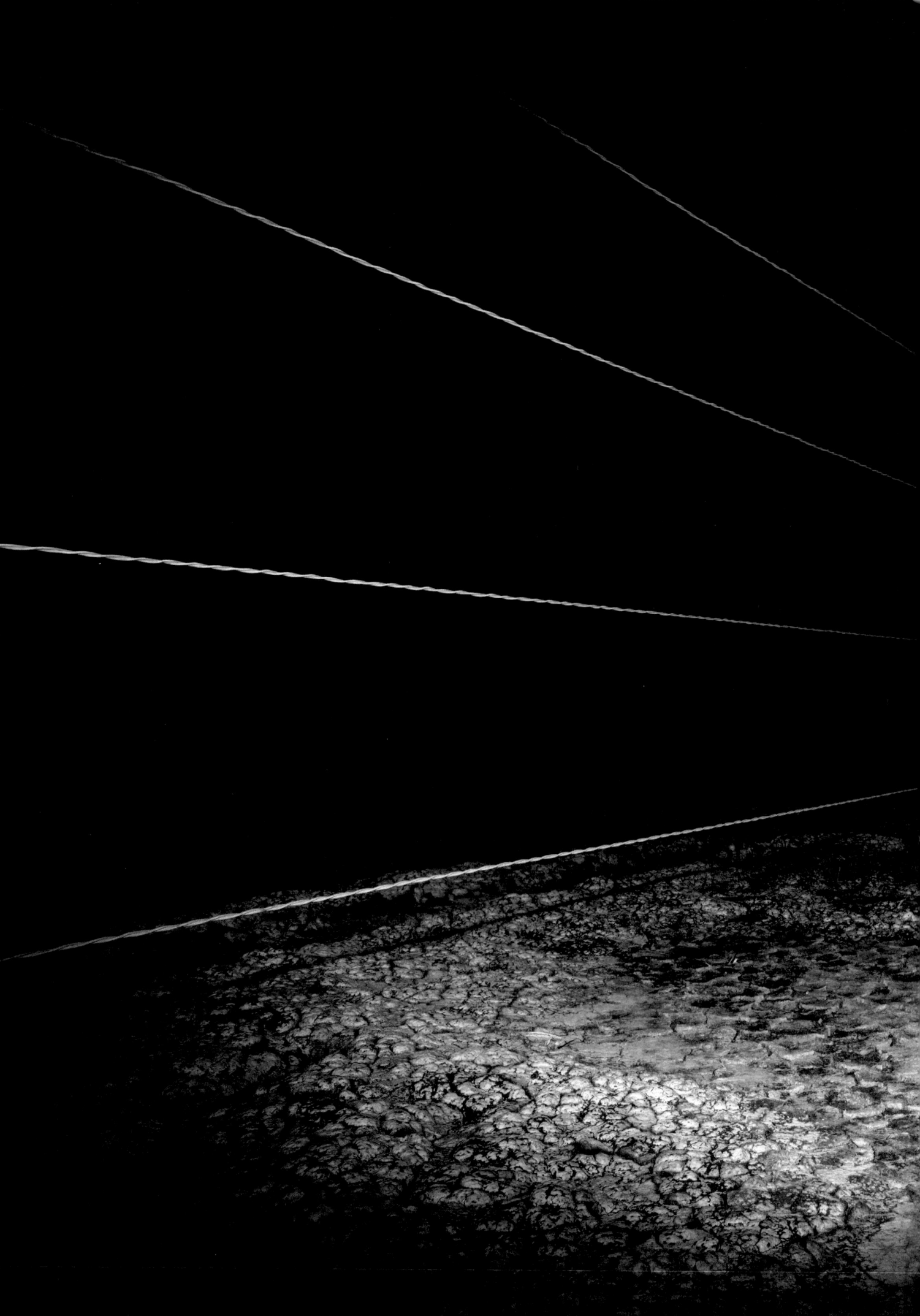

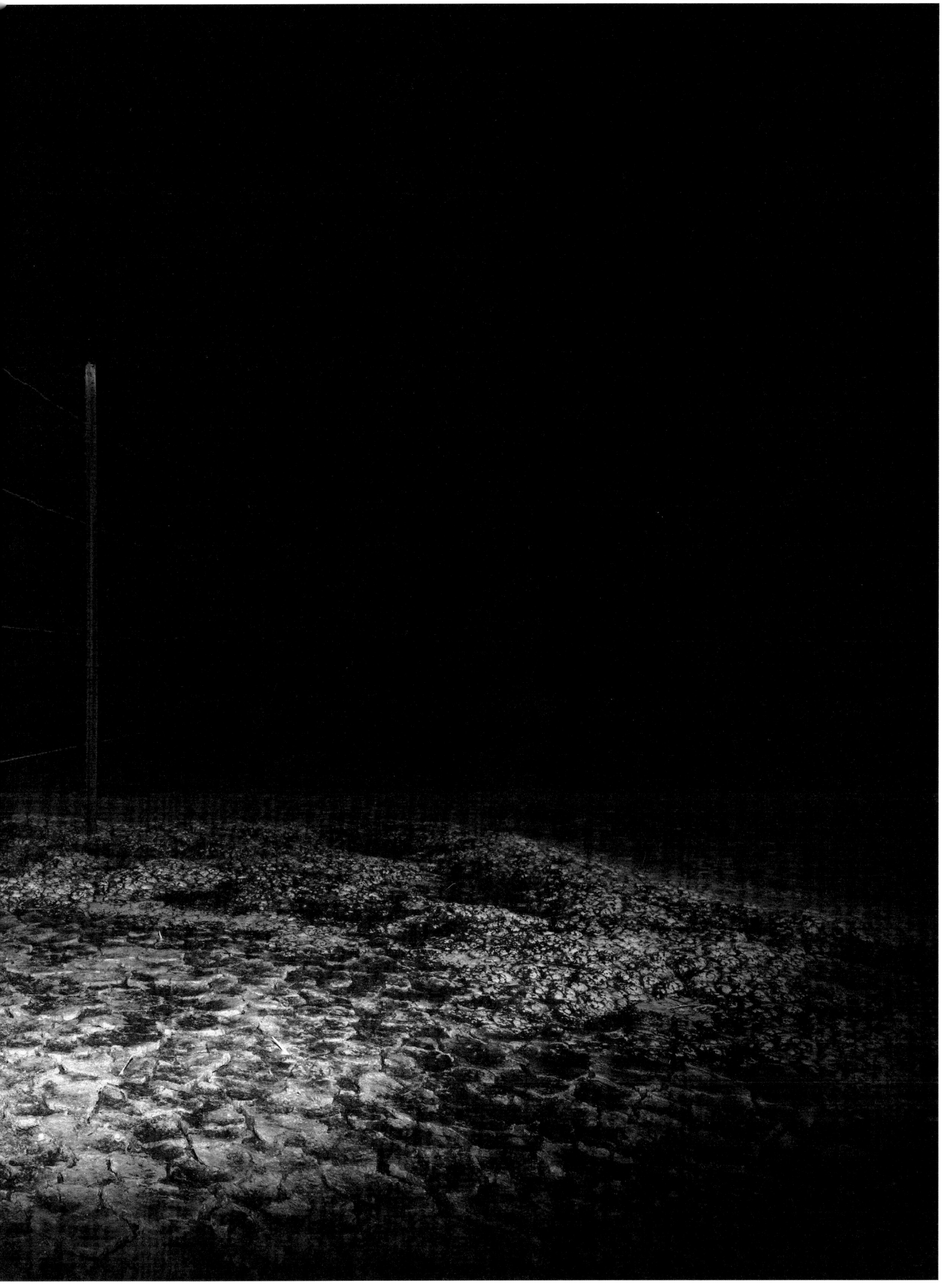

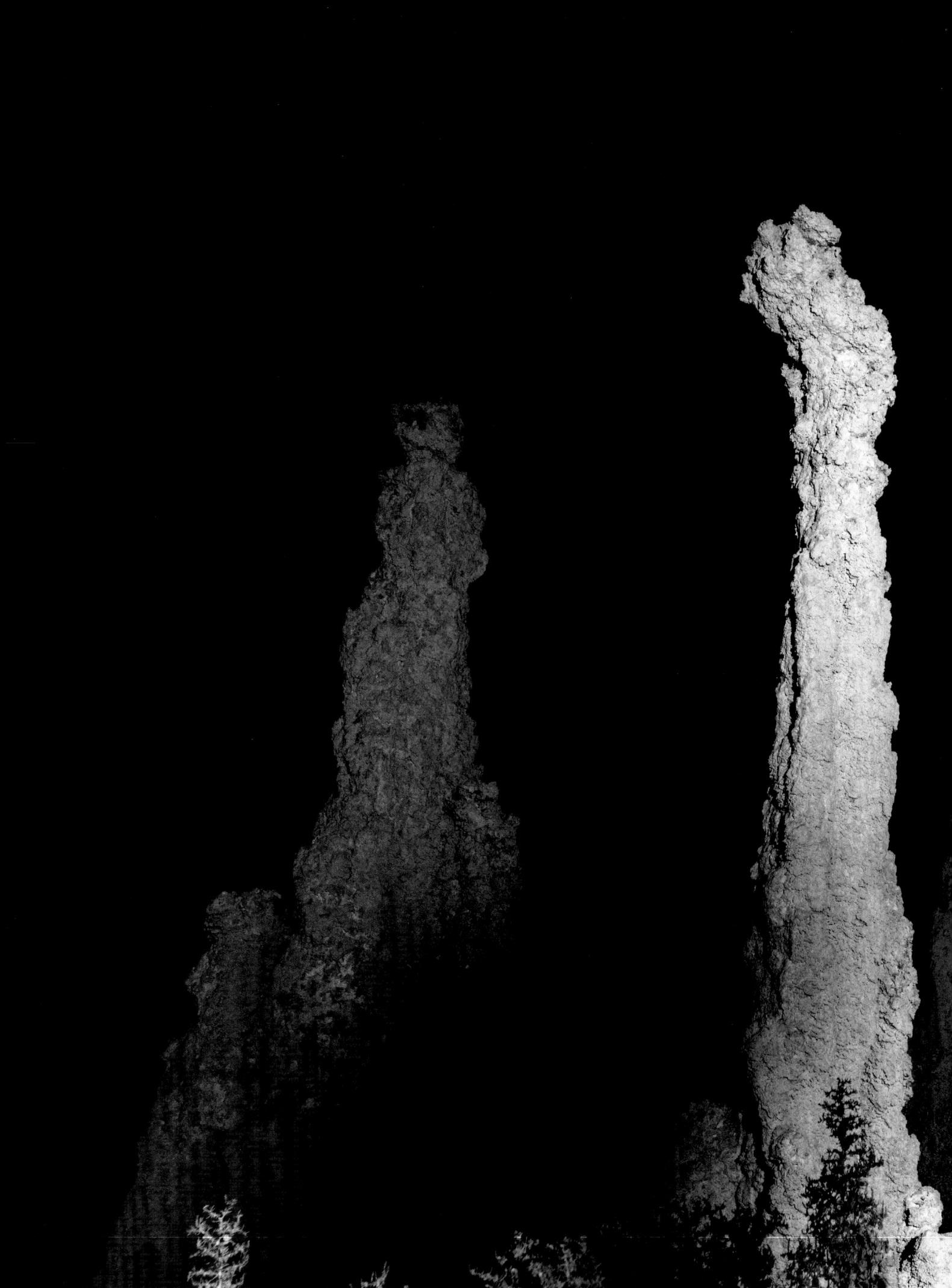

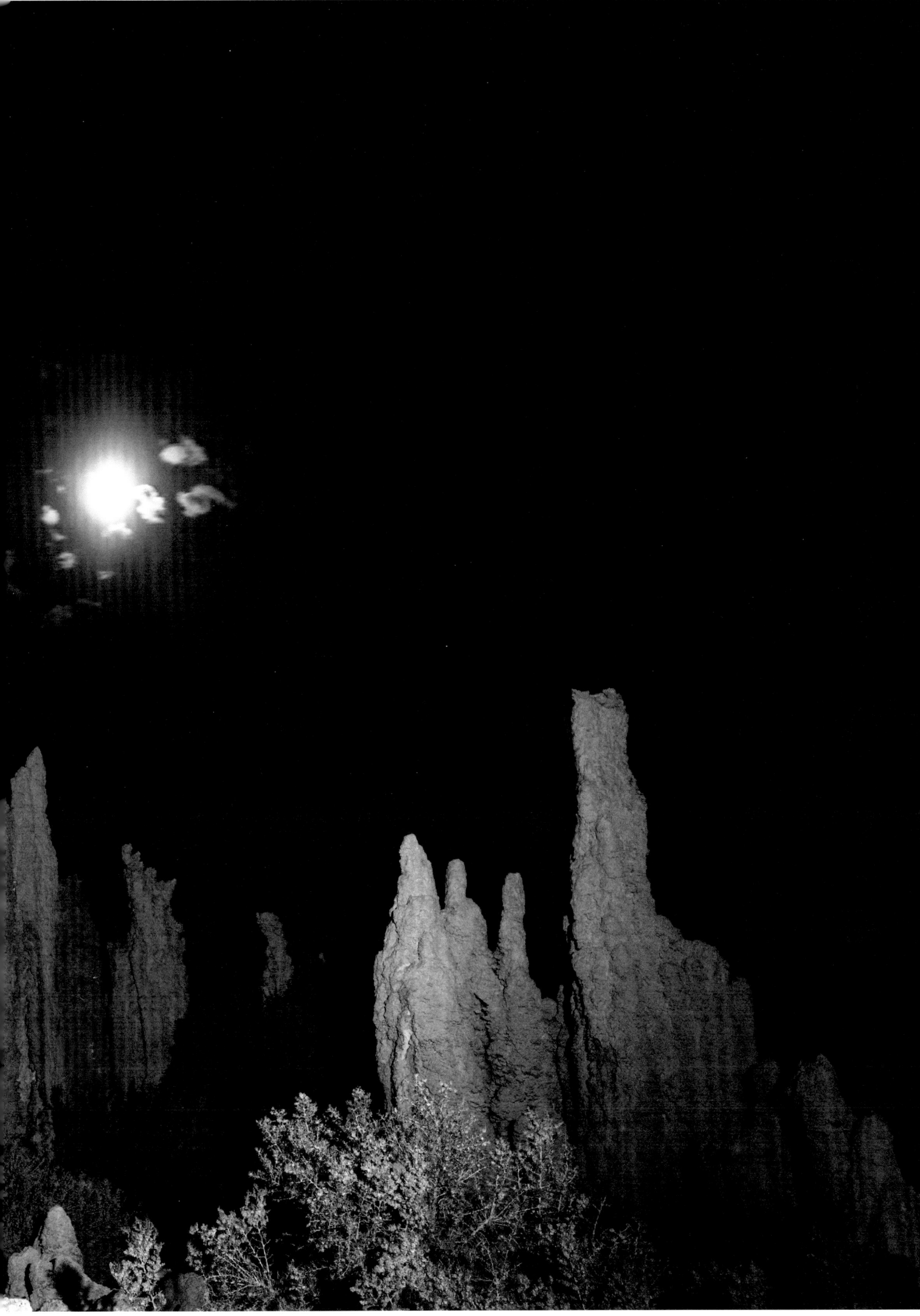

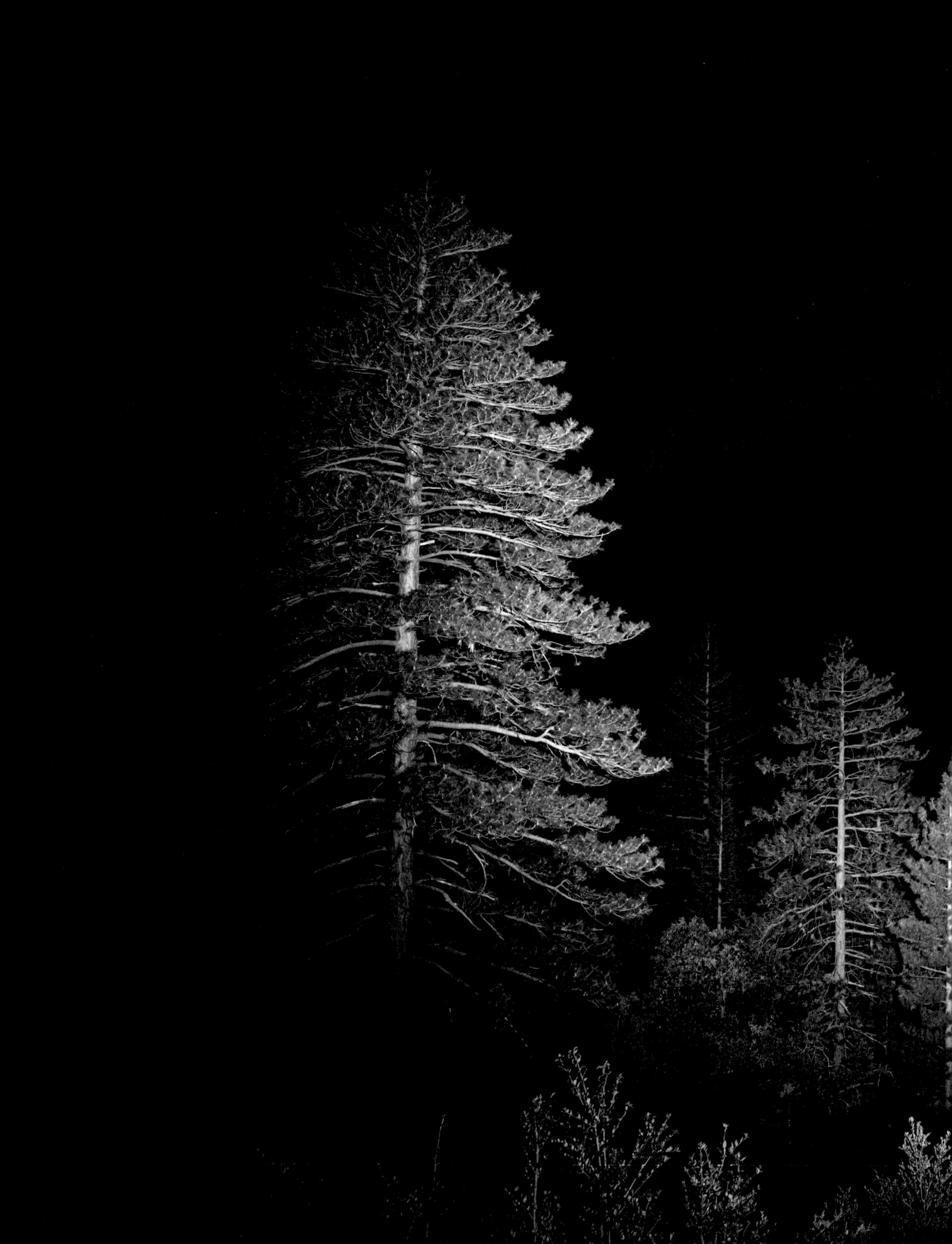

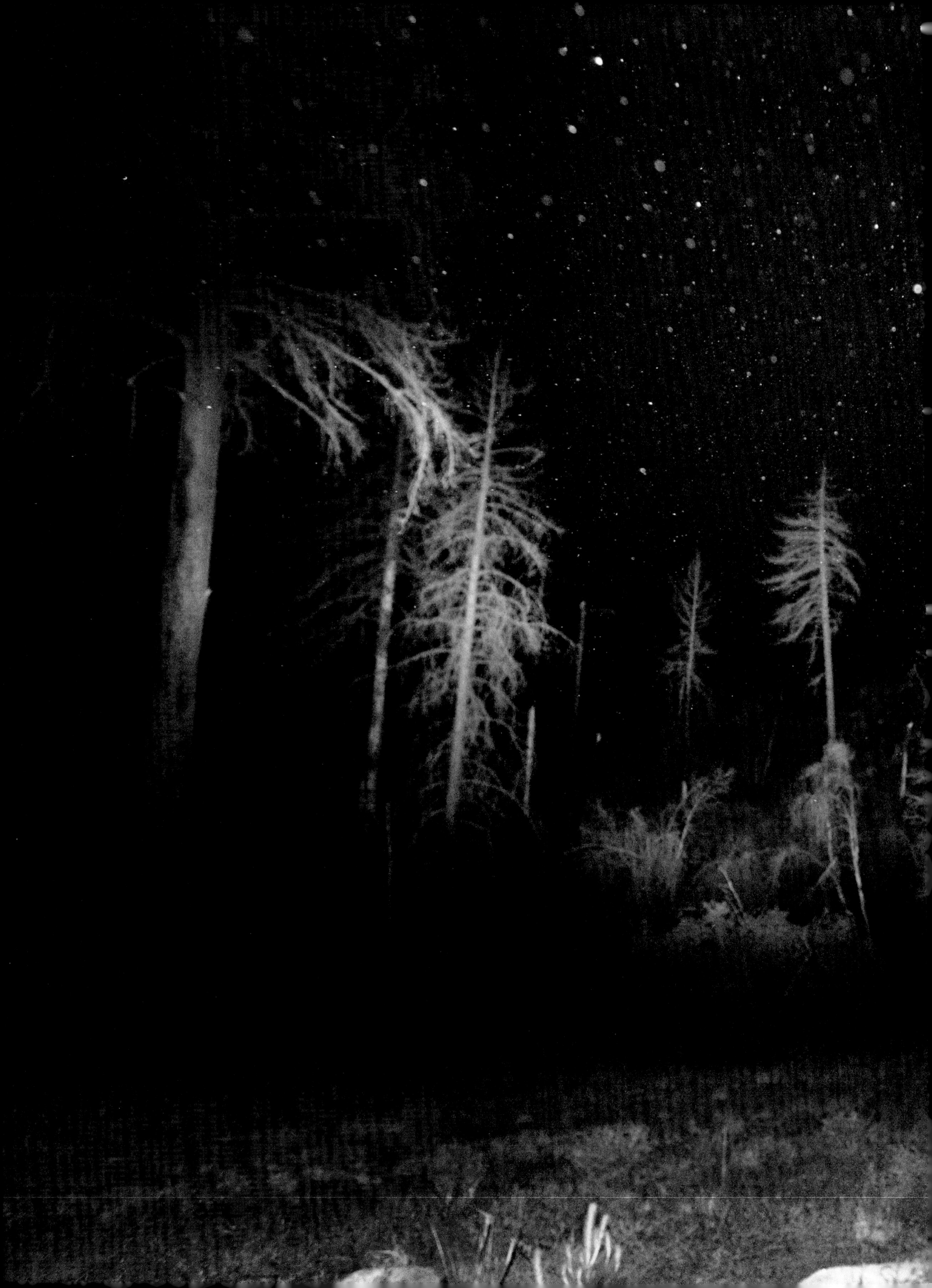

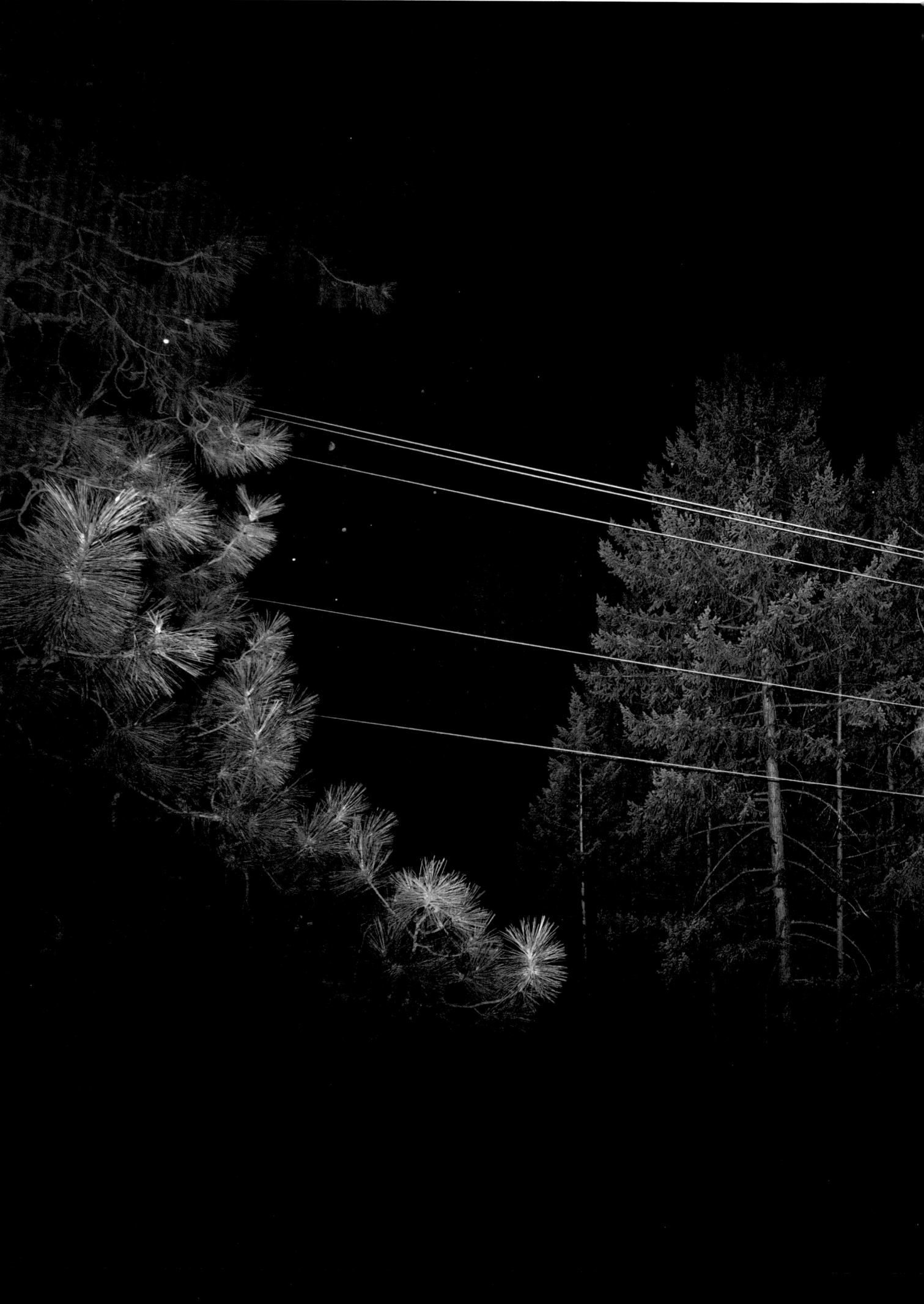

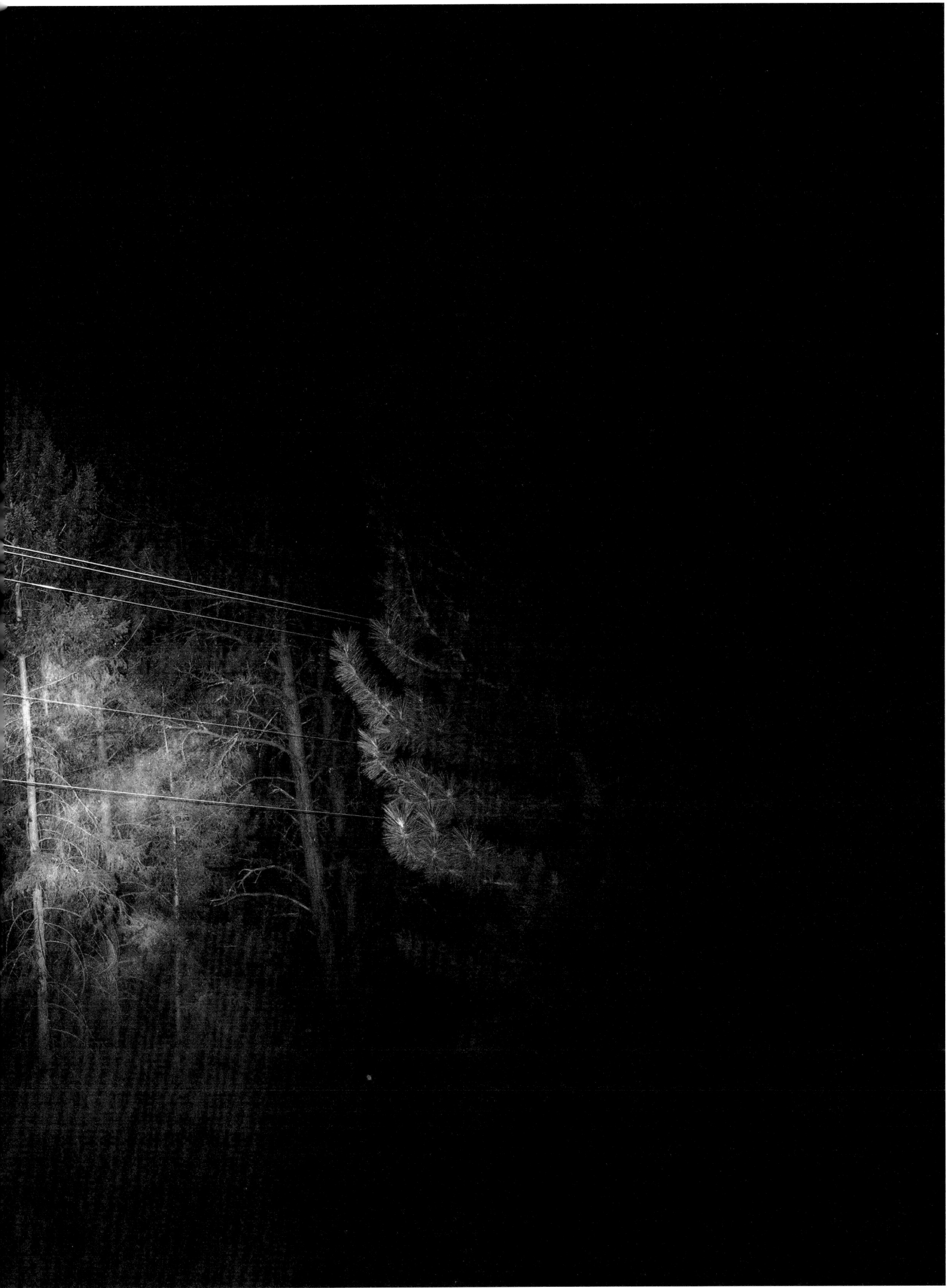

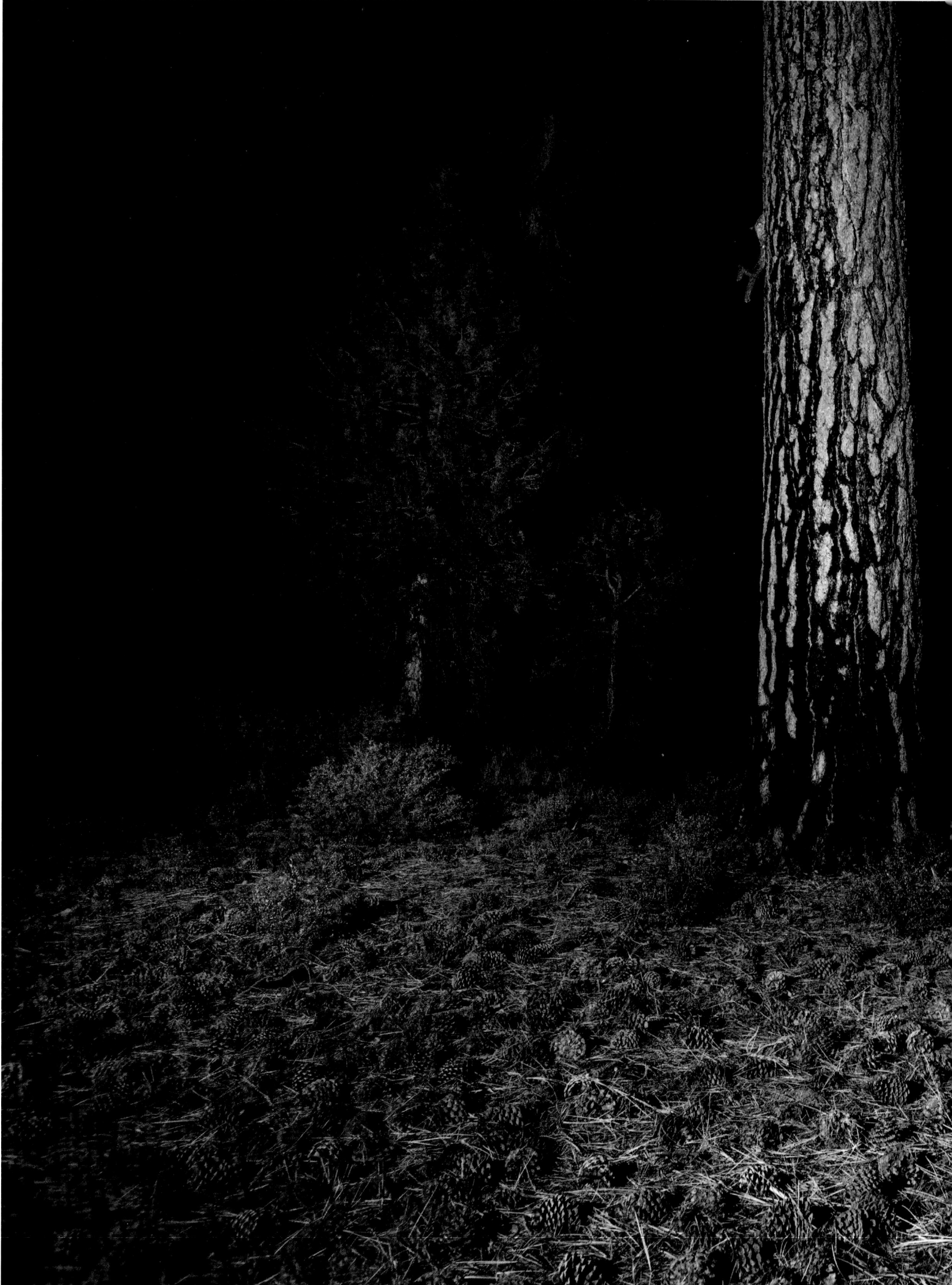

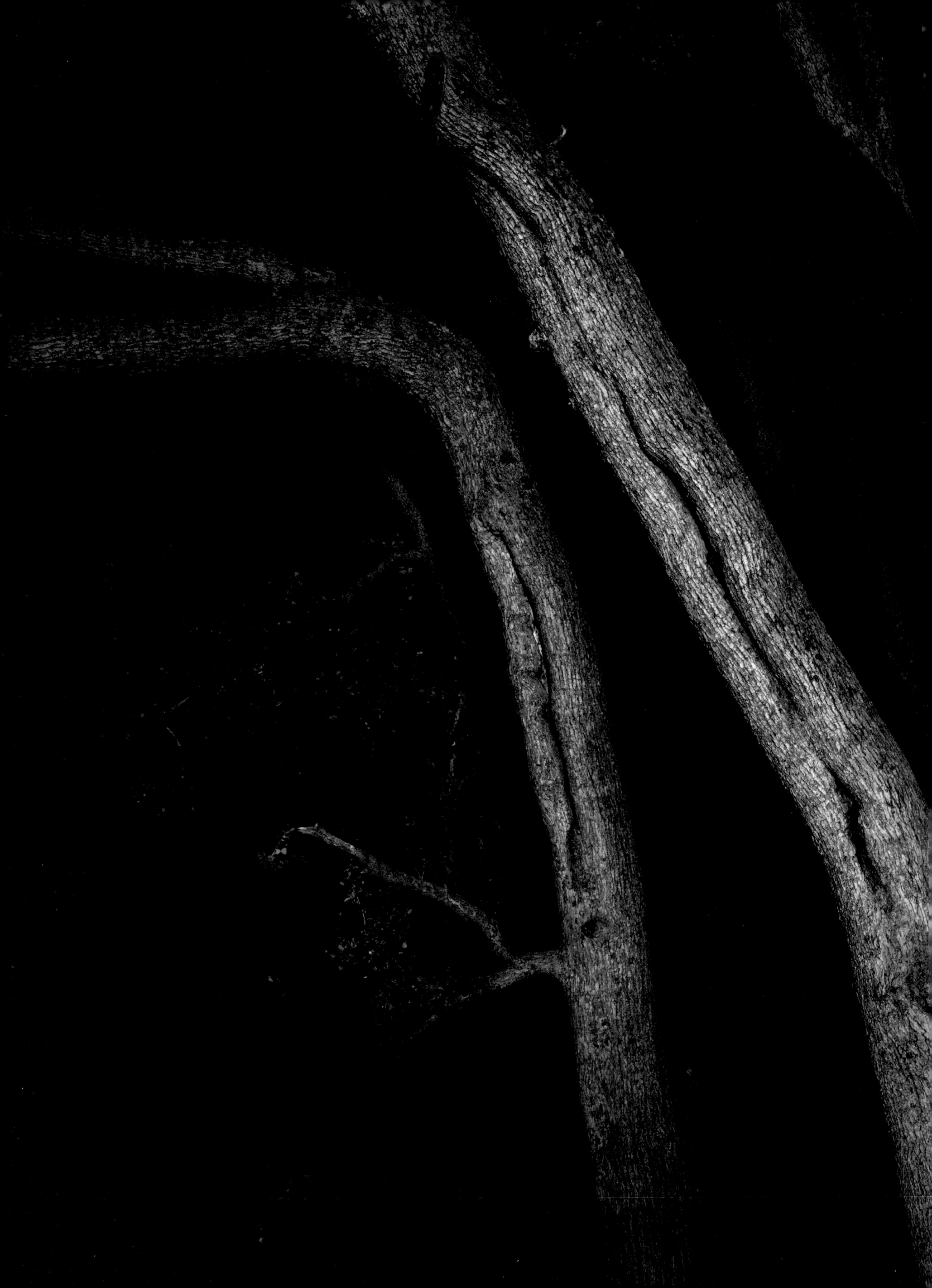

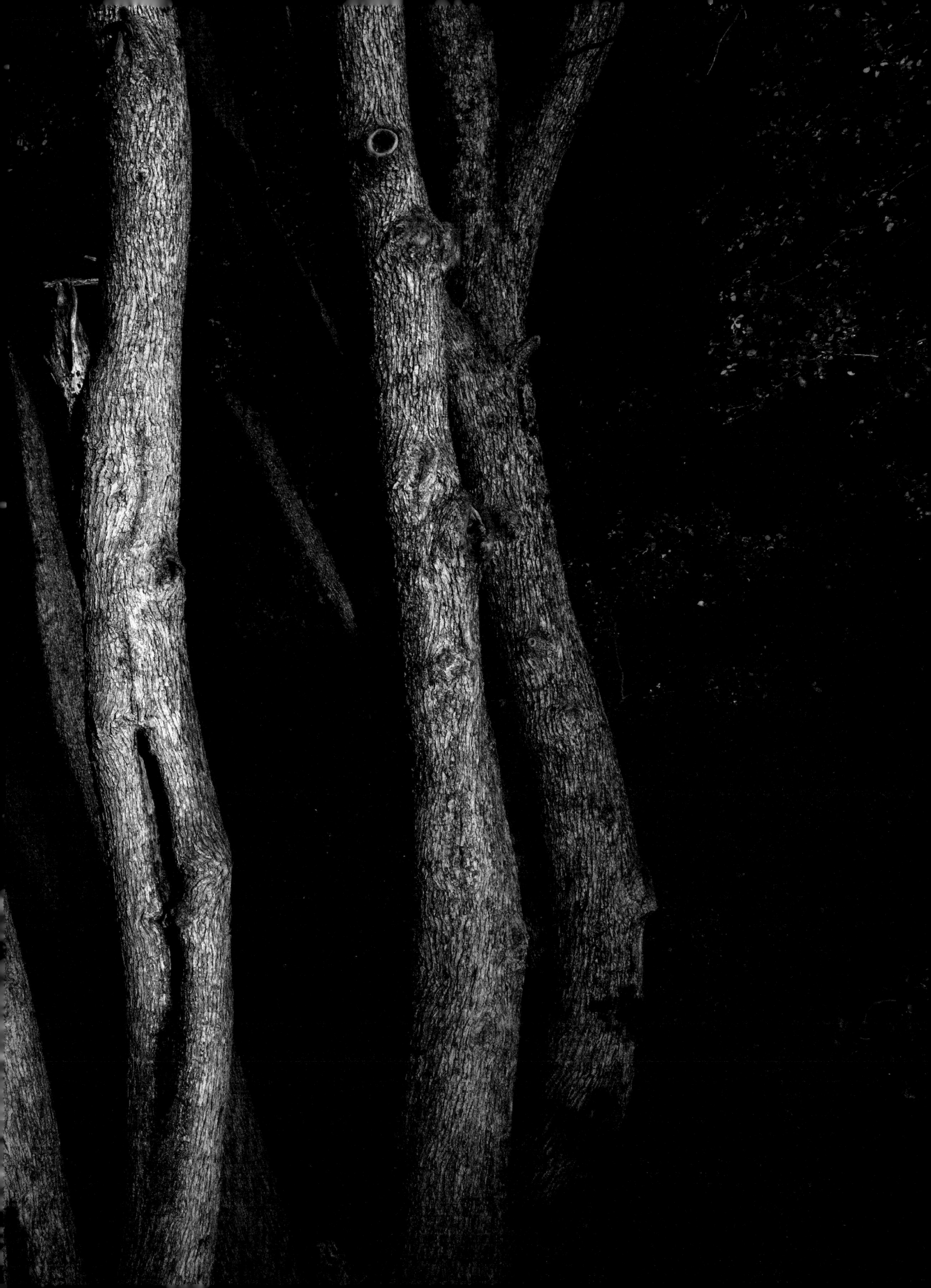

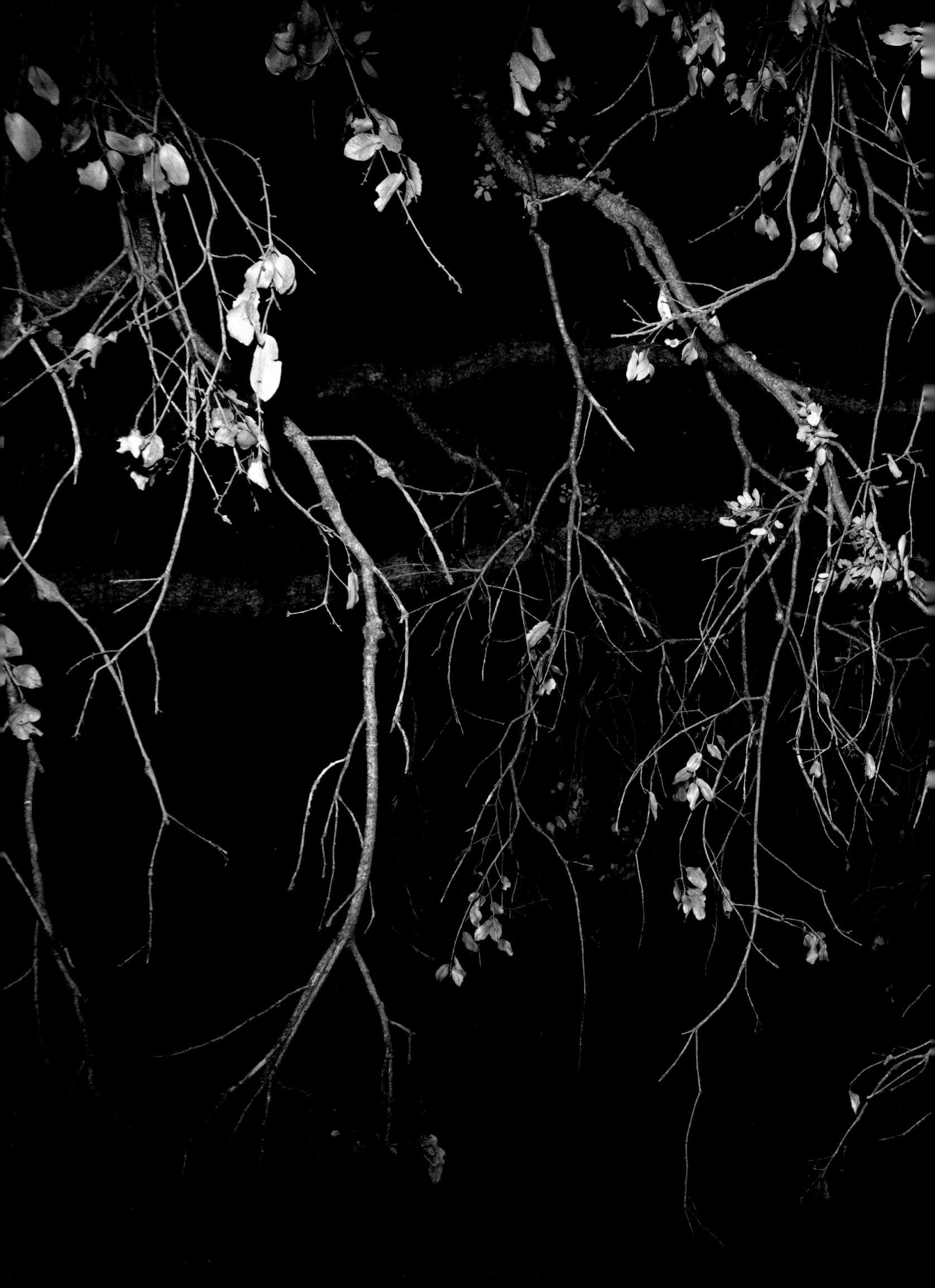

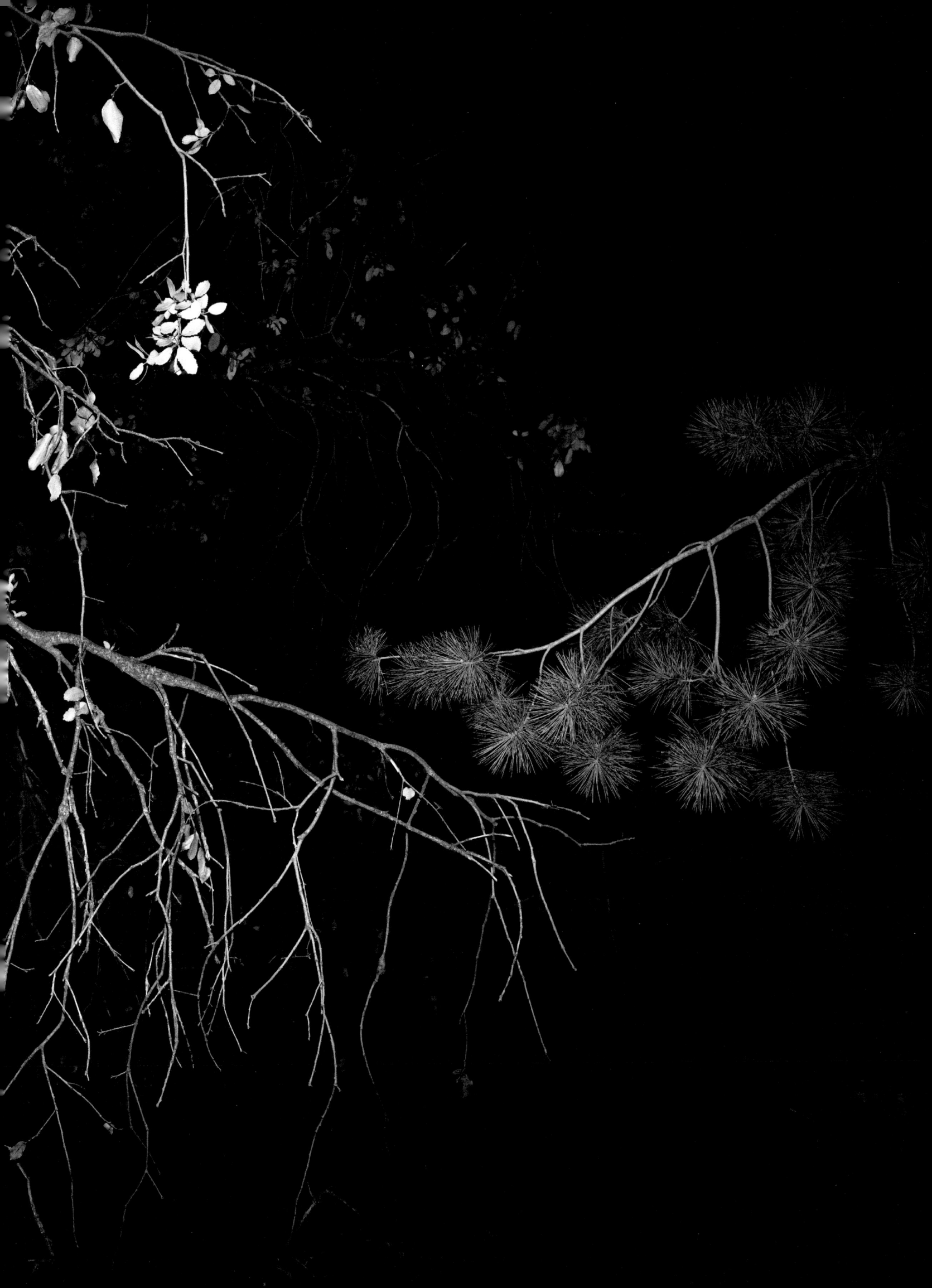

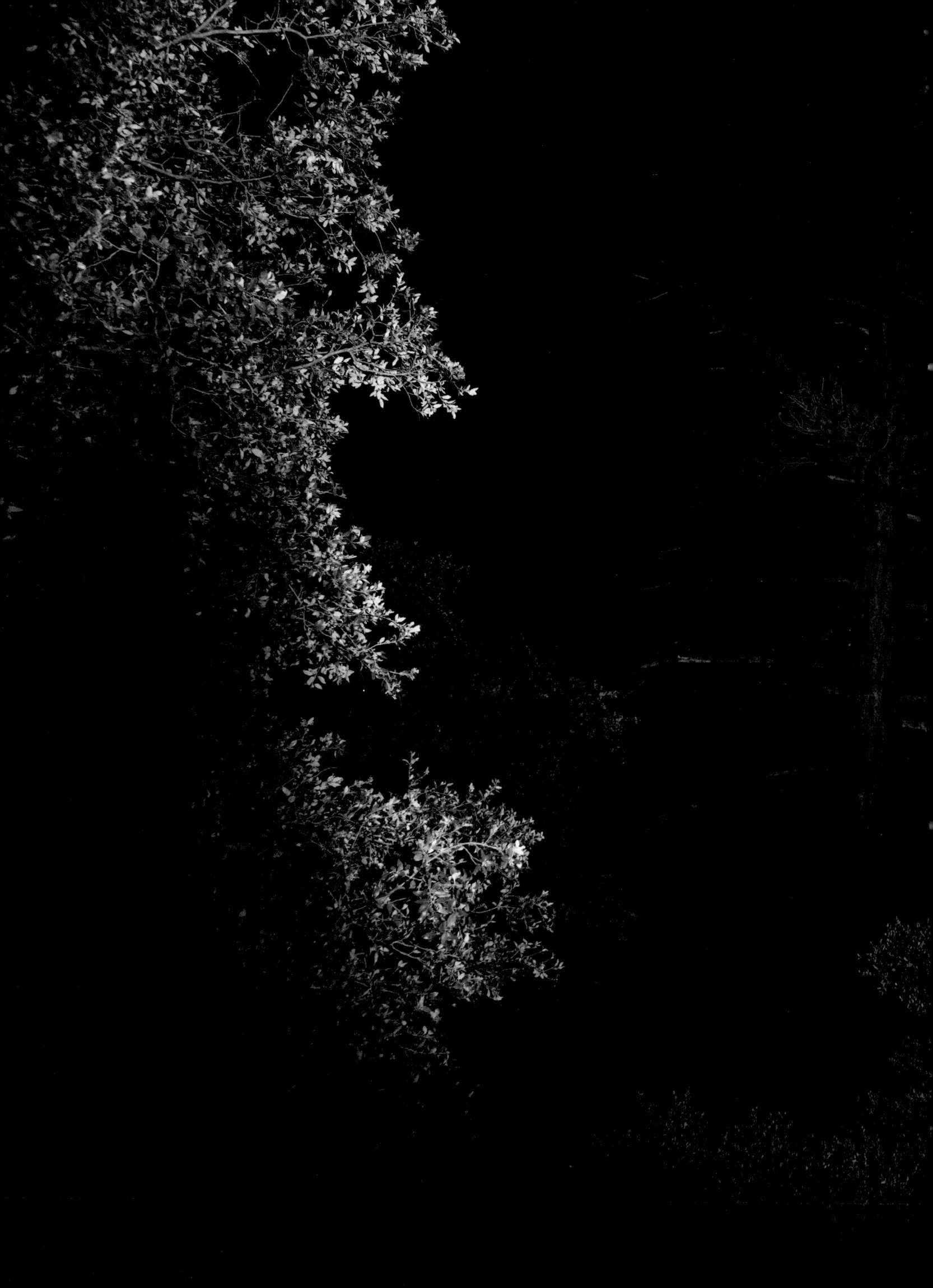

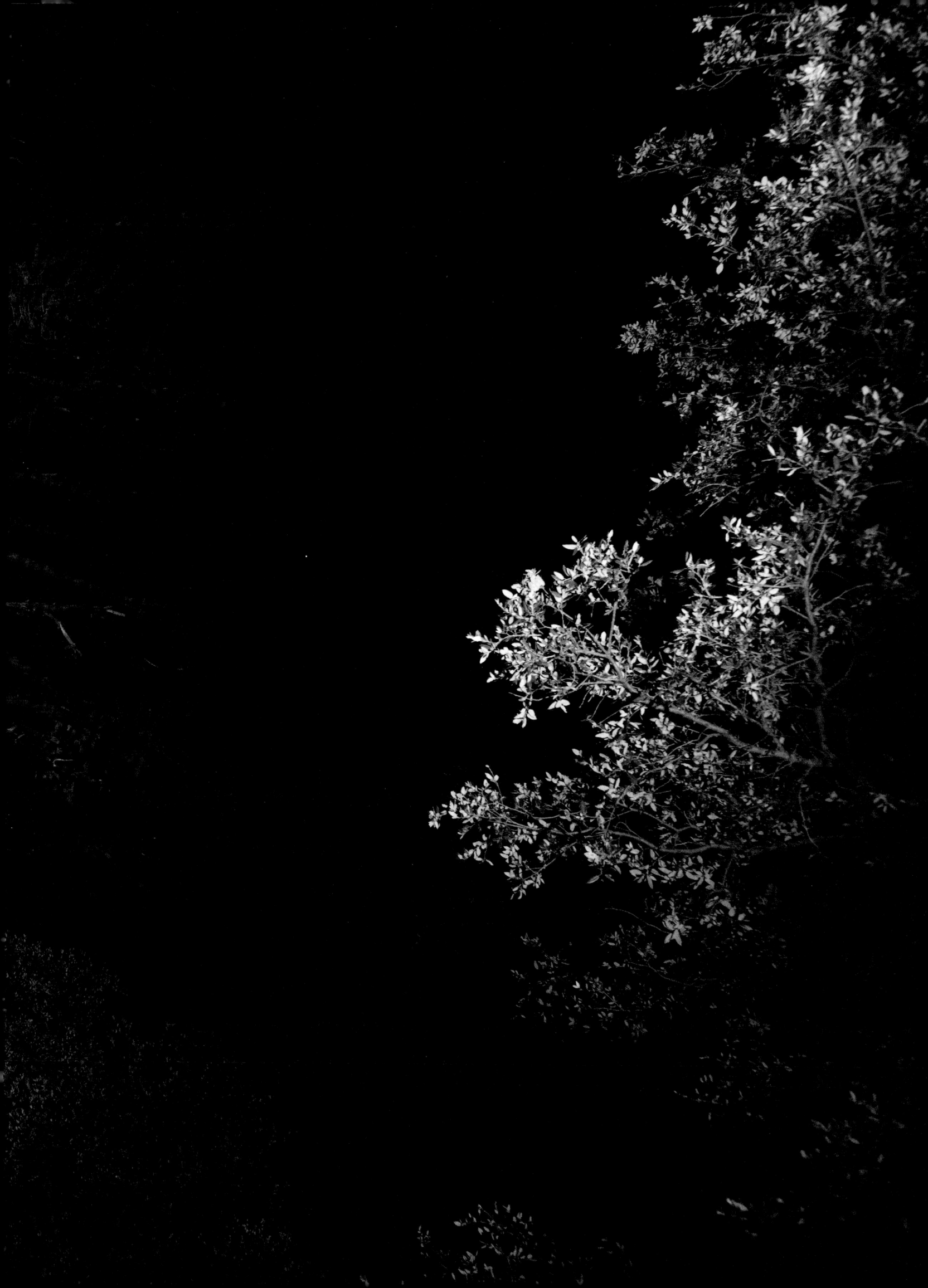

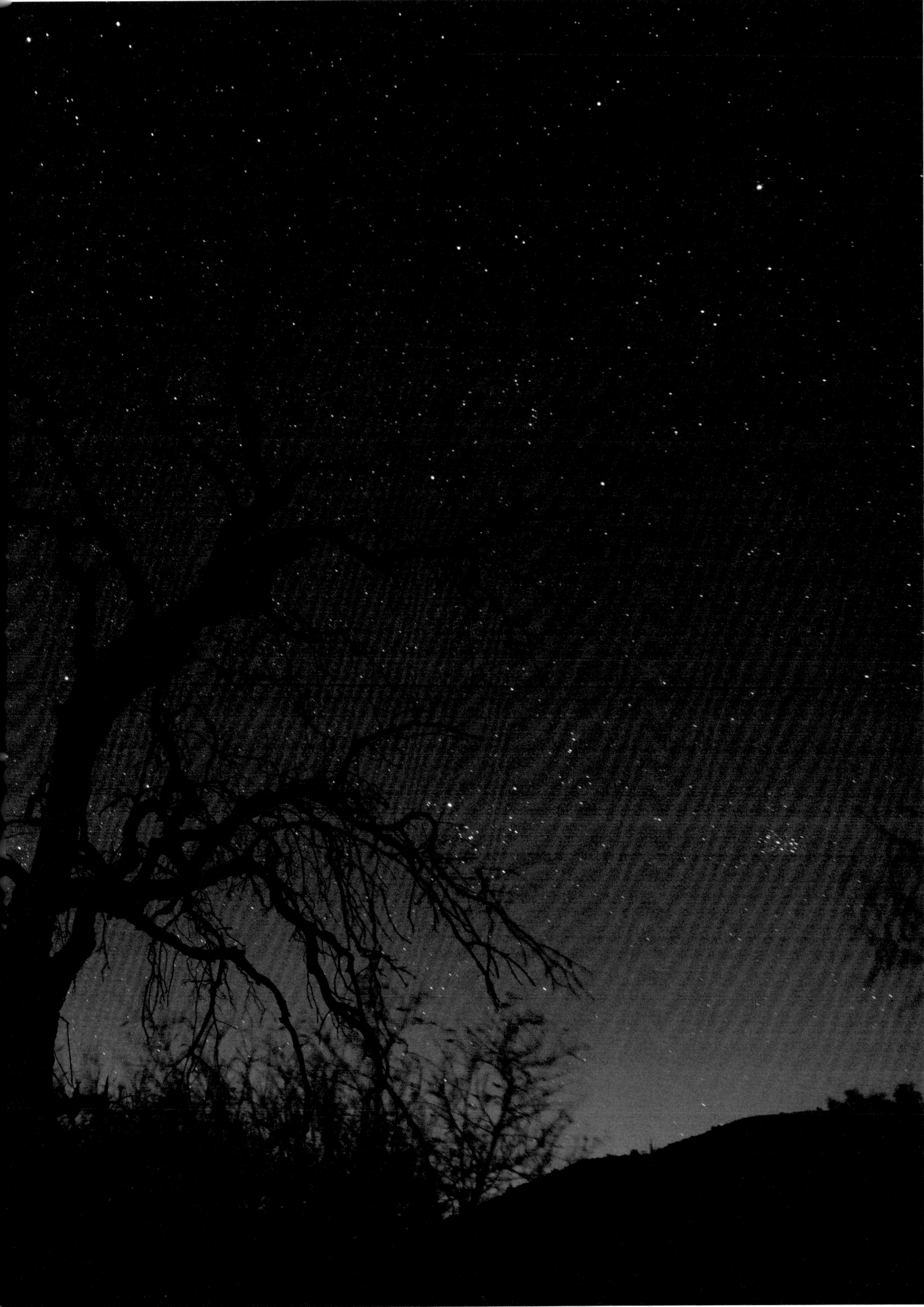

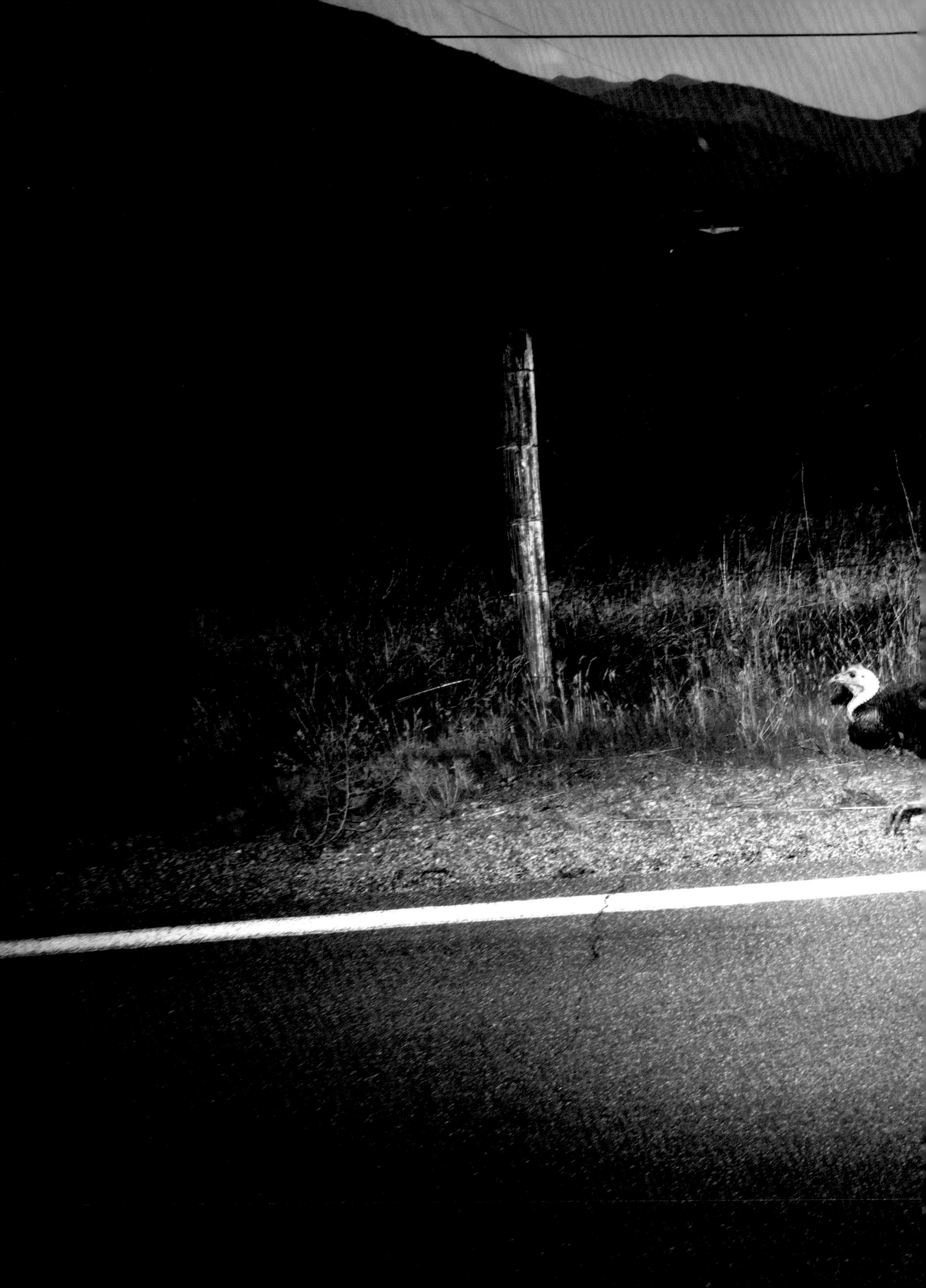

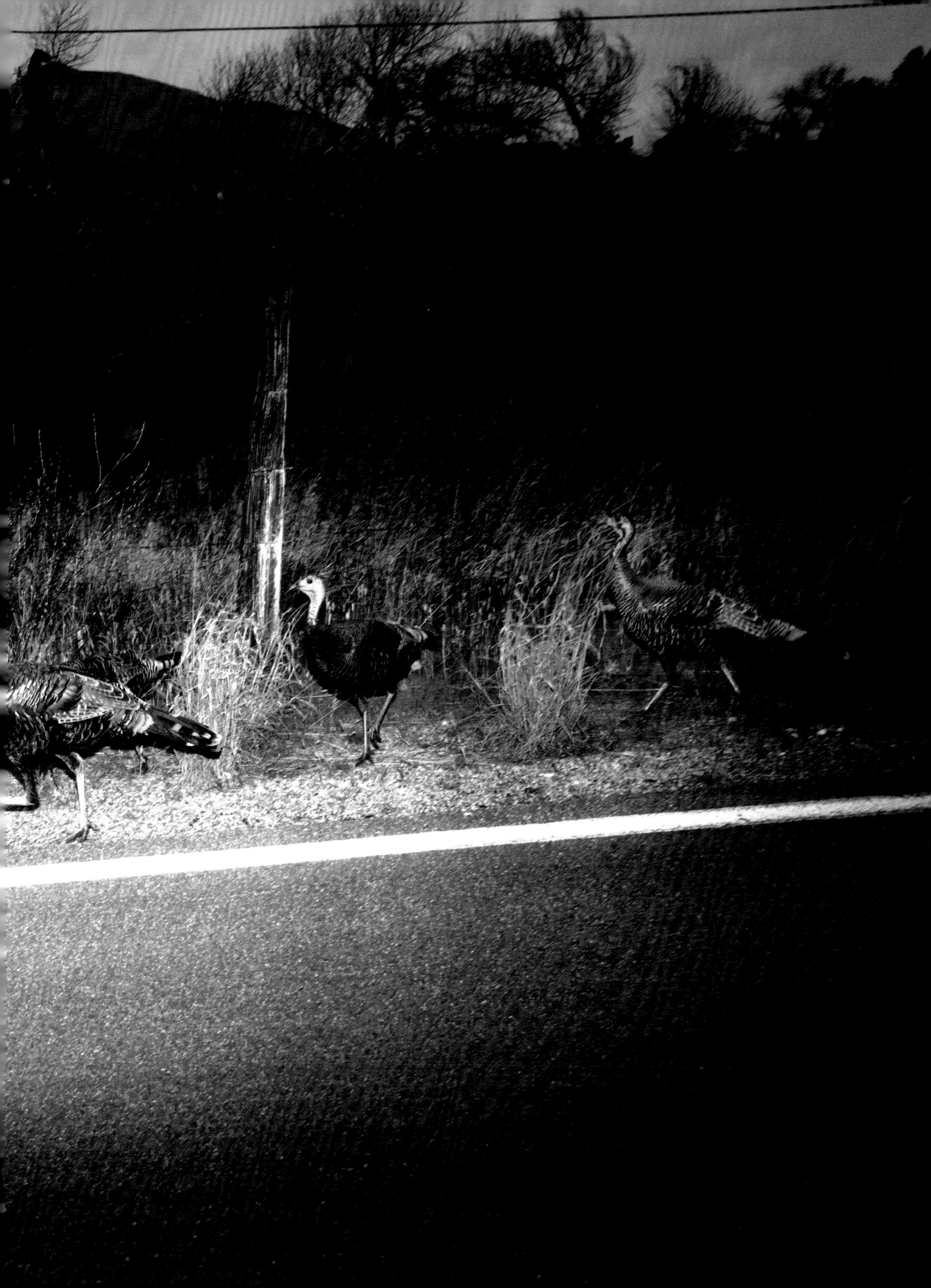

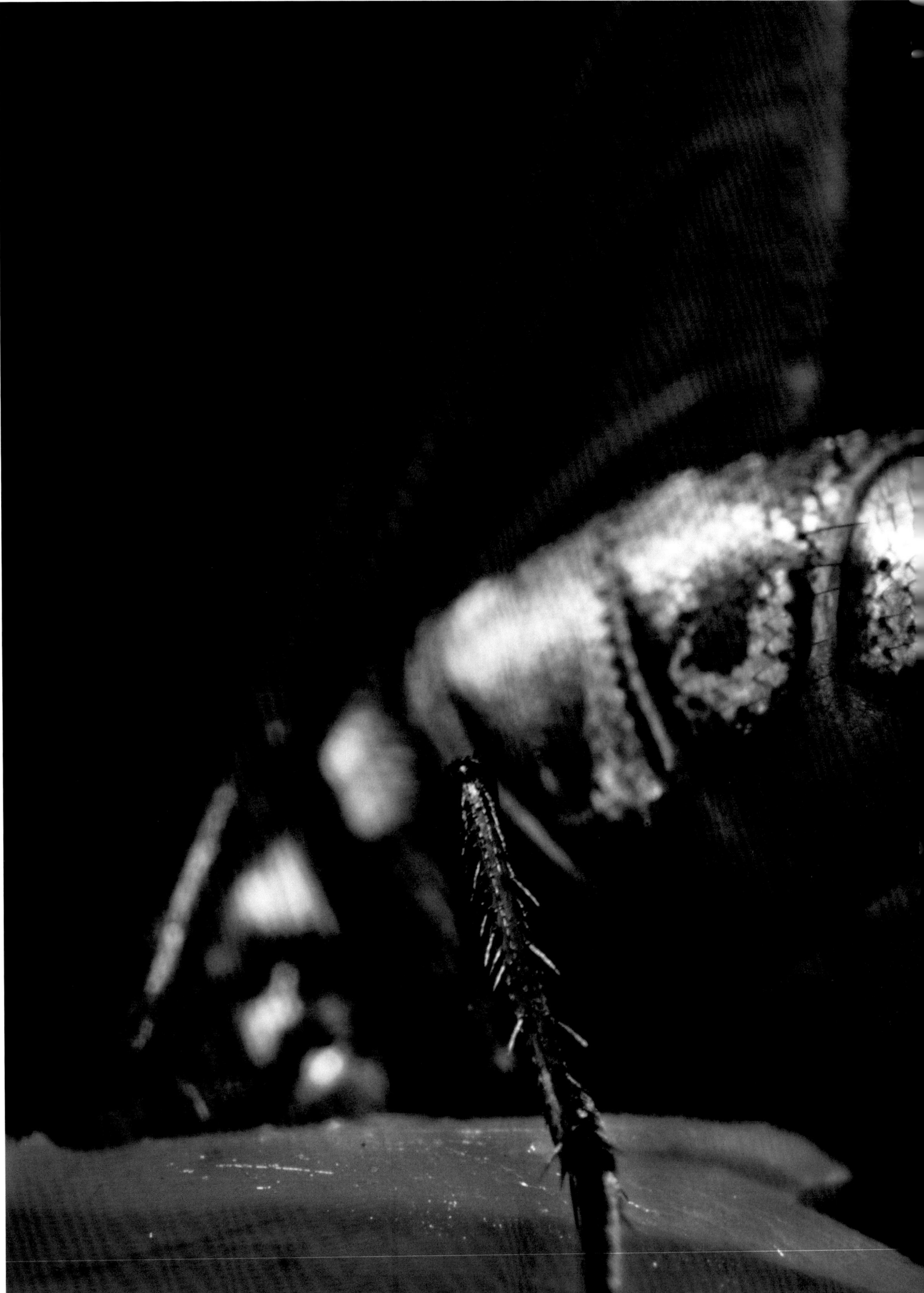

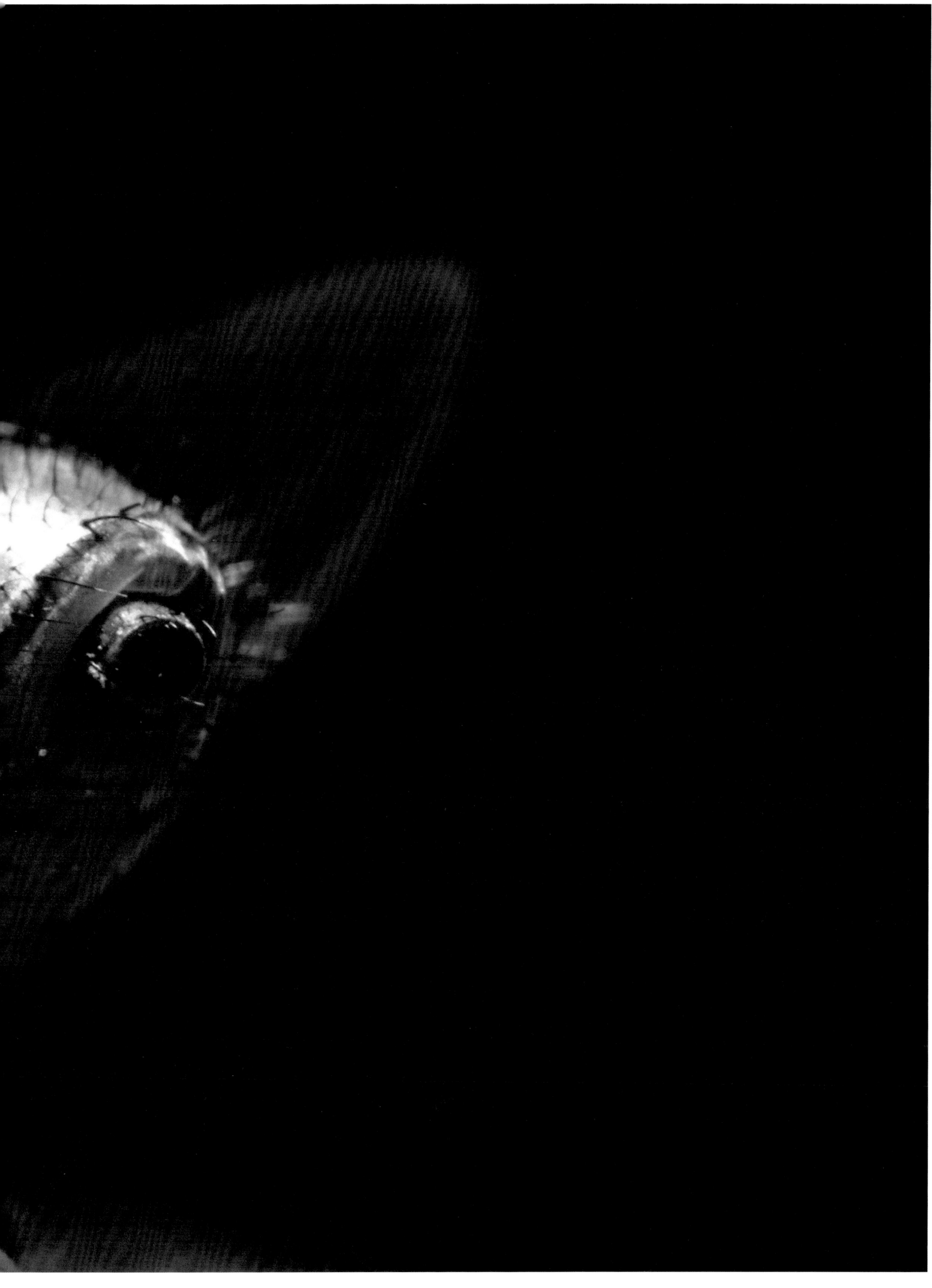

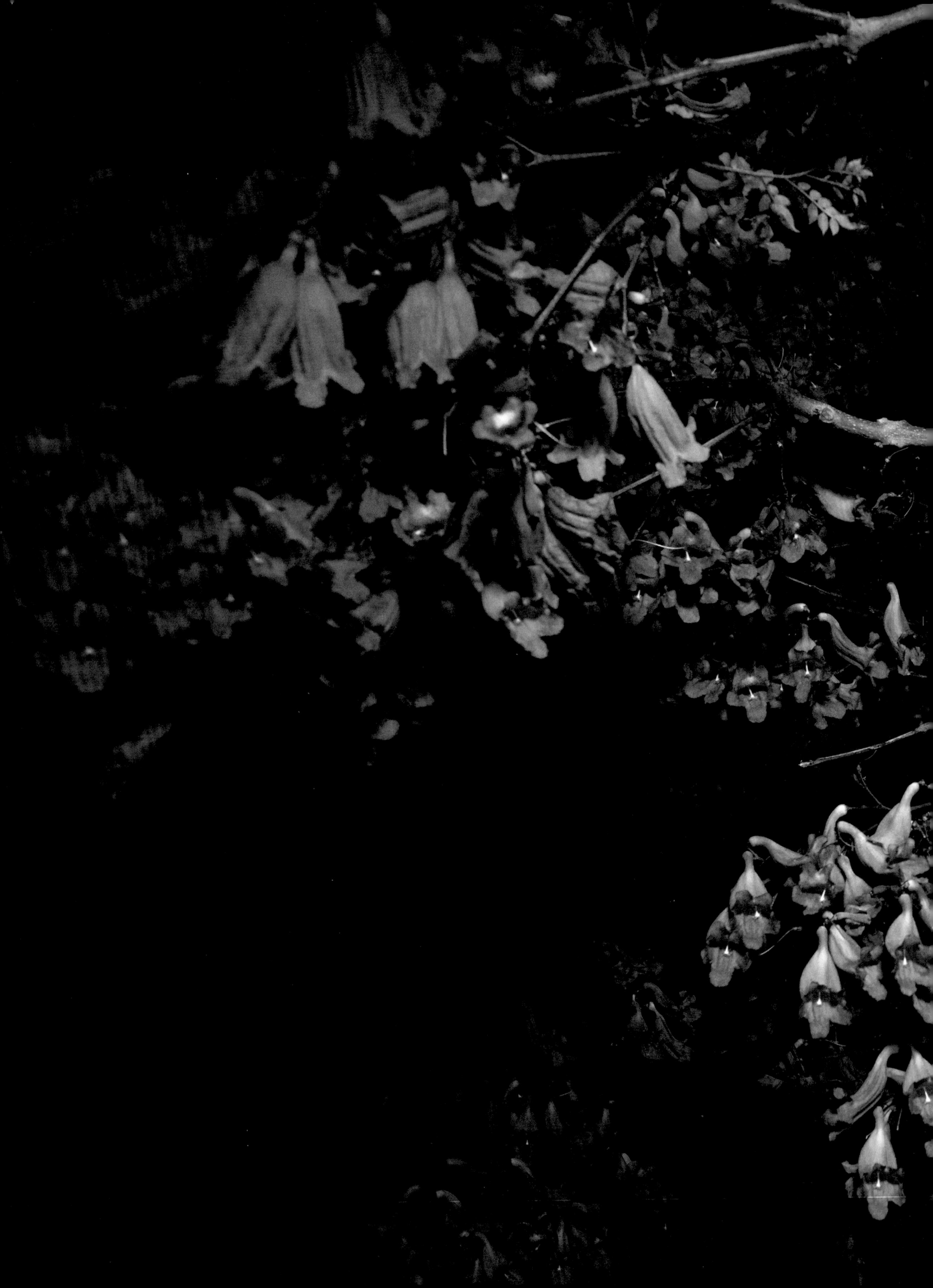

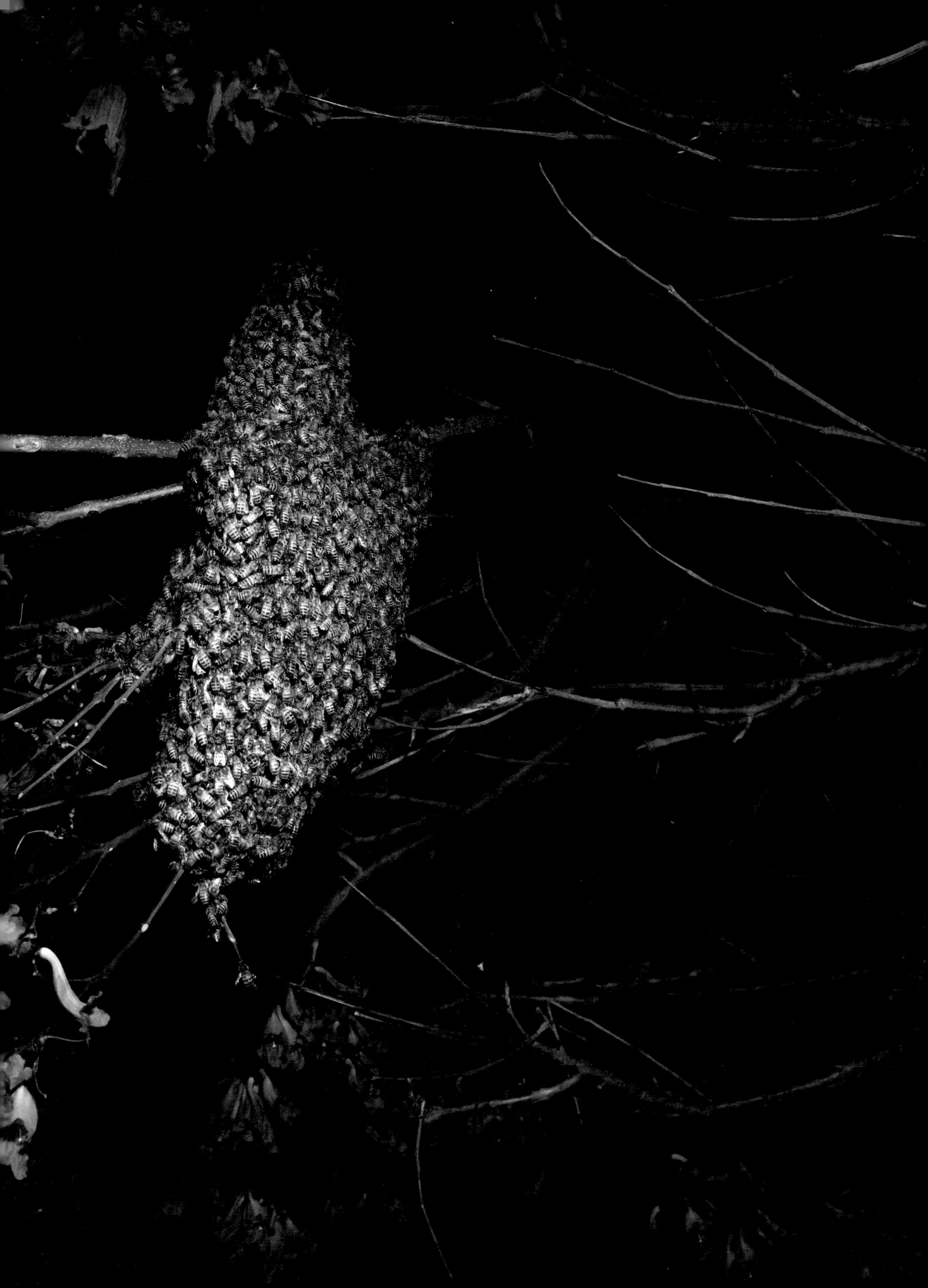

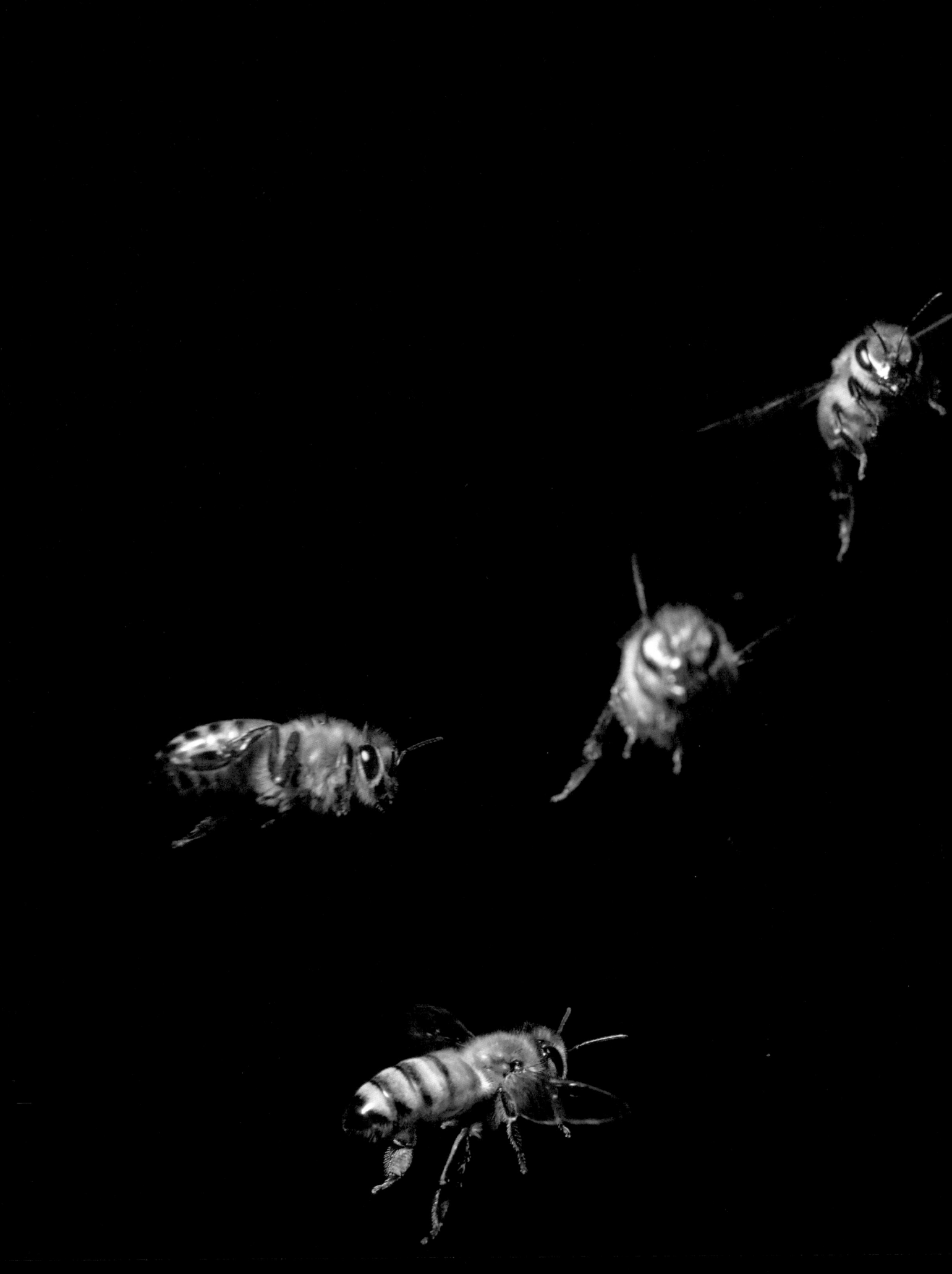

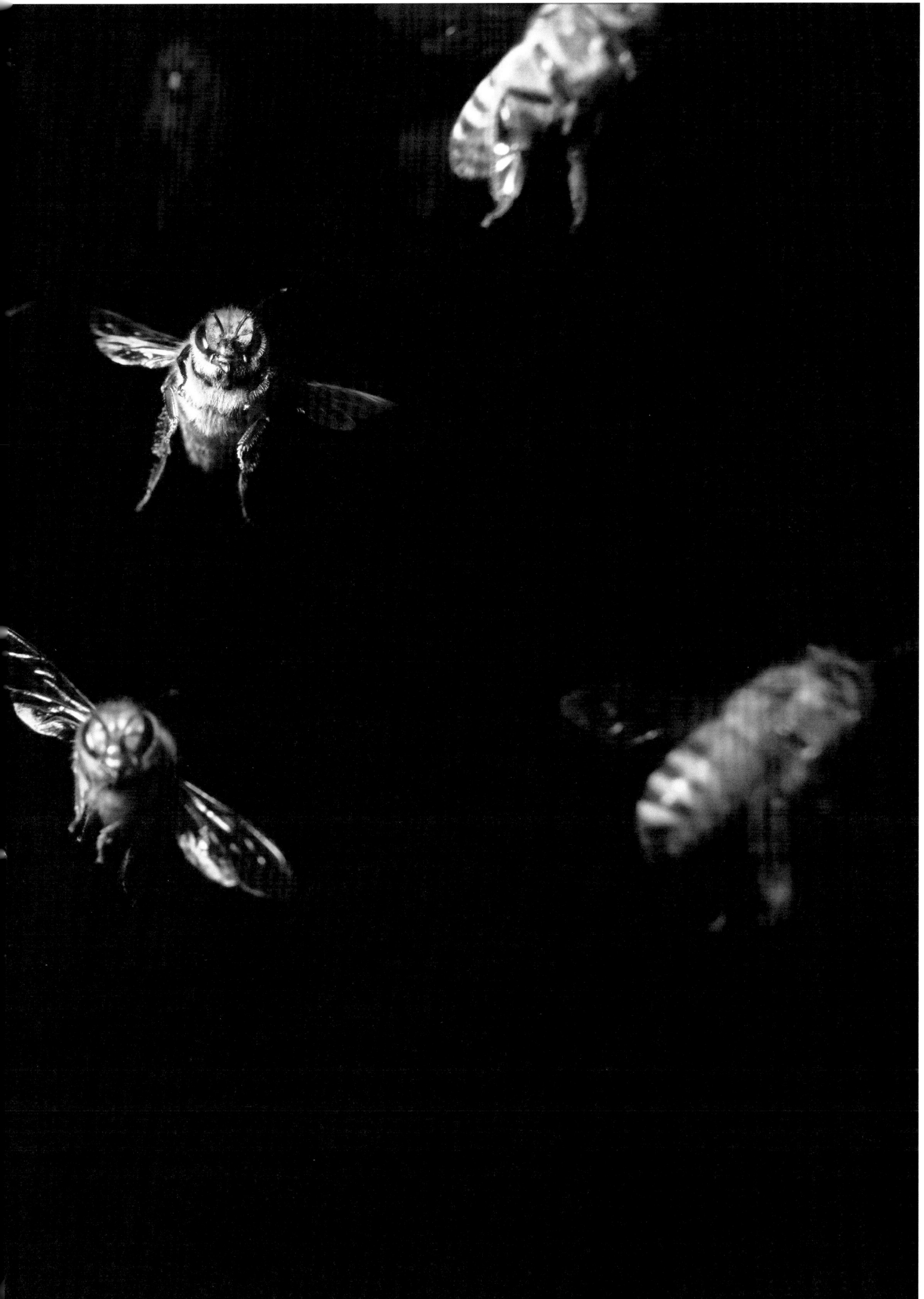

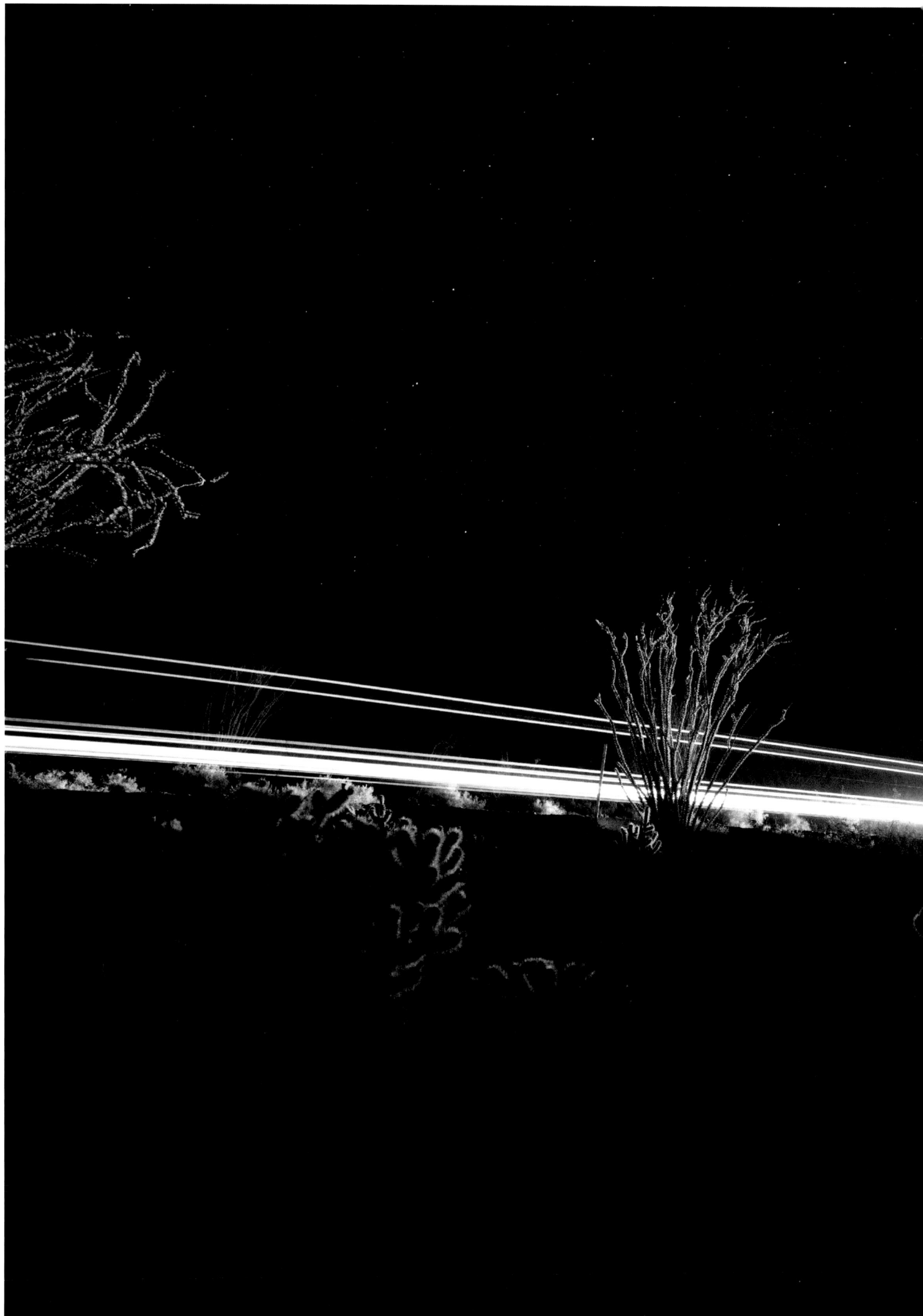

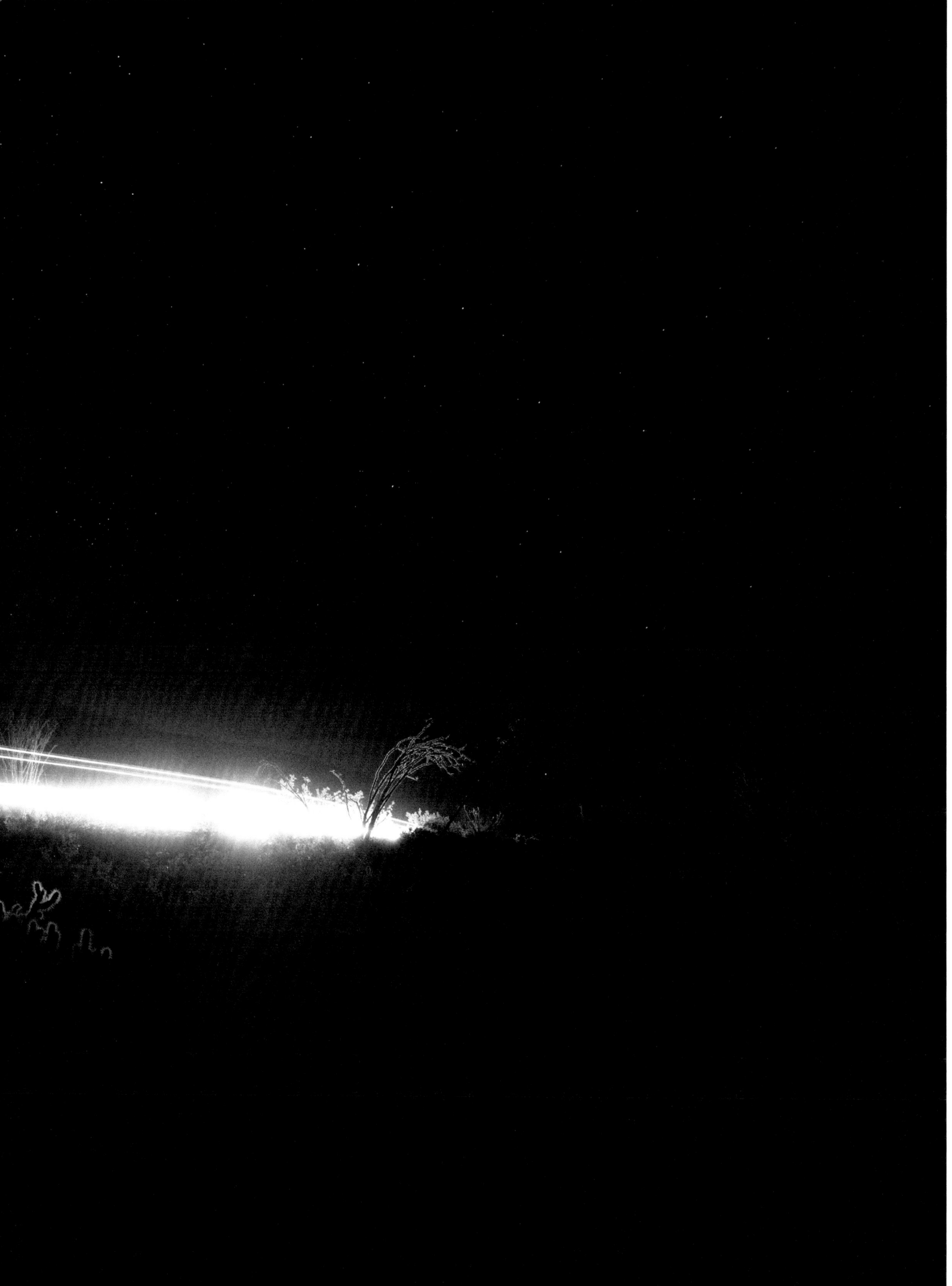

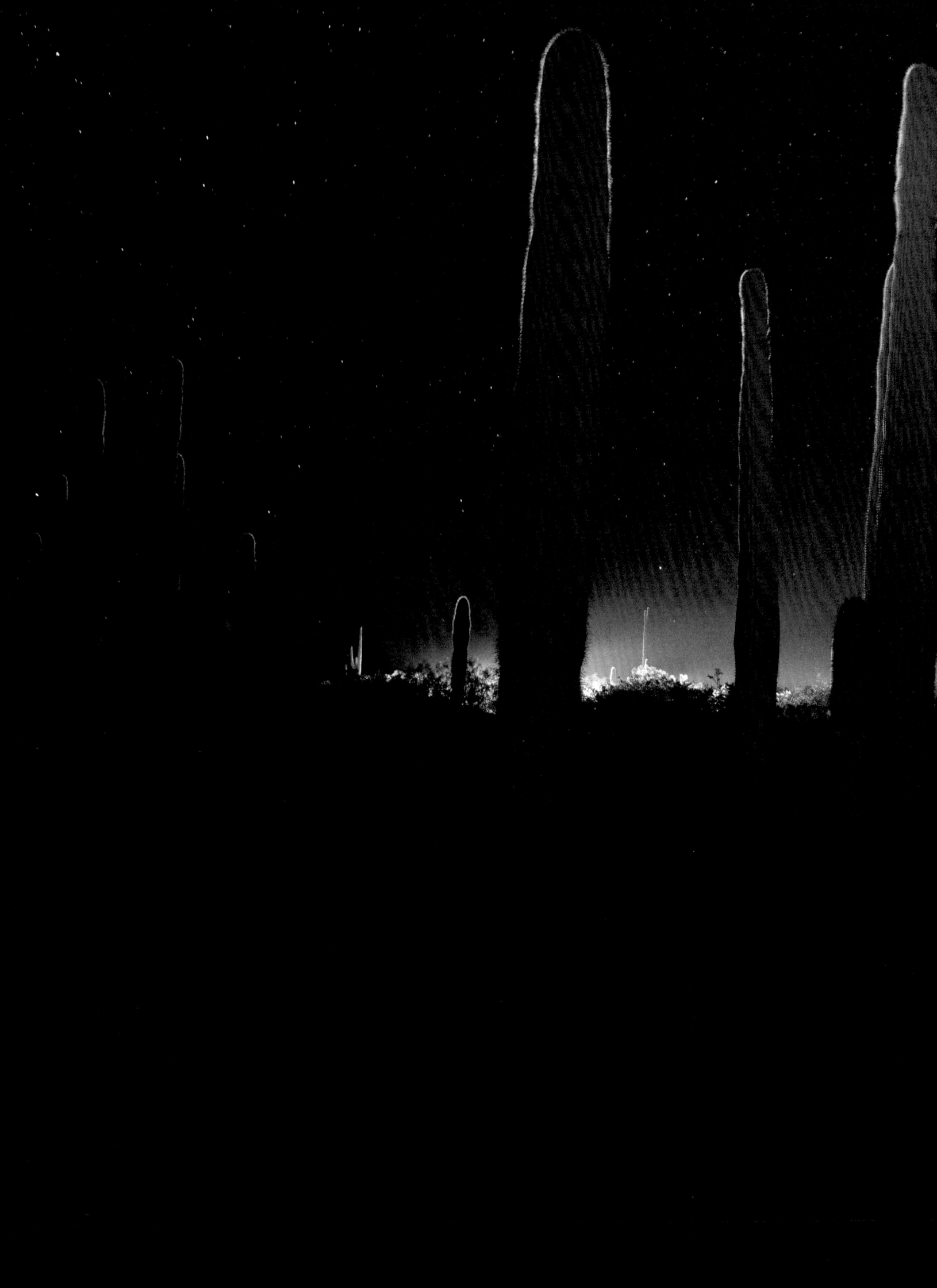

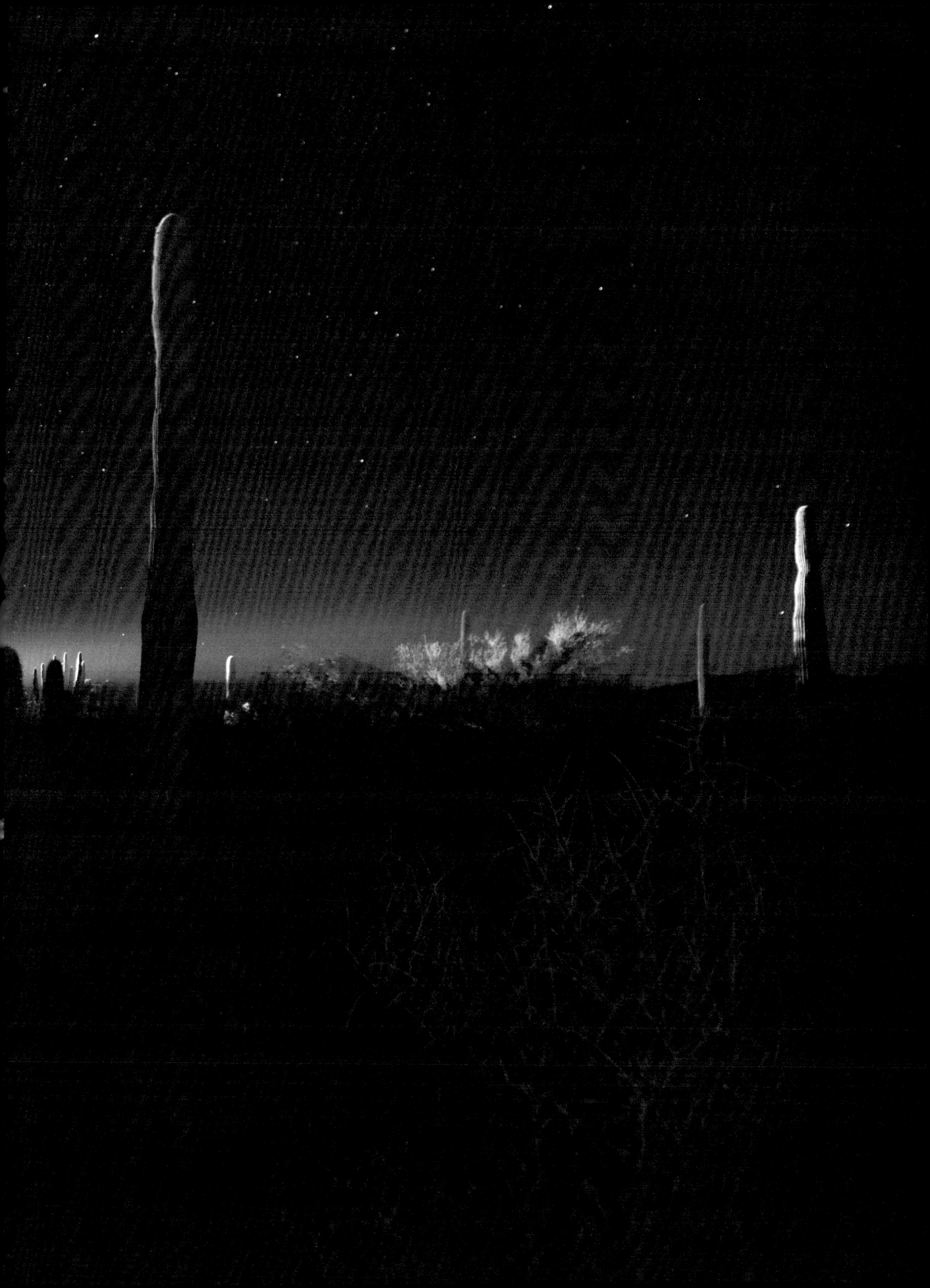

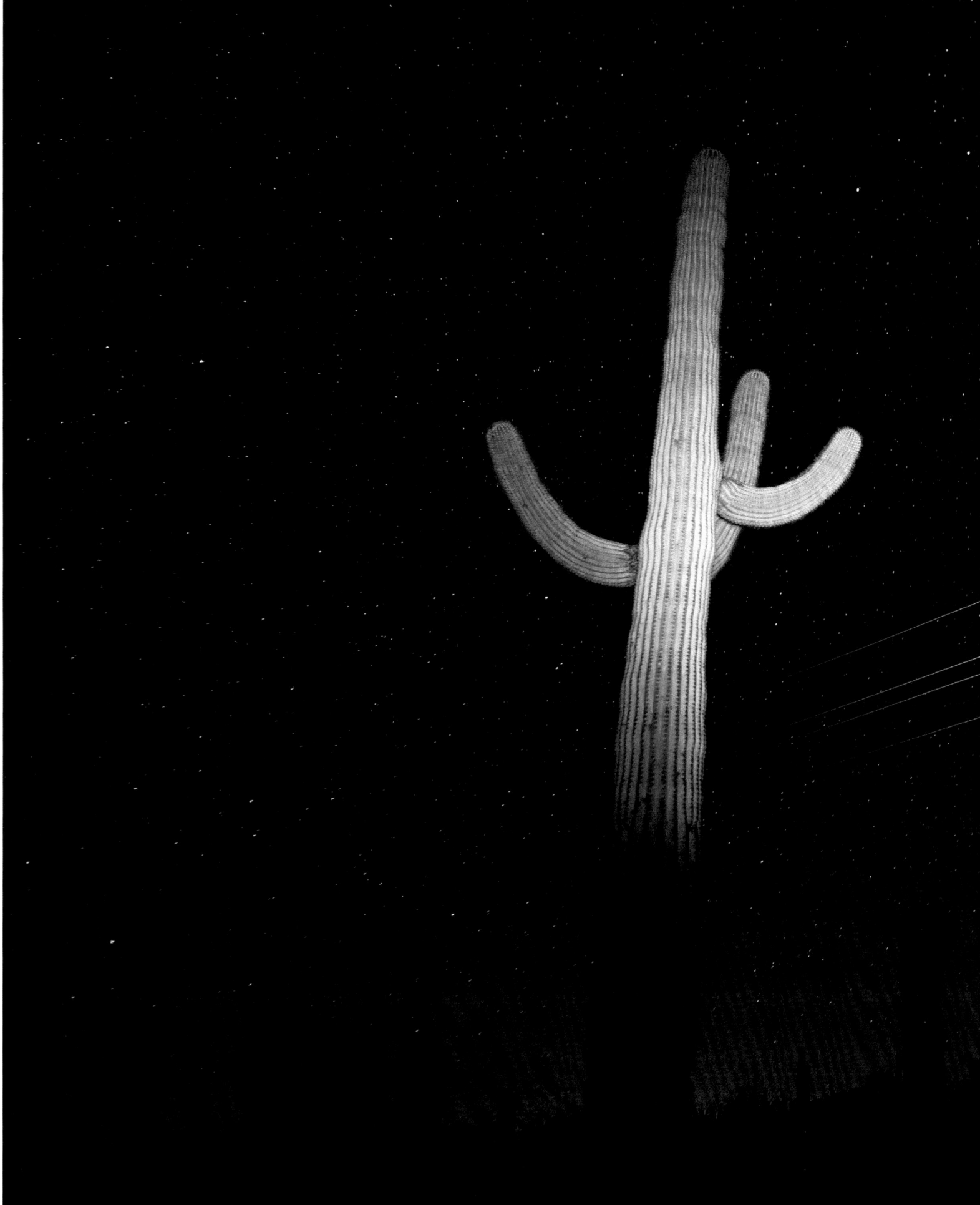

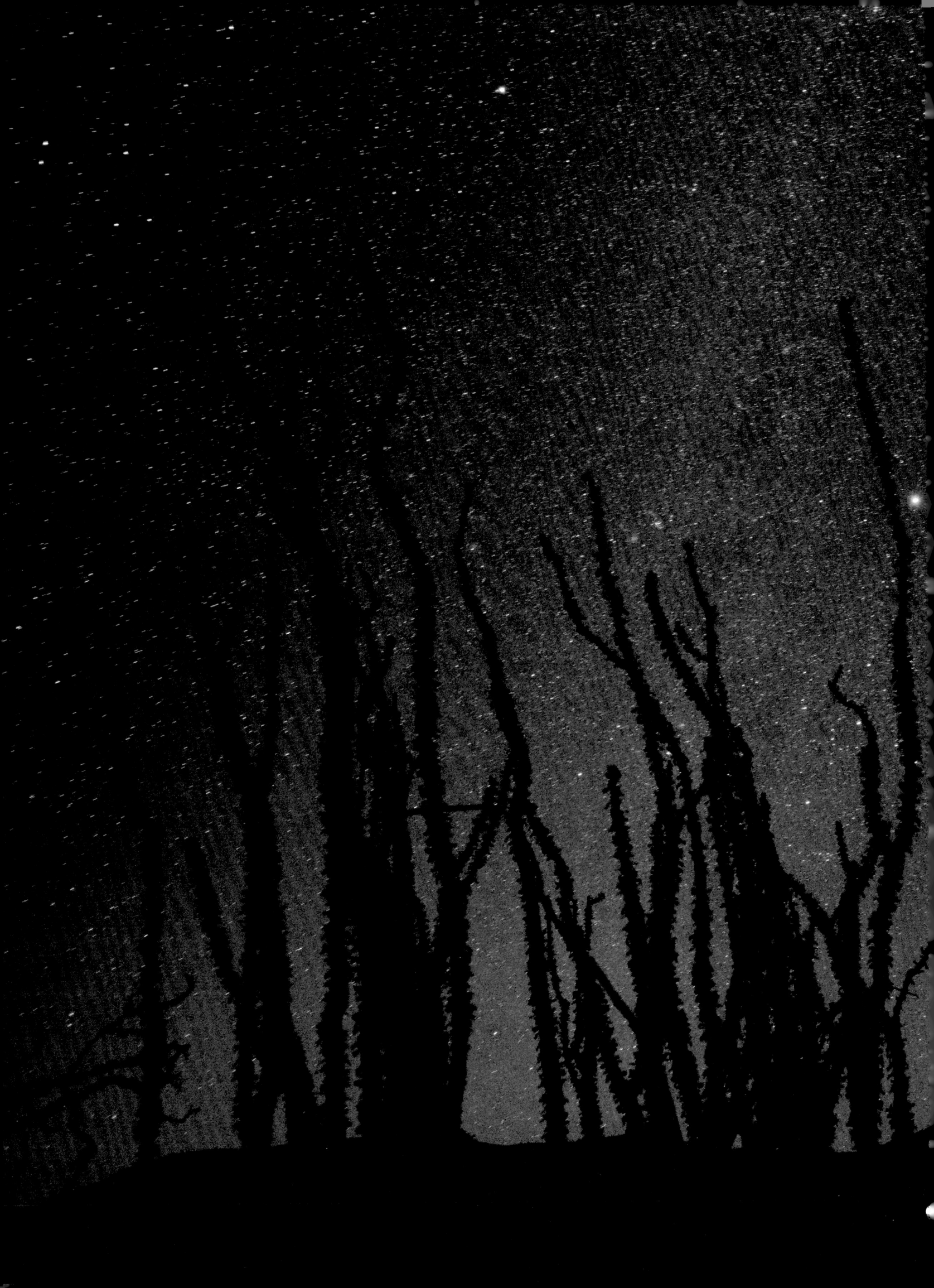

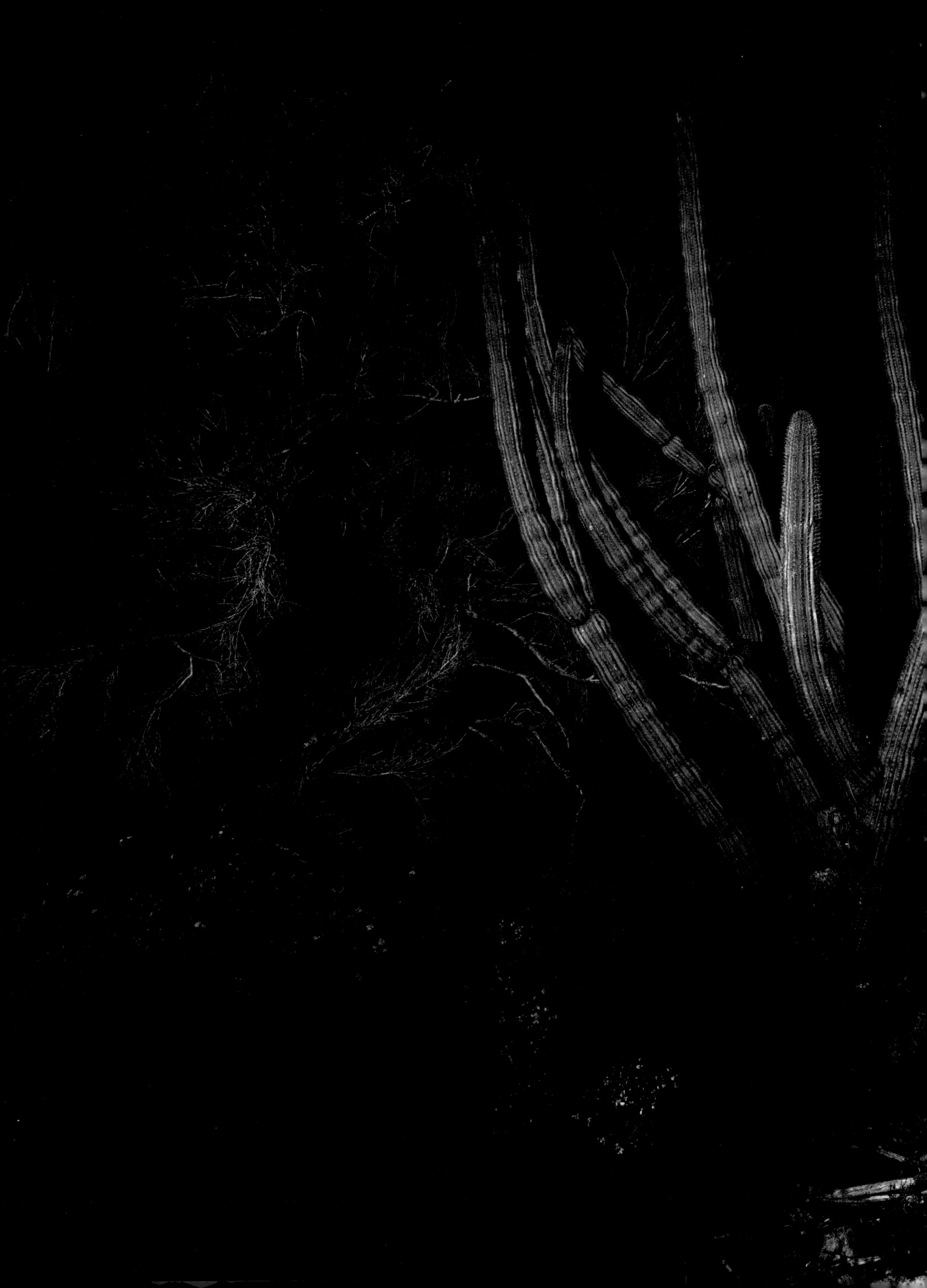

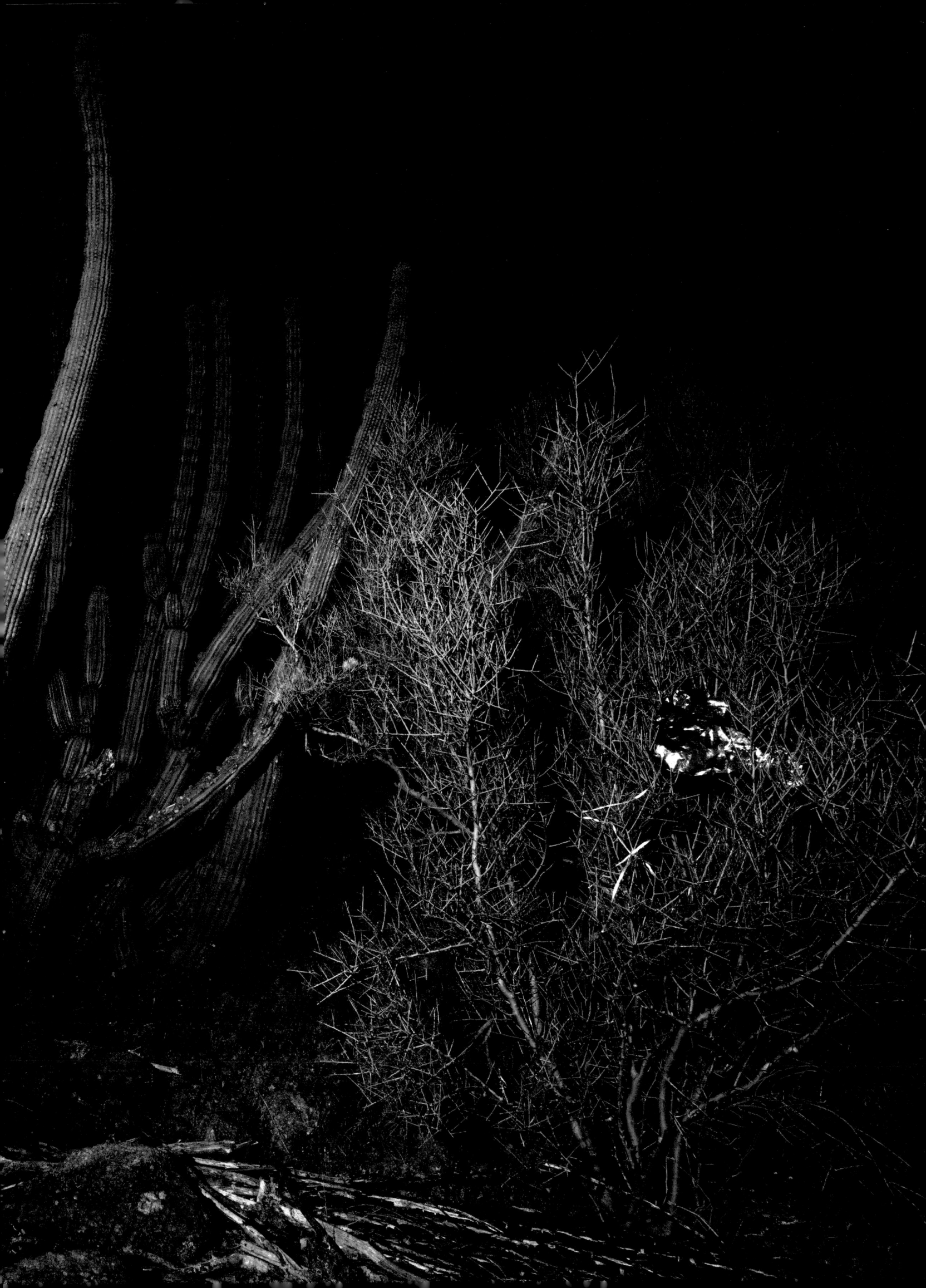

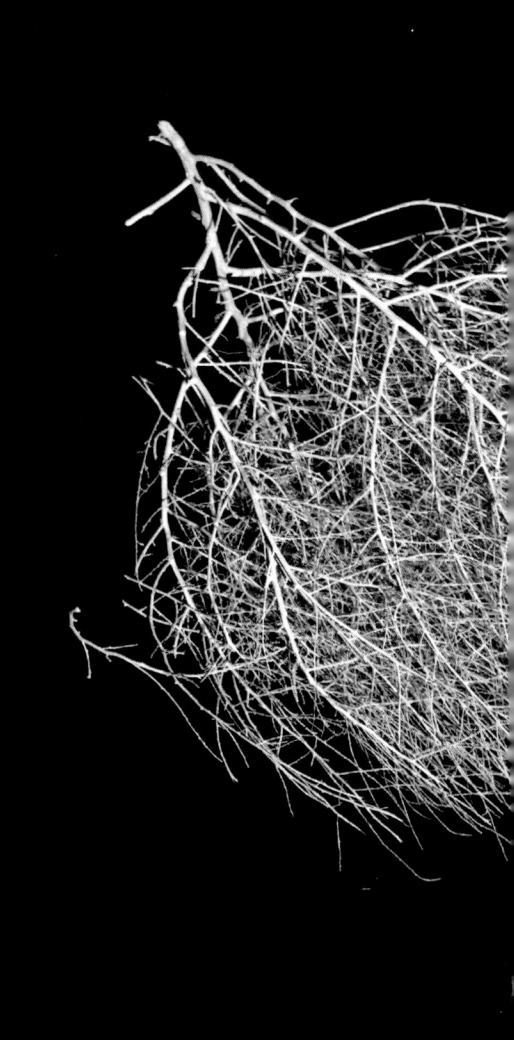

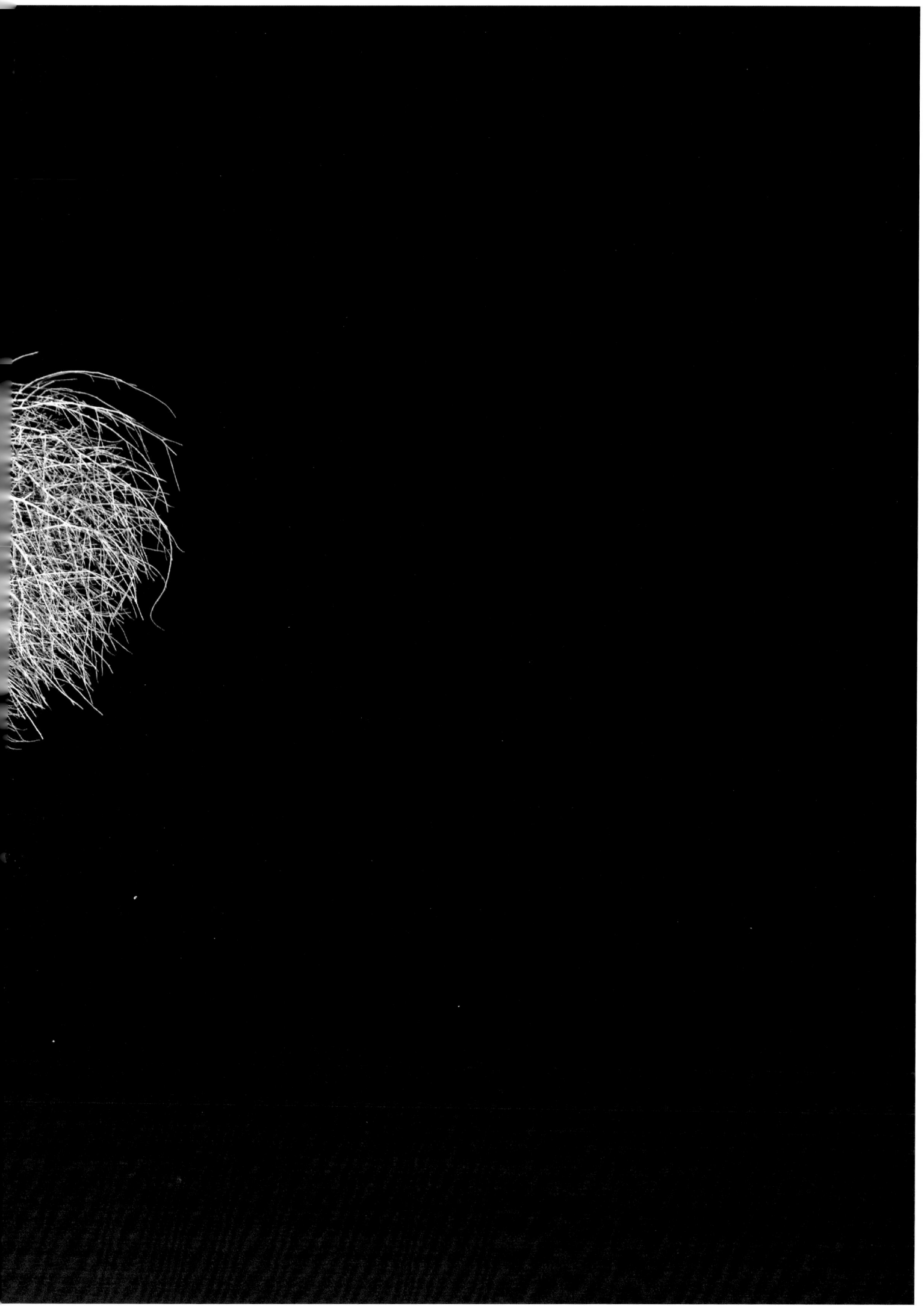

Truck Crossing Sonoran Desert, 2017

Saguaro Forest and Vehicle, 2017

Saguaro, Power Lines, and Bat Trail, 2018

Satellite Crossing Dotted Path of Airplane Between Ocotillo and
   Side View of Milky Way, 2017

Organ Cactus, Mylar Balloon, Sonoran Desert, 2018

Tumbleweed, Invasive Russian Thistle, 2019

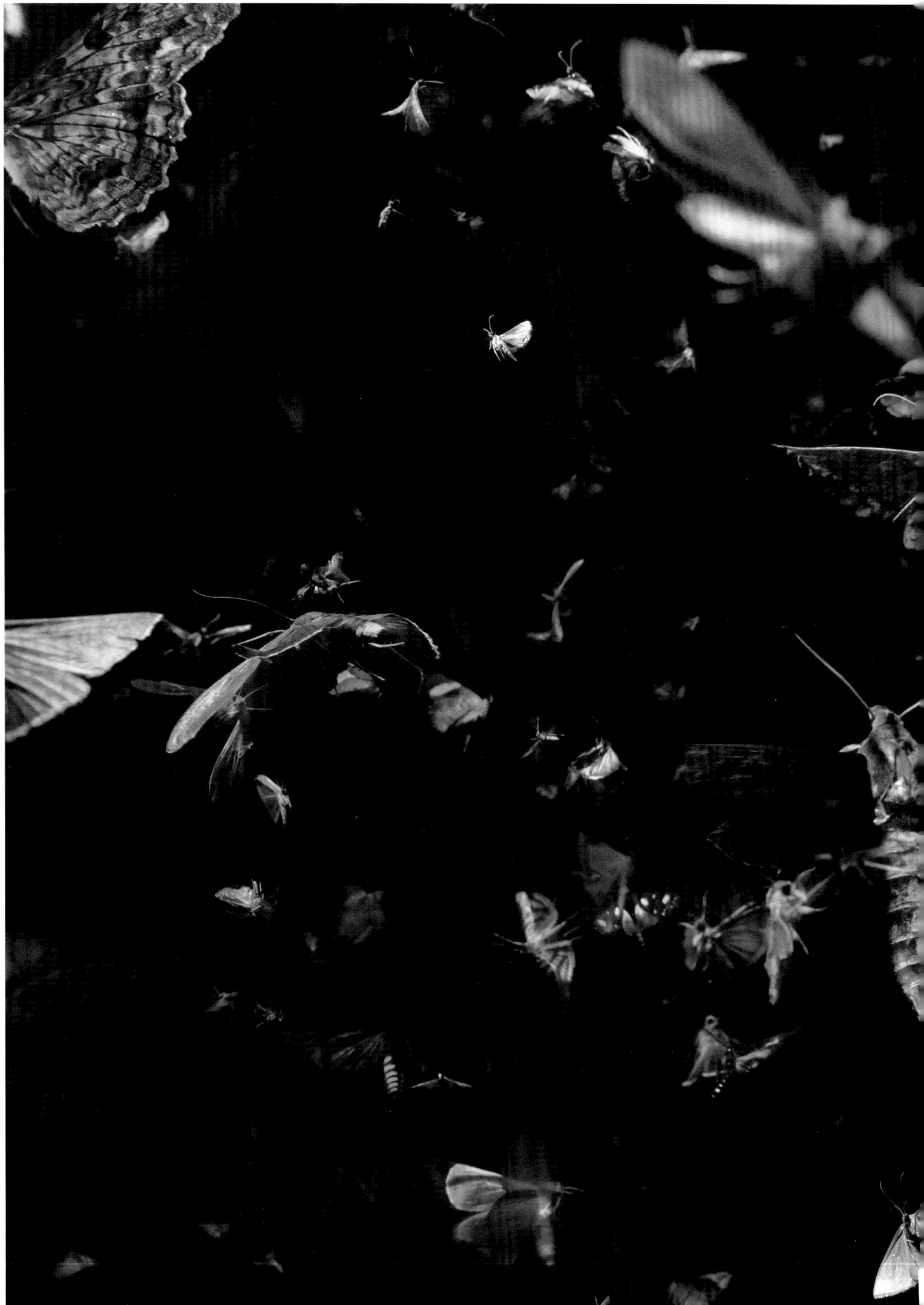

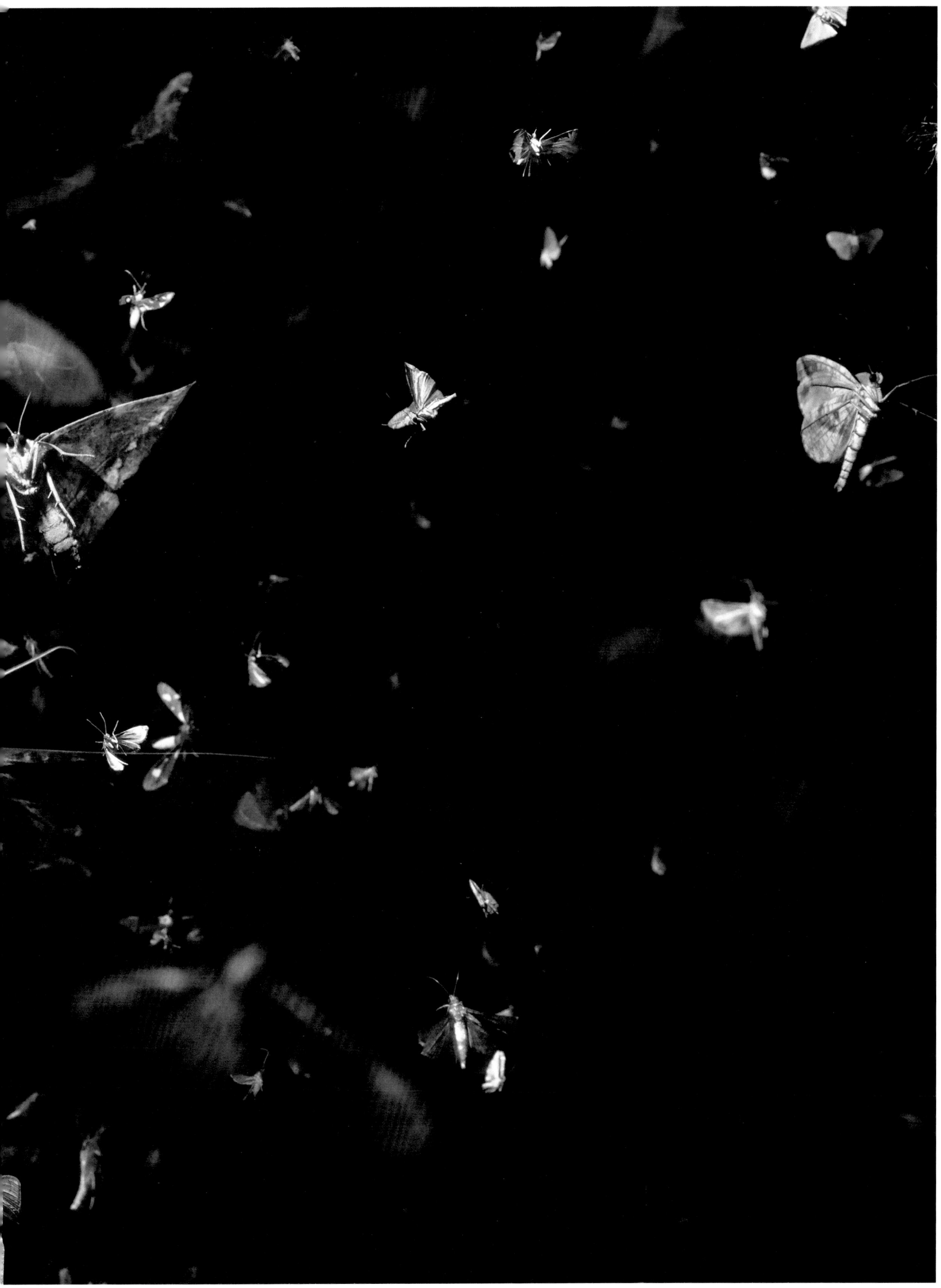

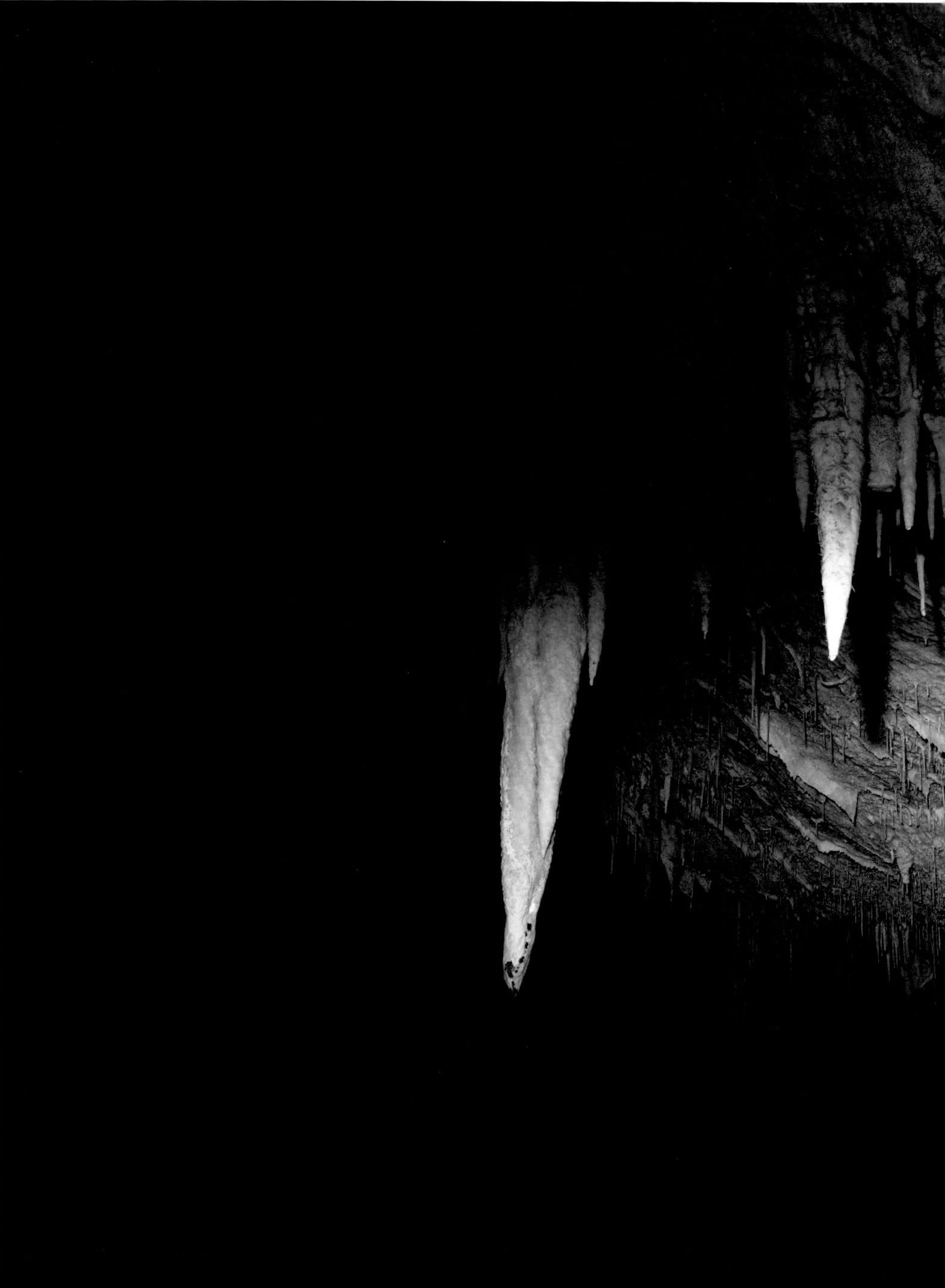

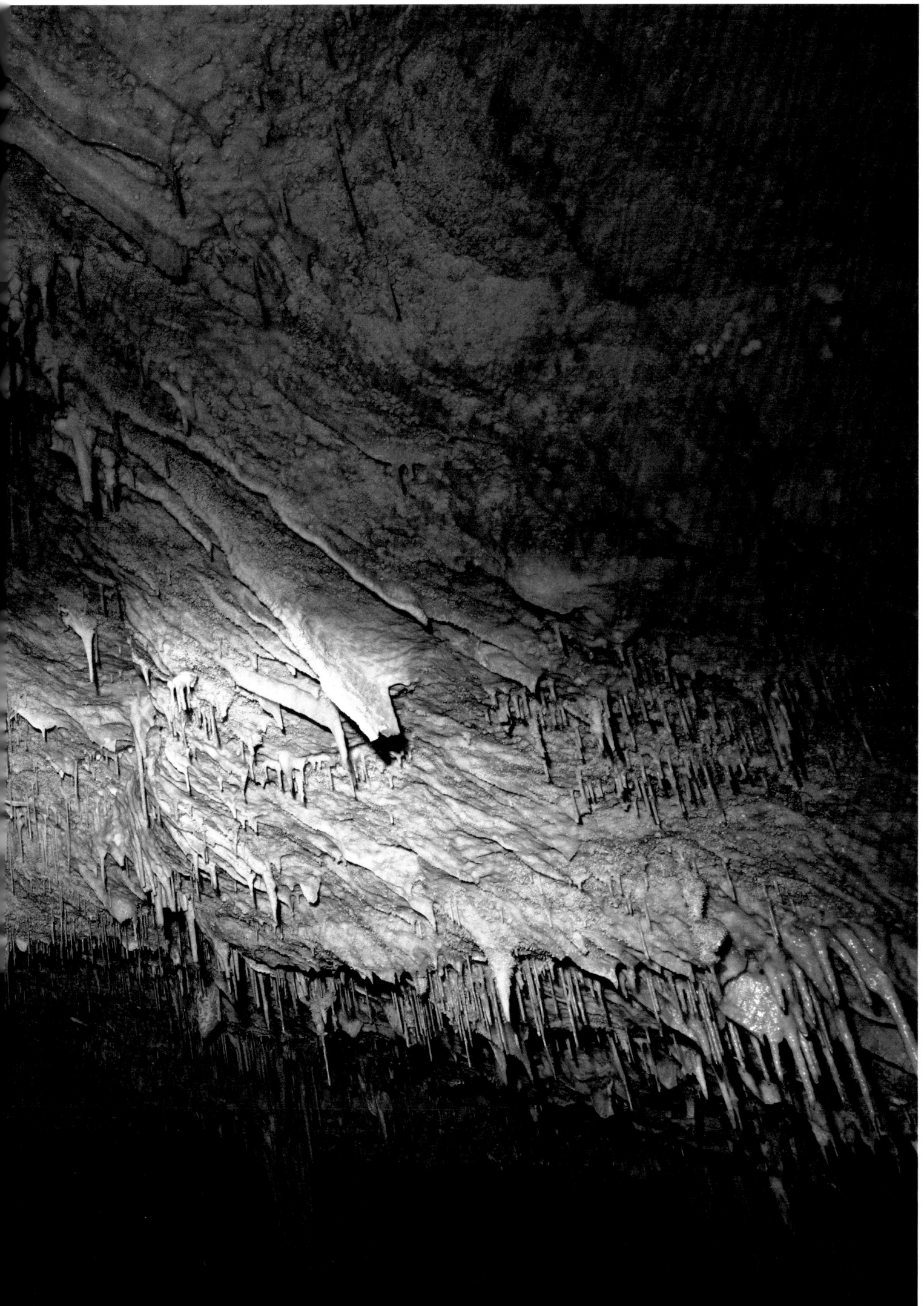

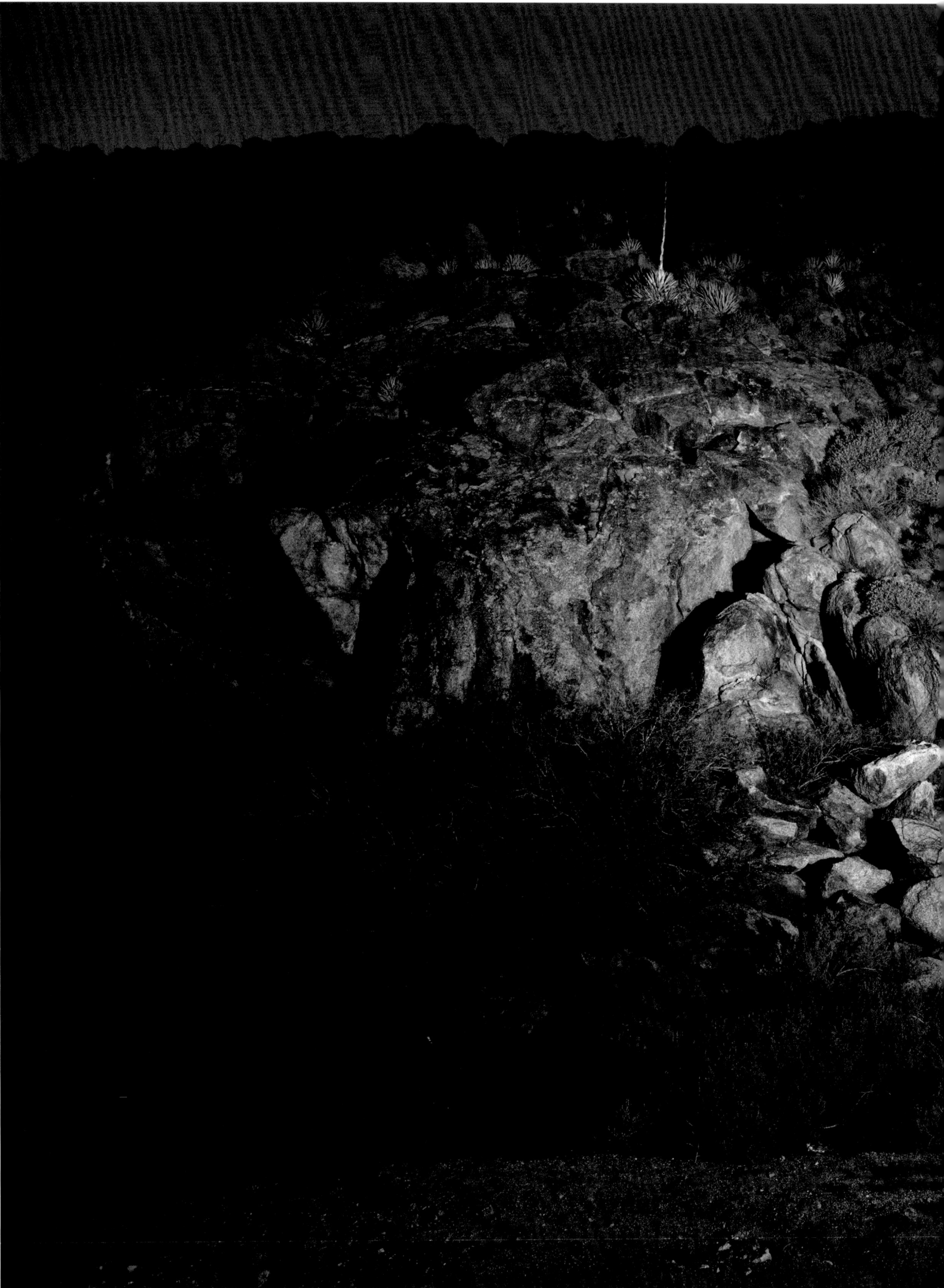

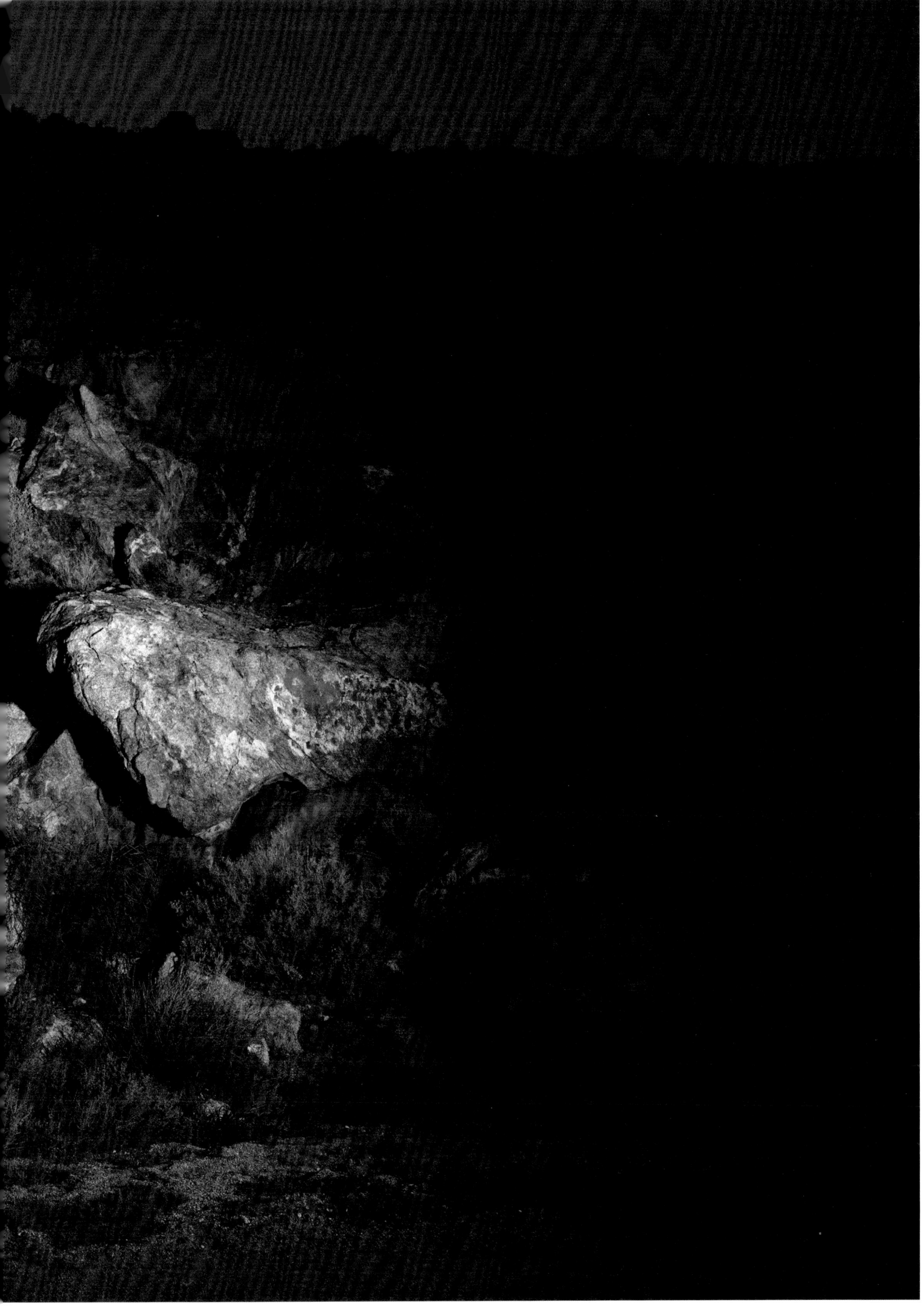

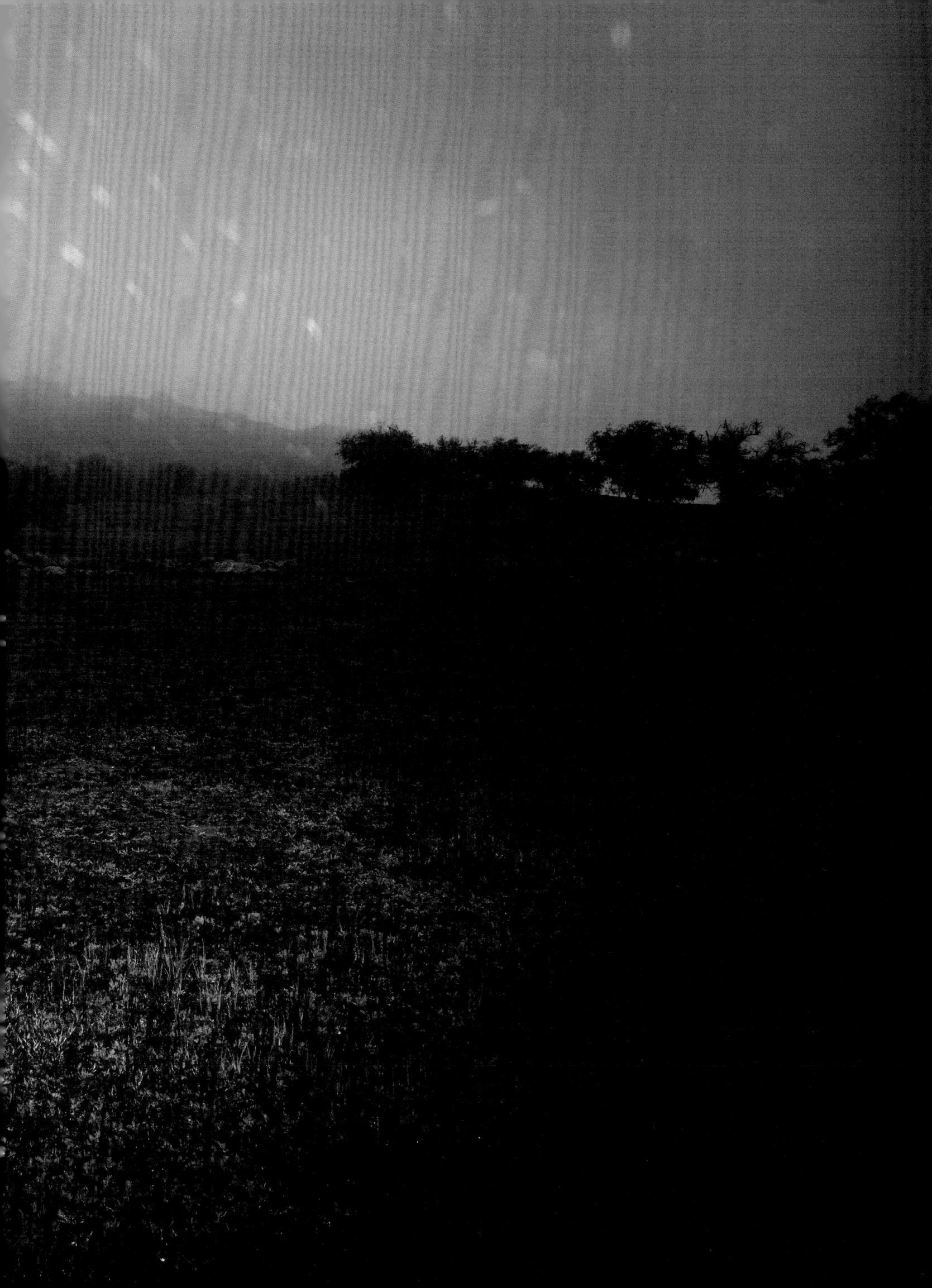

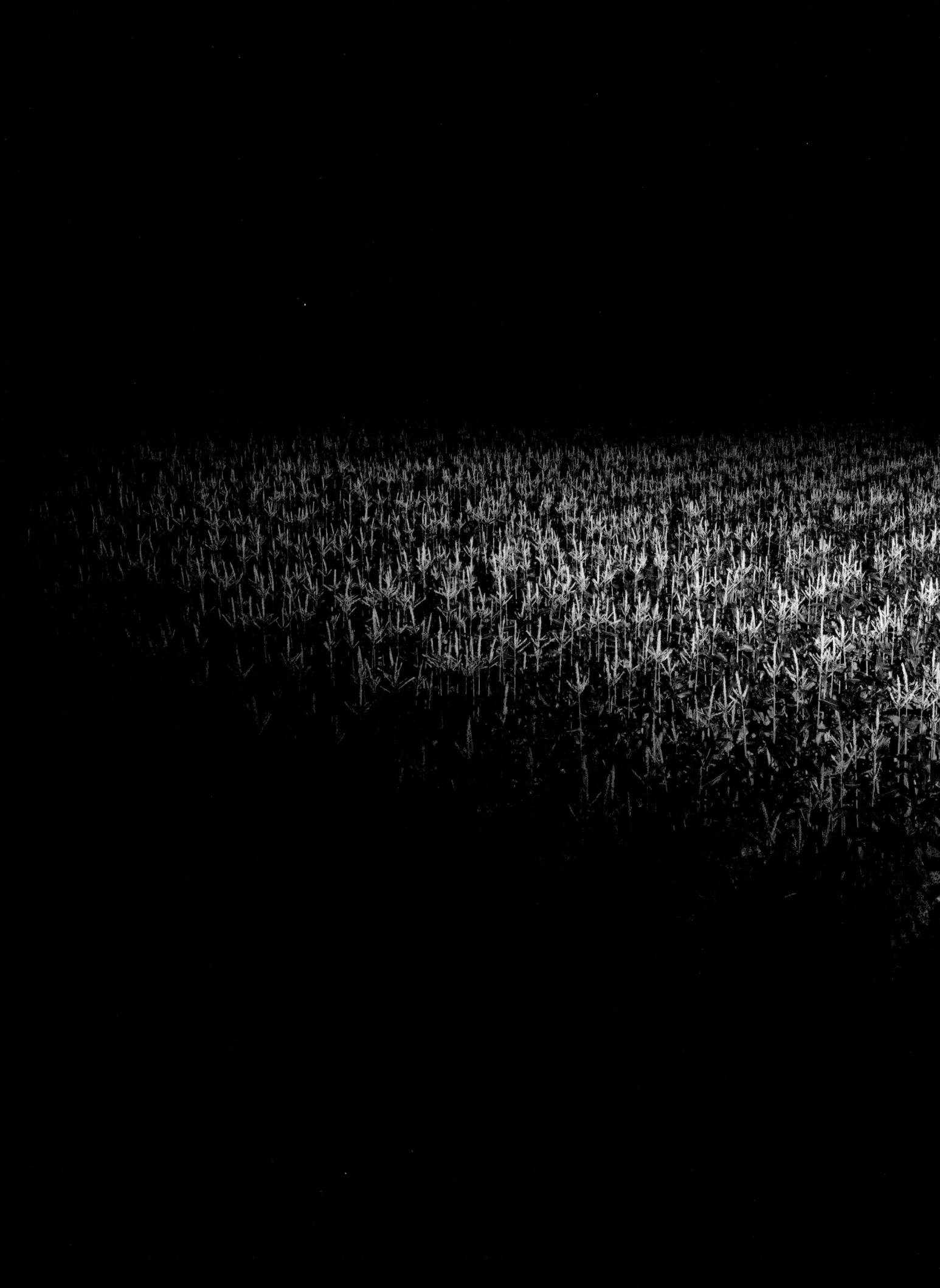

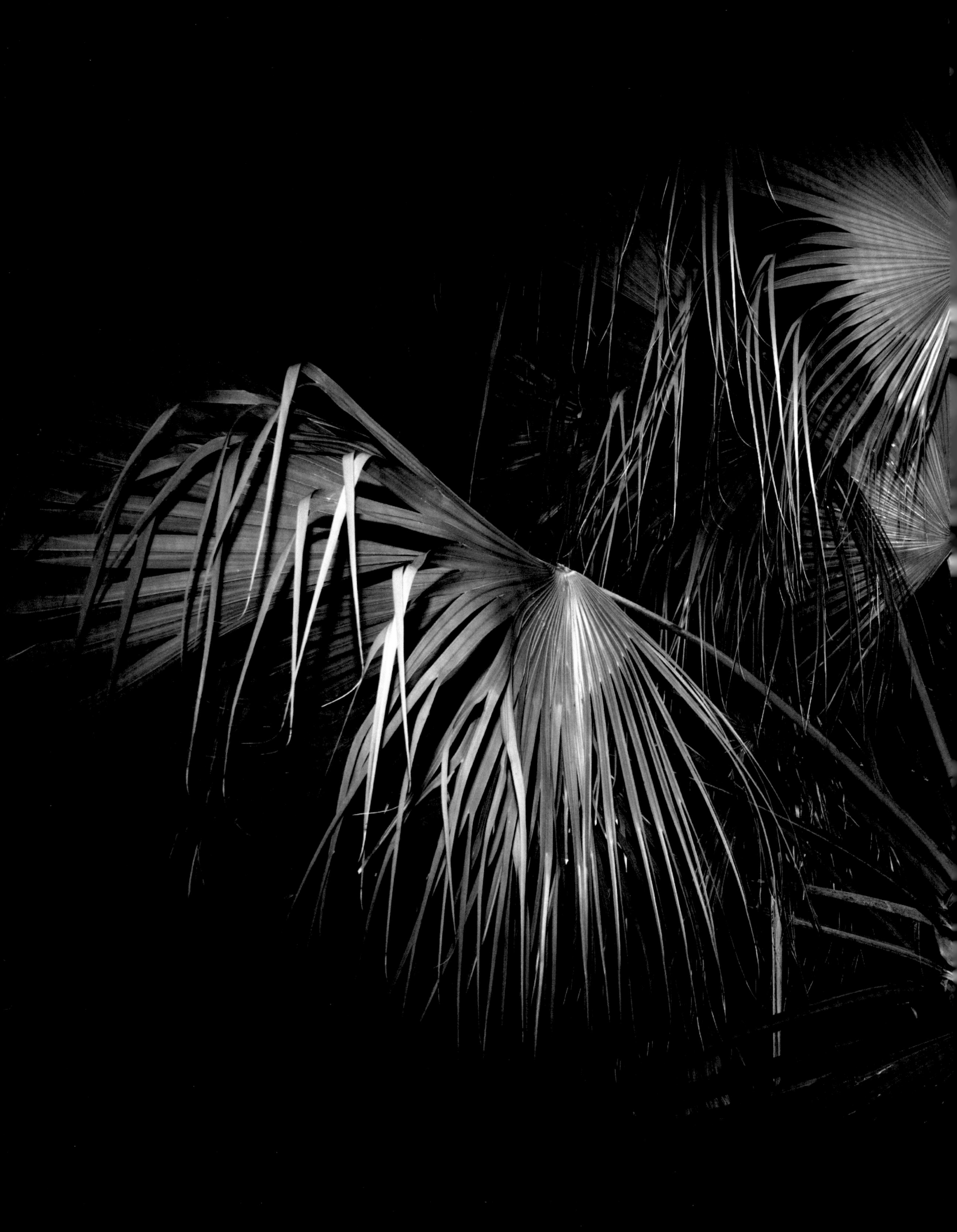

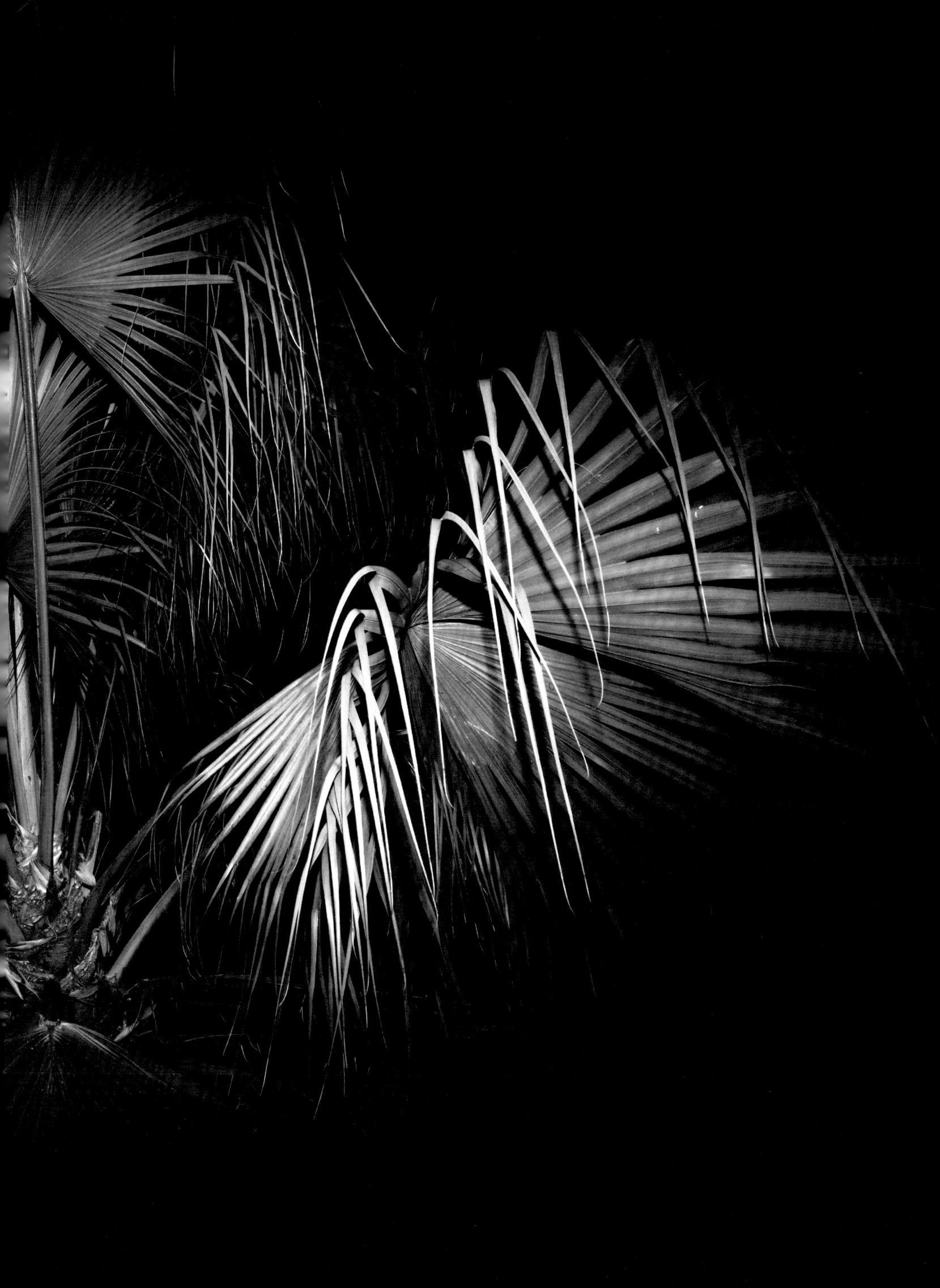

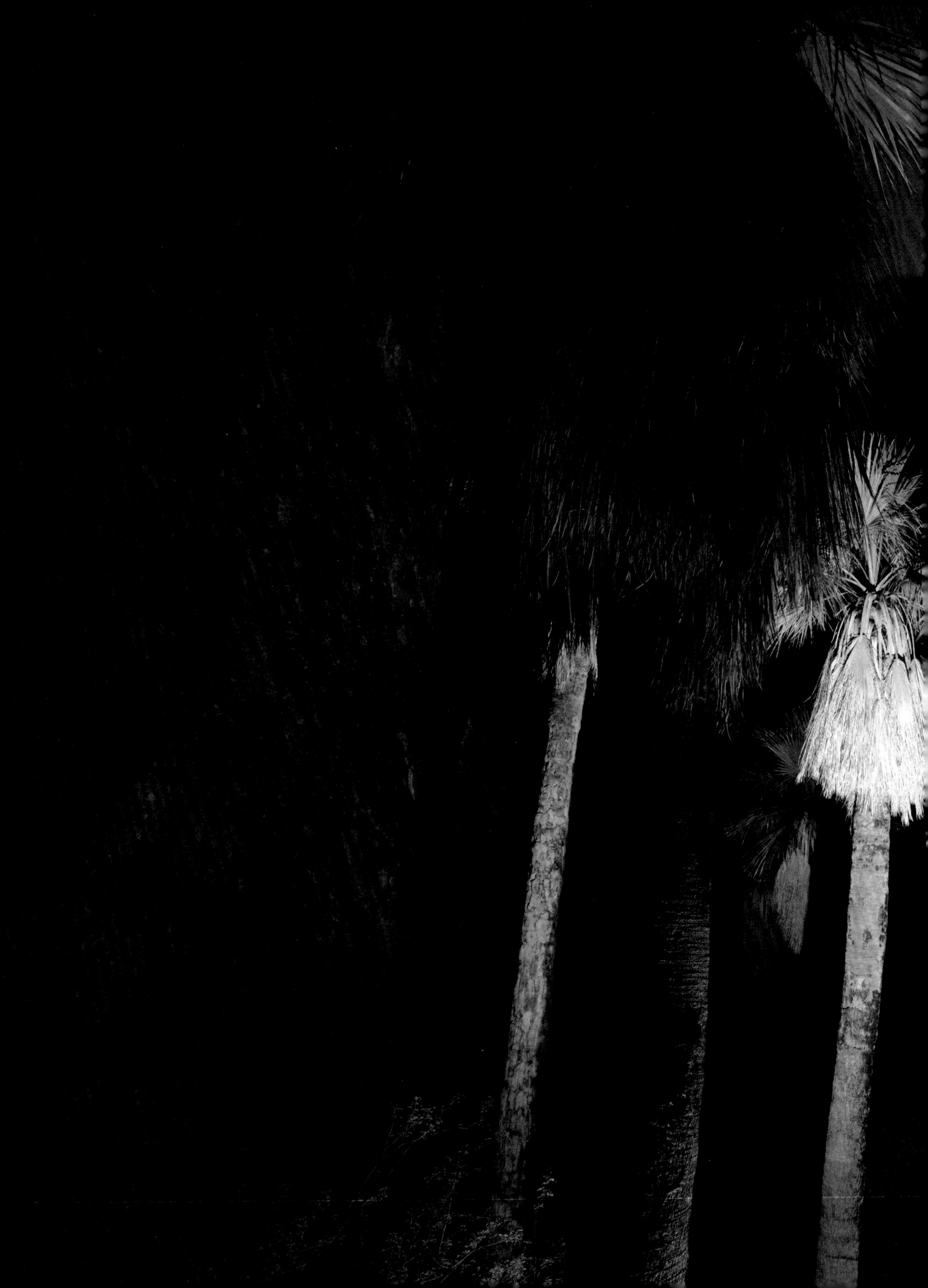

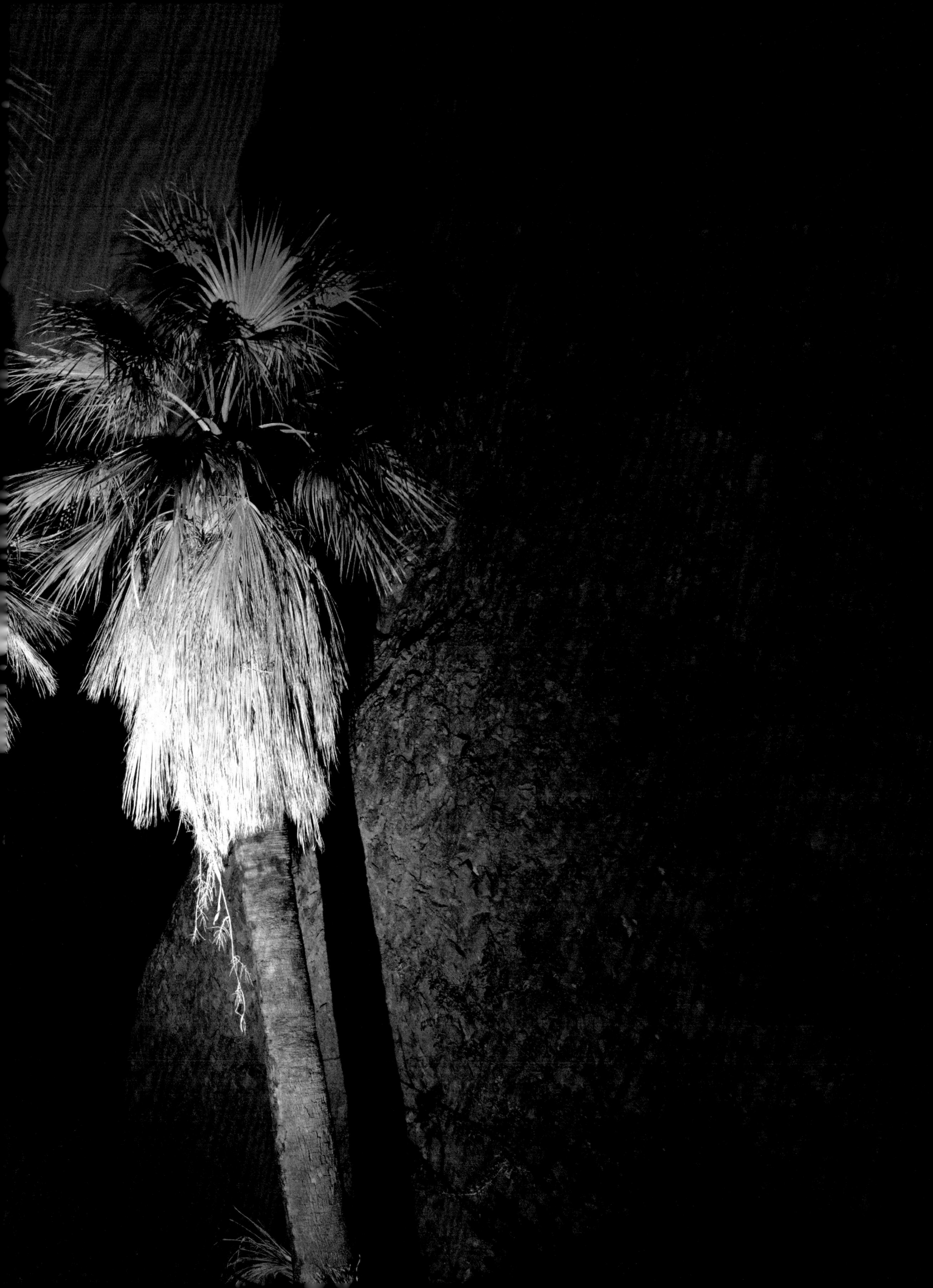

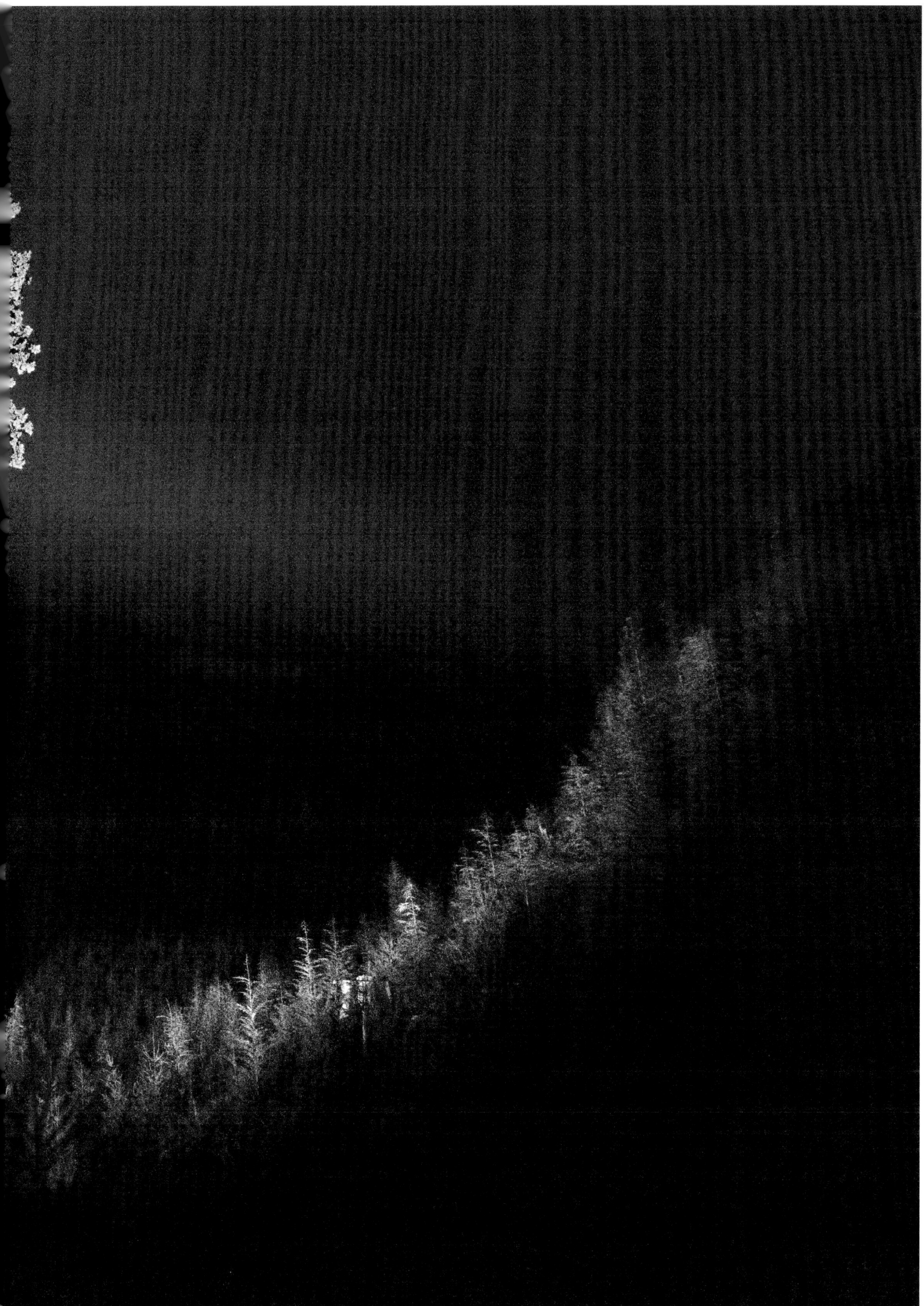

Insects Swarming Artificial Light Near Equator, Panama, 2019

Whole and Molested Stalactites, Carribean Cave, 2018

Road Blasting Site, 2017

Cleared Grazing Land, West Coast, 2017

Cornfield, Sonoran Desert, 2019

Endangered Bermuda Palmetto, 2018

Only Existing Grove of Natural Native Palms in Arizona, High in
   Mountain Ravine, 2018

Second-Largest Douglas Fir in Canada Surrounded by Clear-cut, 2019

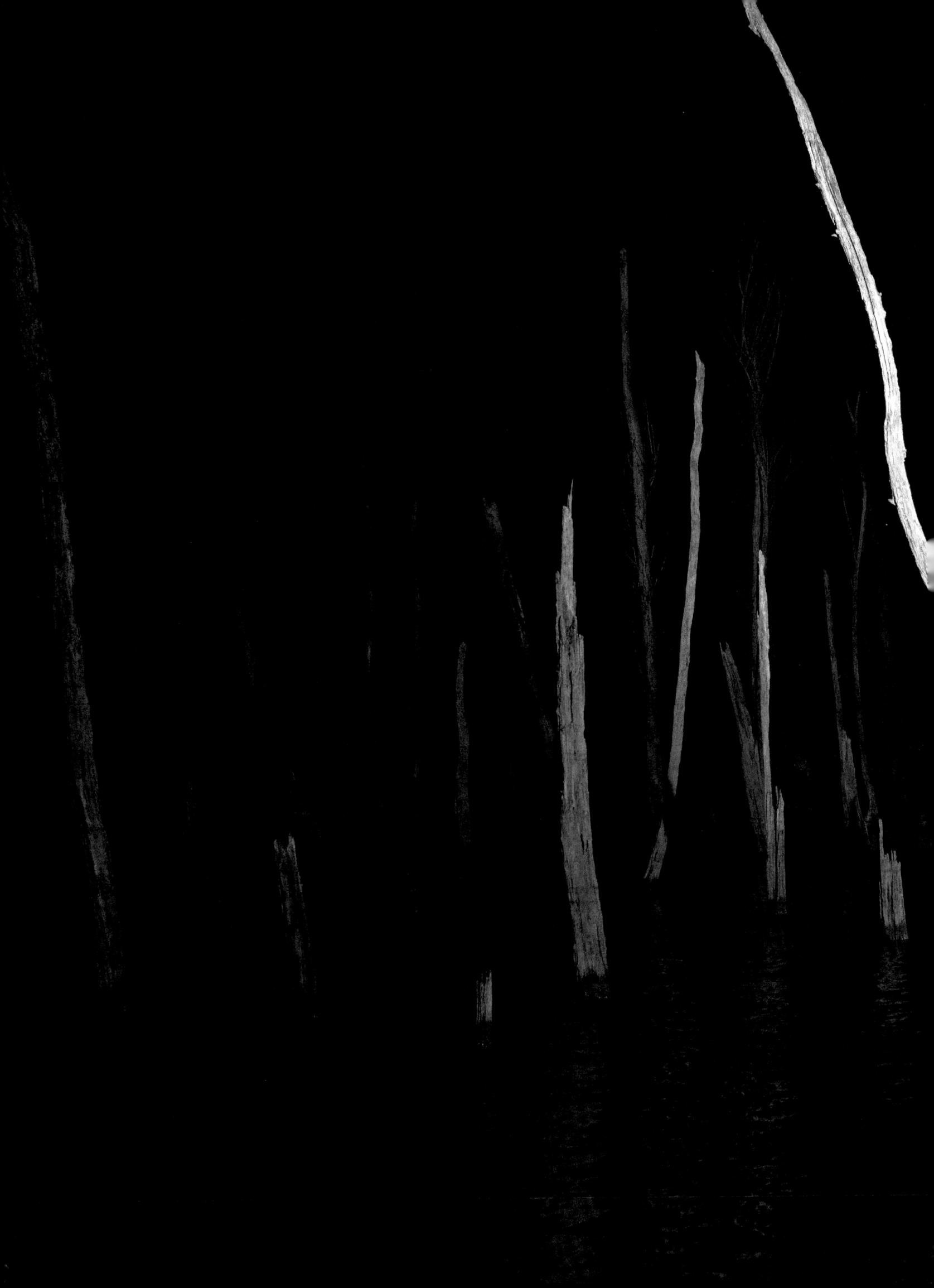

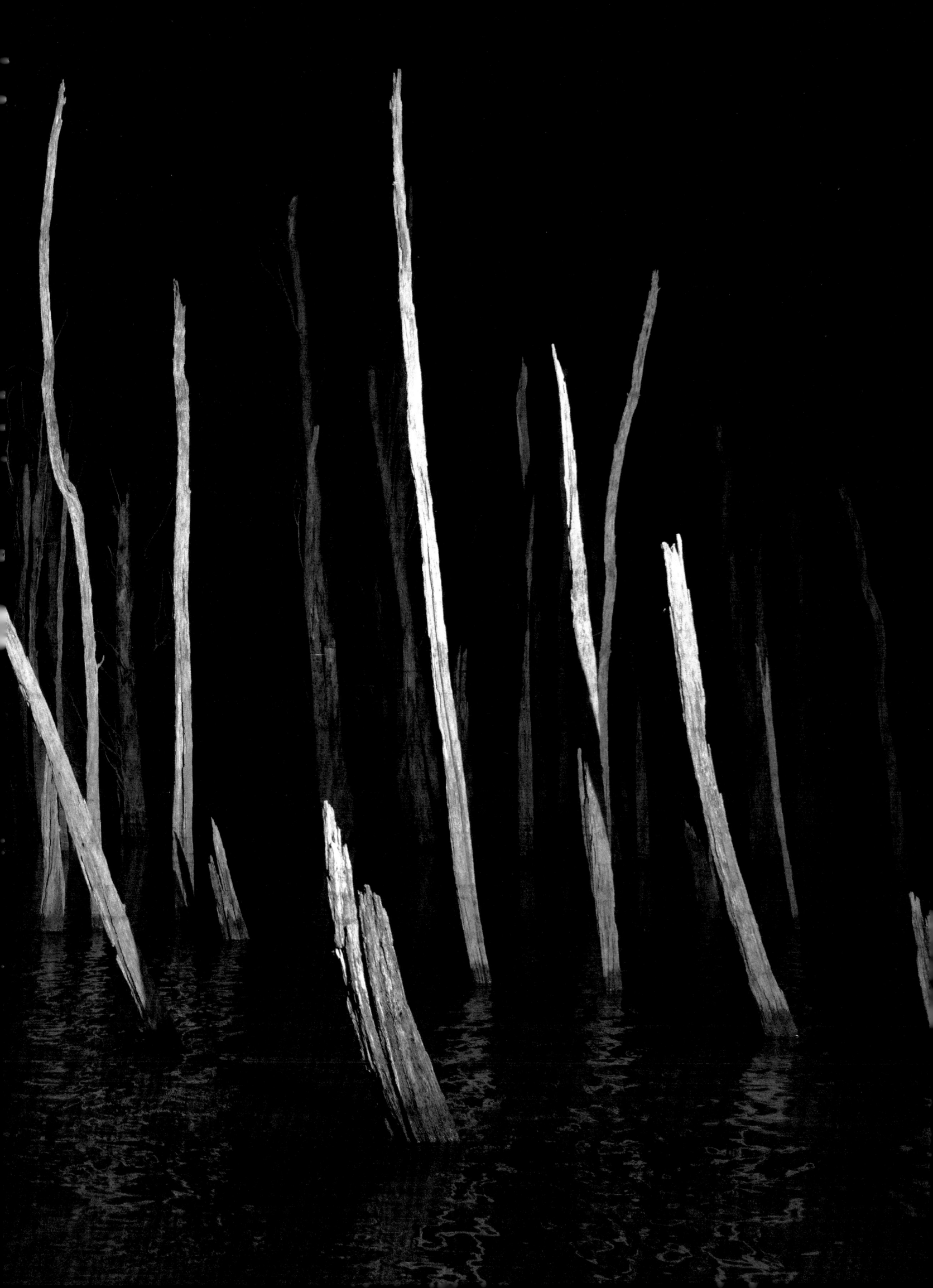

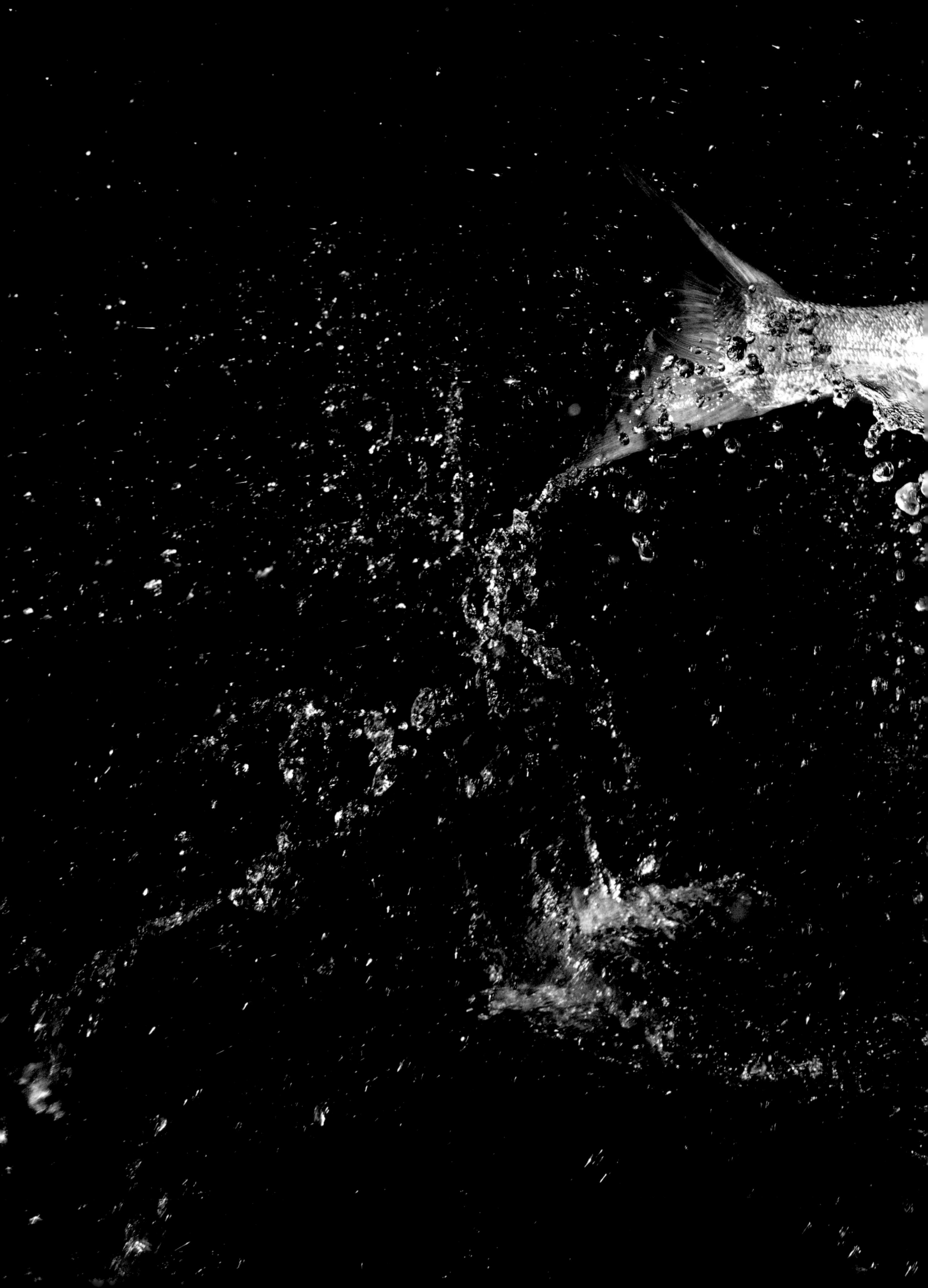

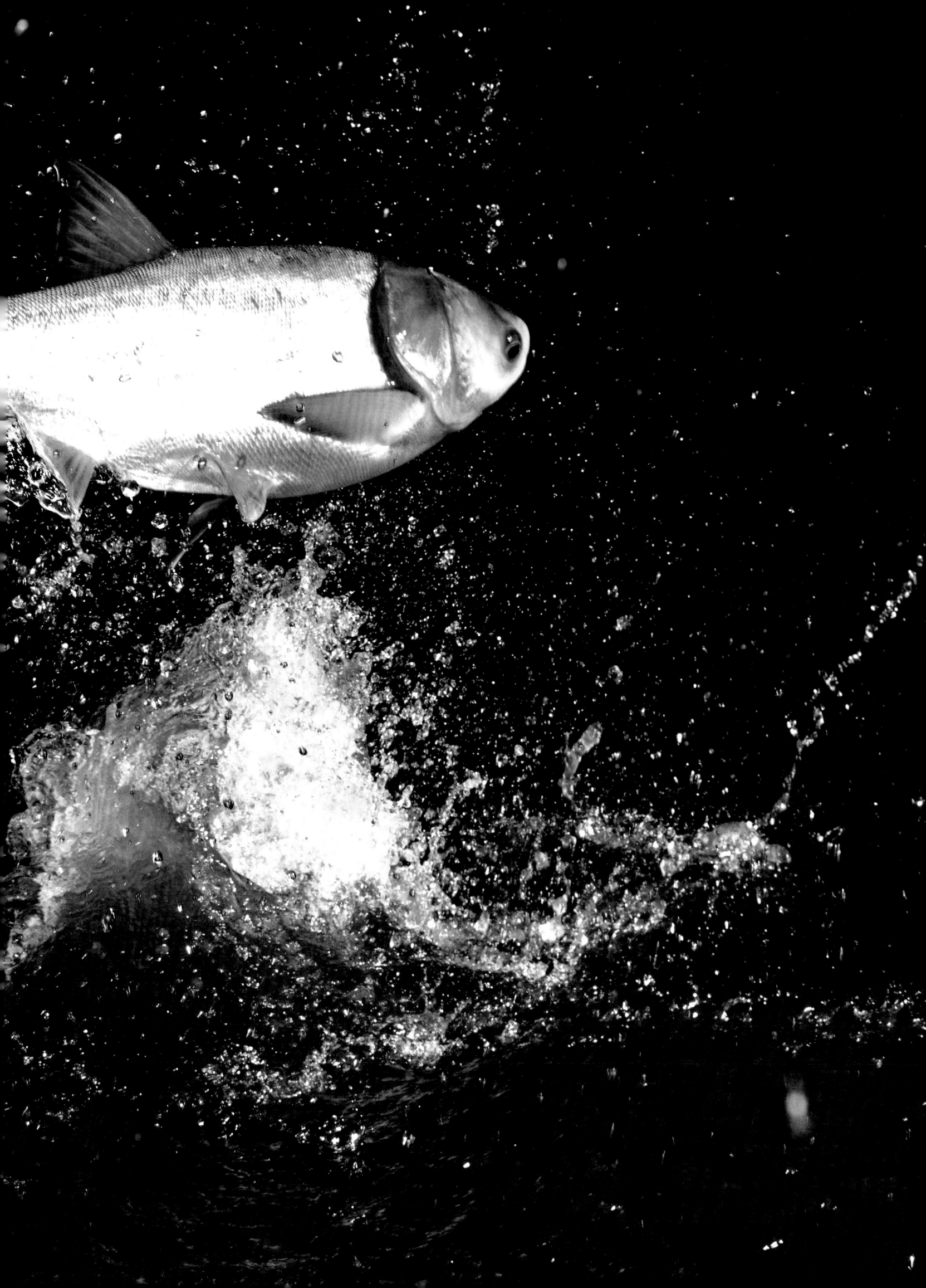

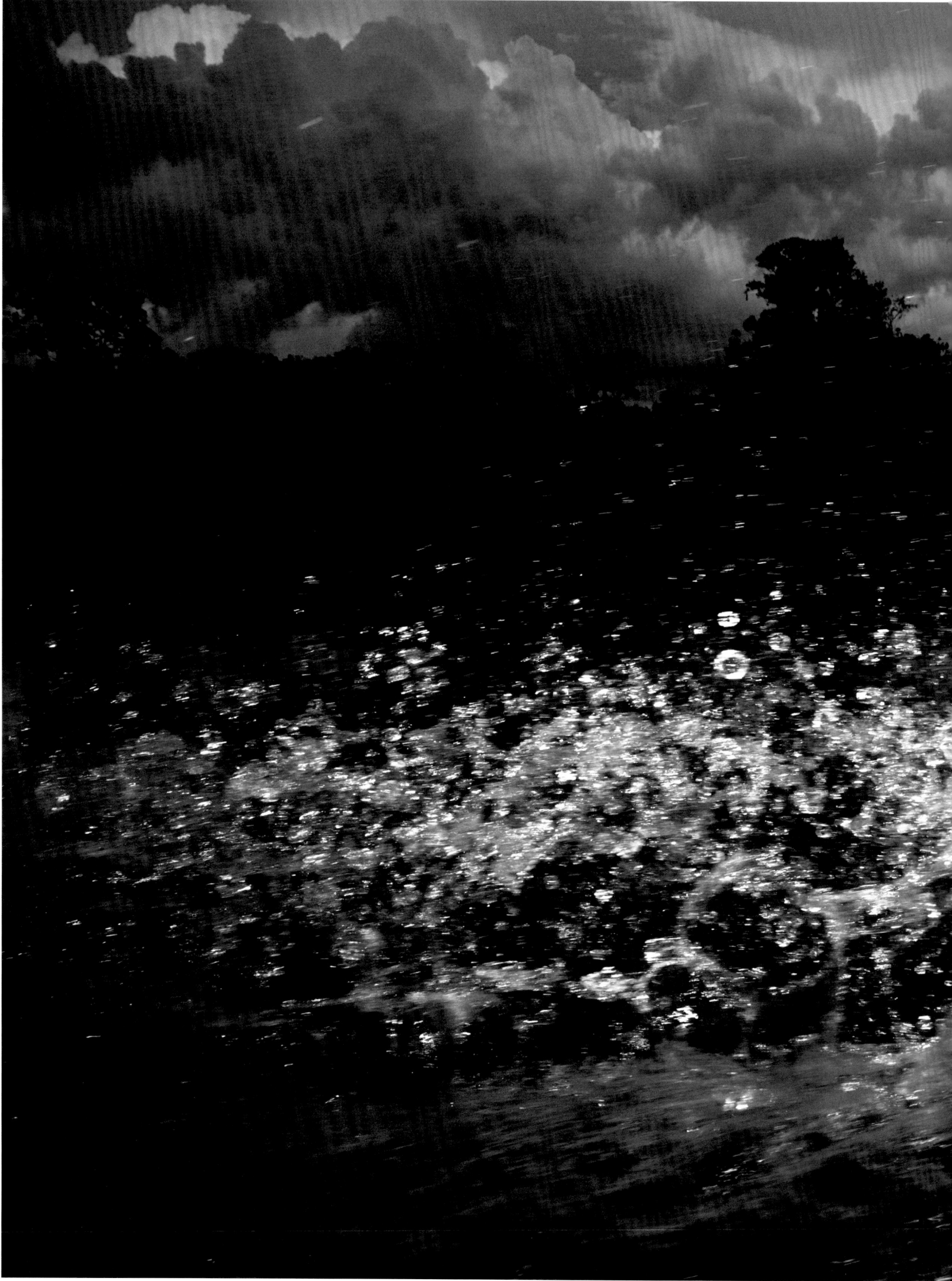

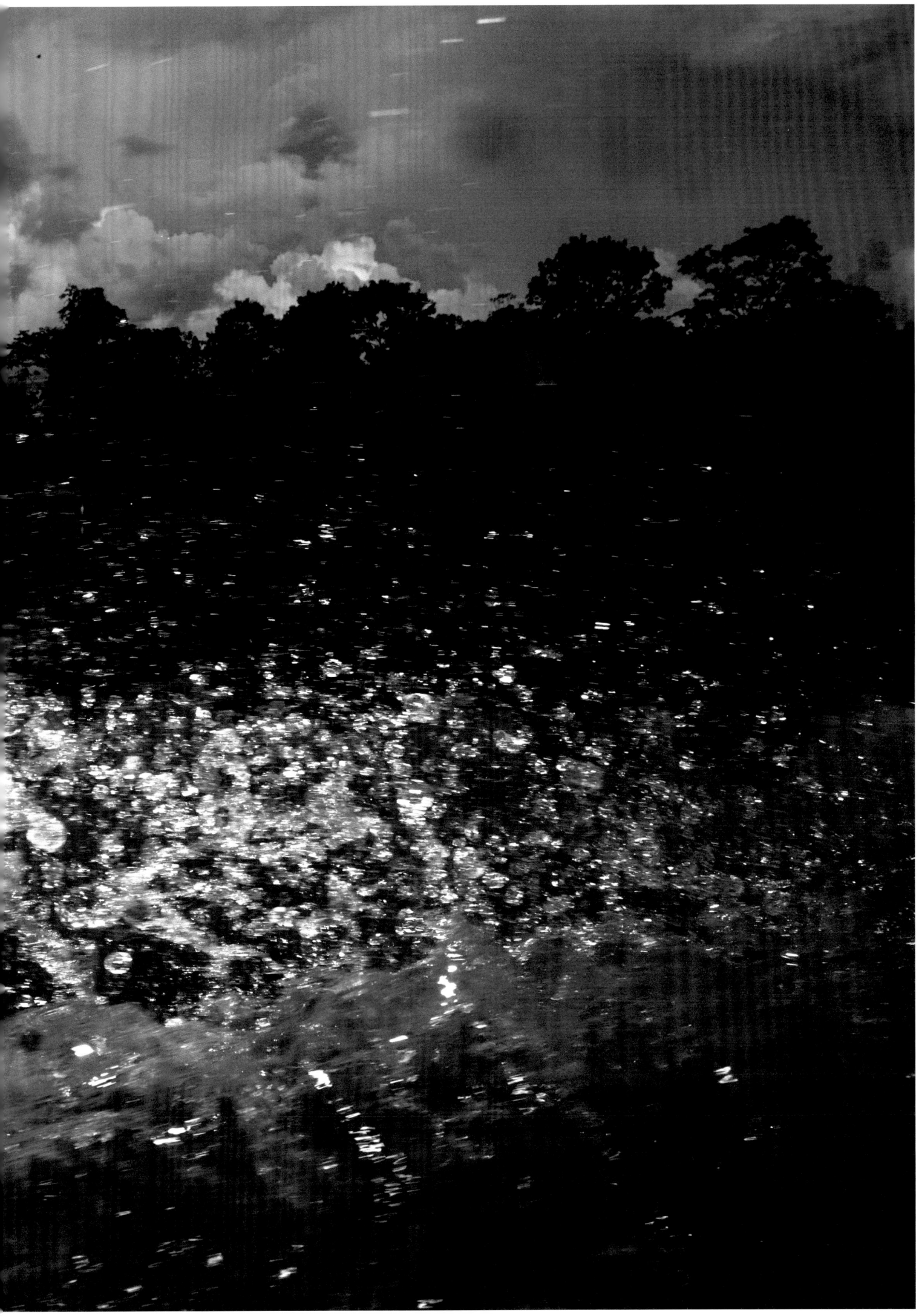

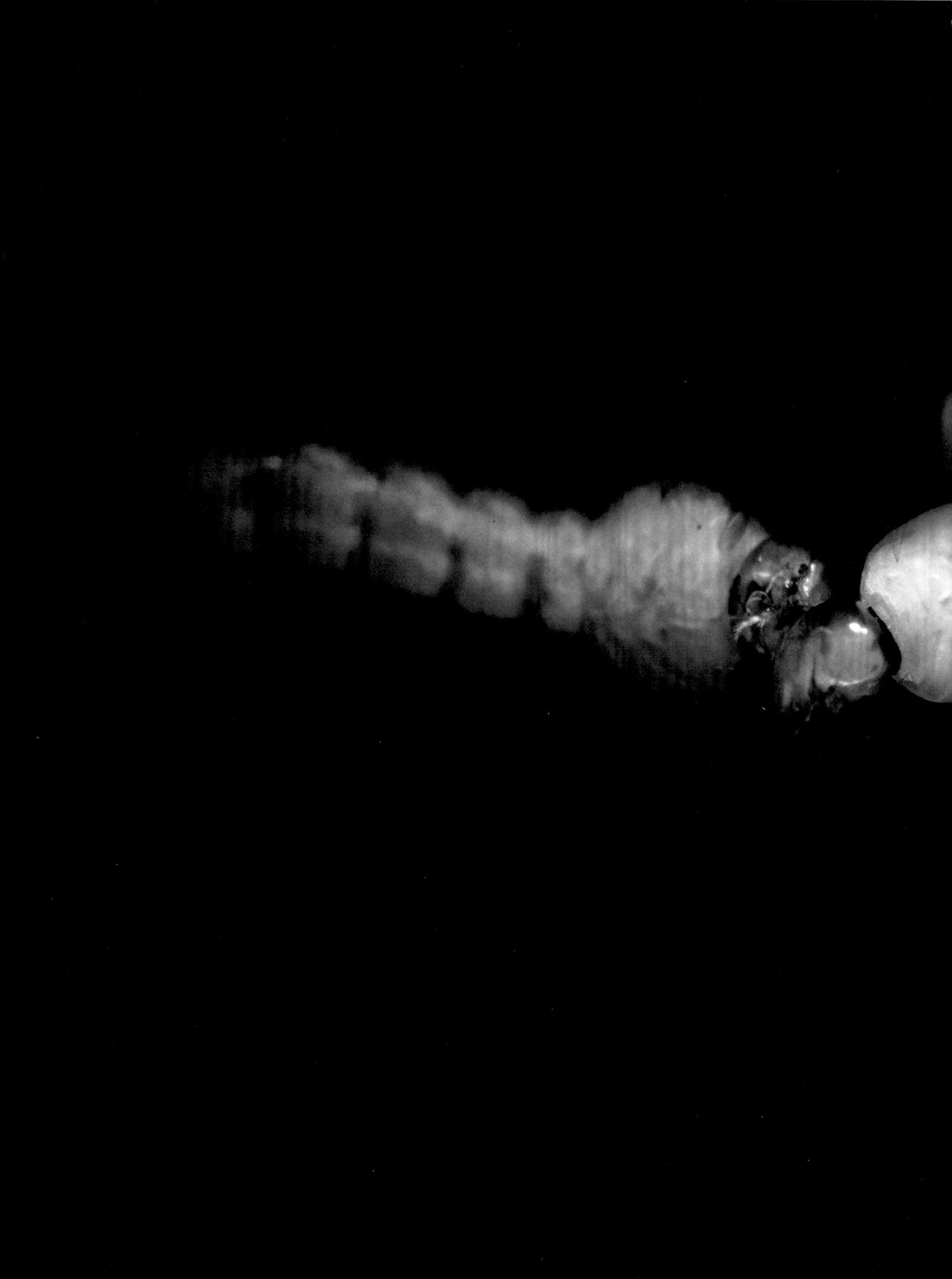

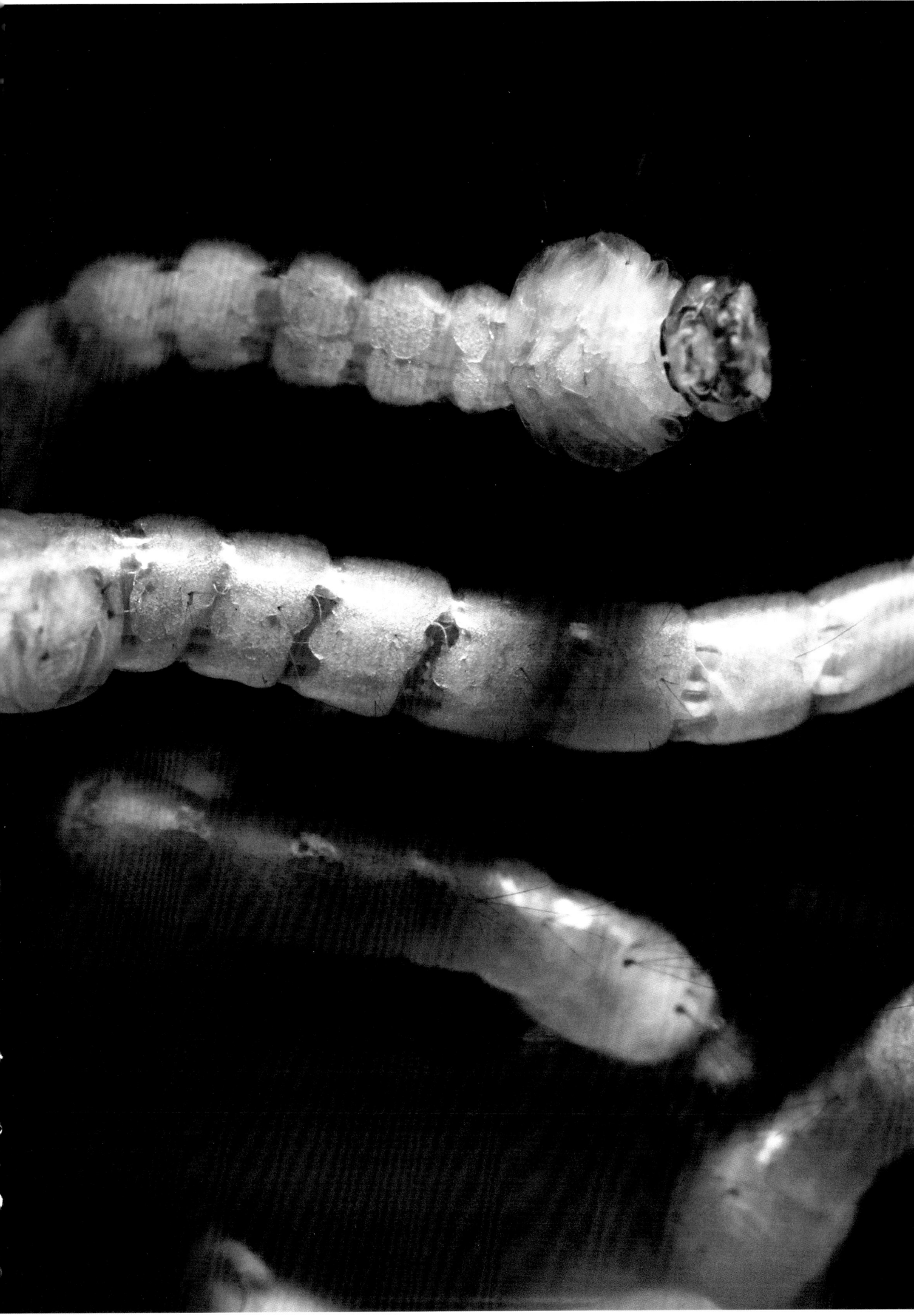

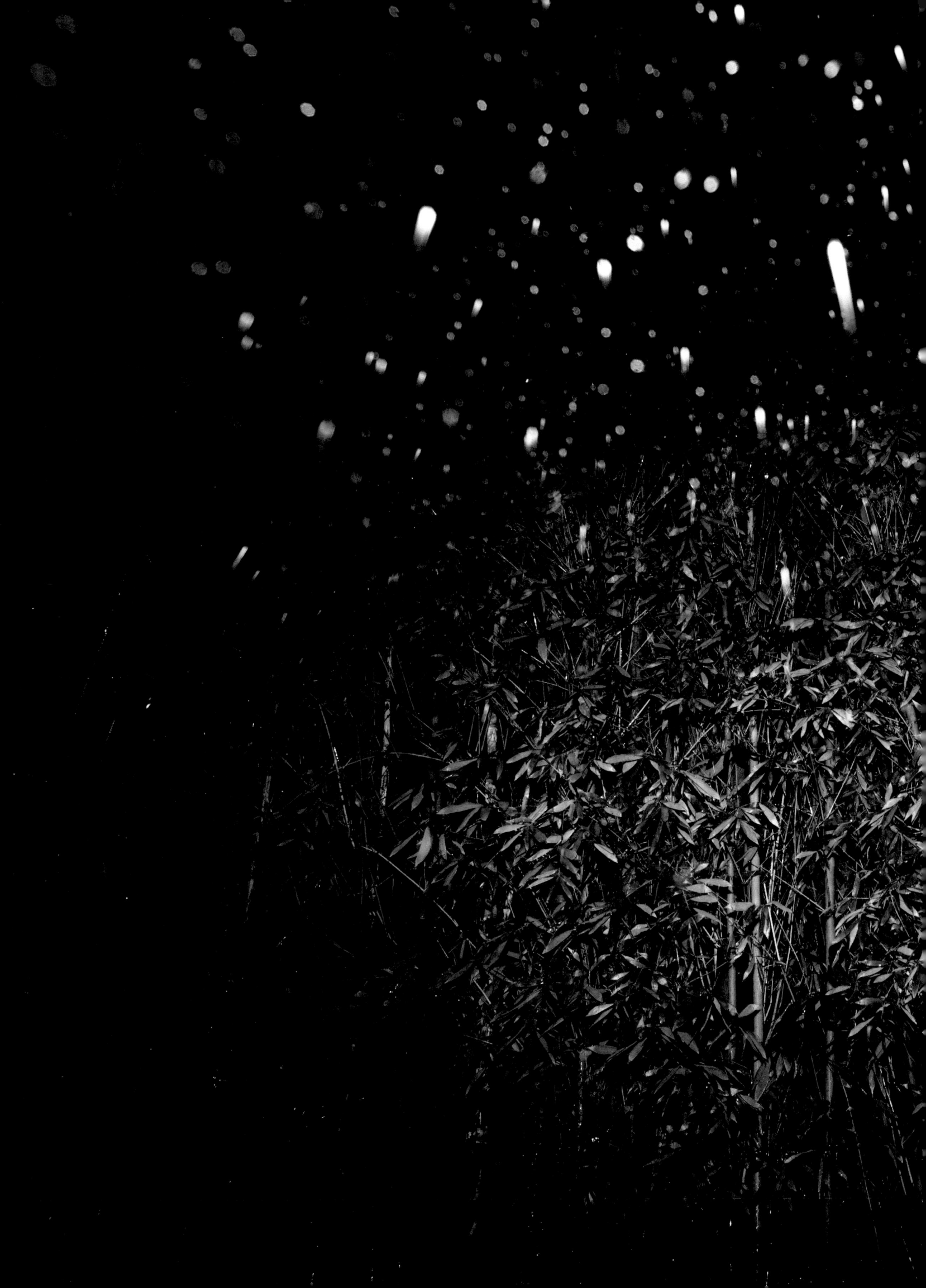

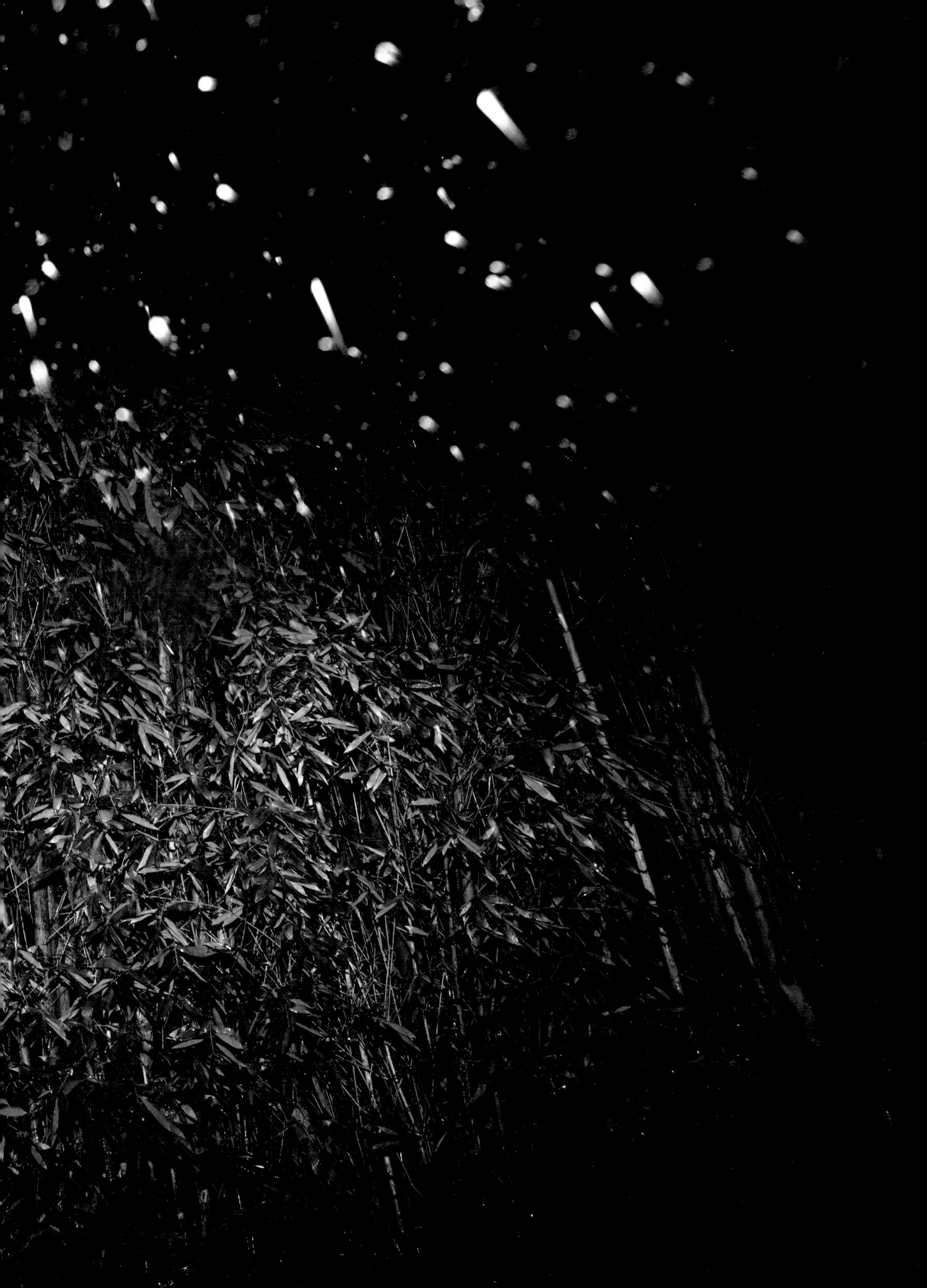

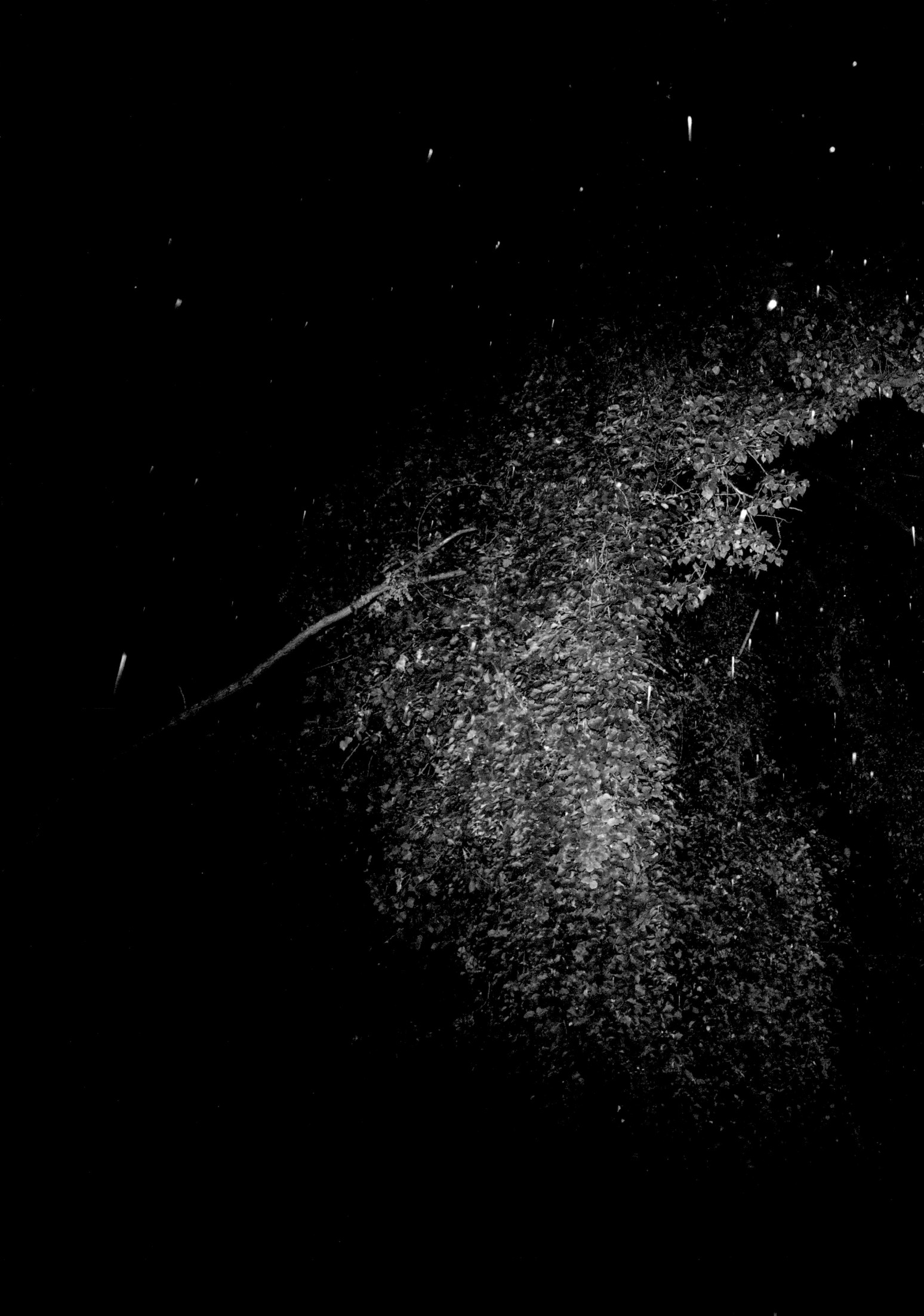

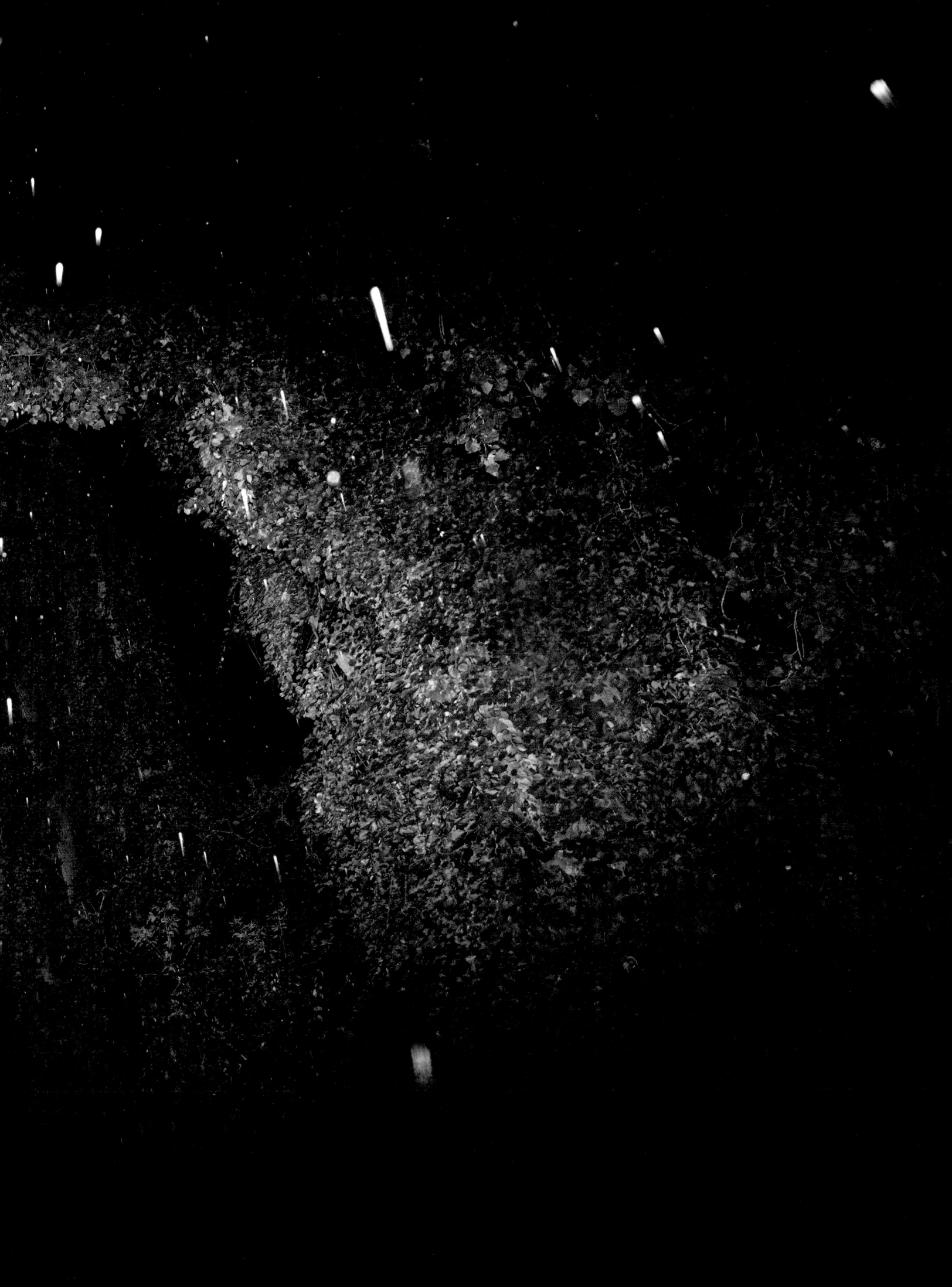

Dead Trees in Oxbow Lake, Mississippi Delta, 2018

Invasive (Asian) Silver Carp, Mississippi Delta, 2018

Boat Spray, Cargo Ship, Amazon River, 2017

Genetically Modified Invasive Mosquito Larvae, California, 2017

Nonnative Bamboo in Rainstorm, 2017

Invasive Oriental Bittersweet Strangling Native Trees on
   Hudson River, 2017

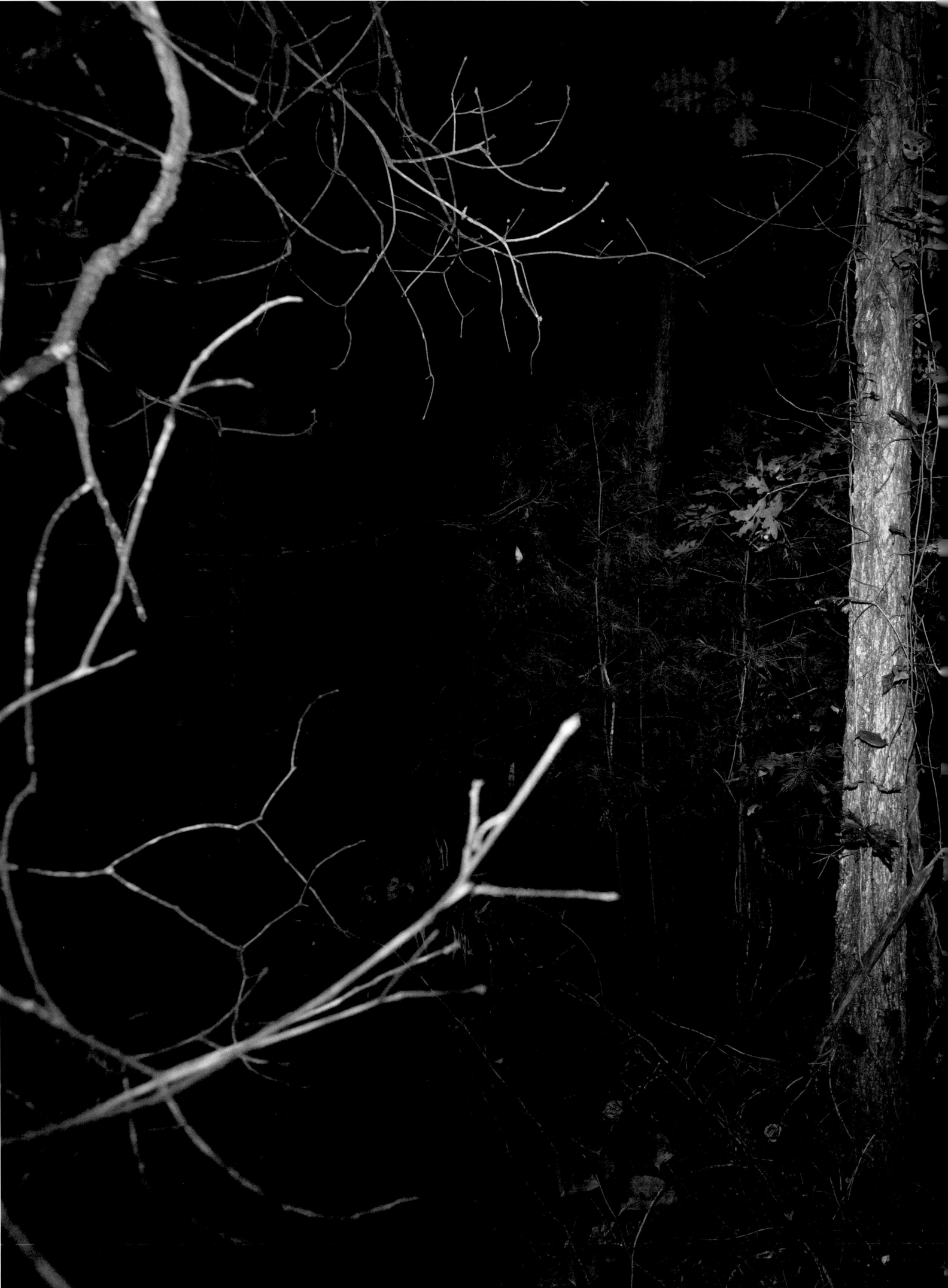

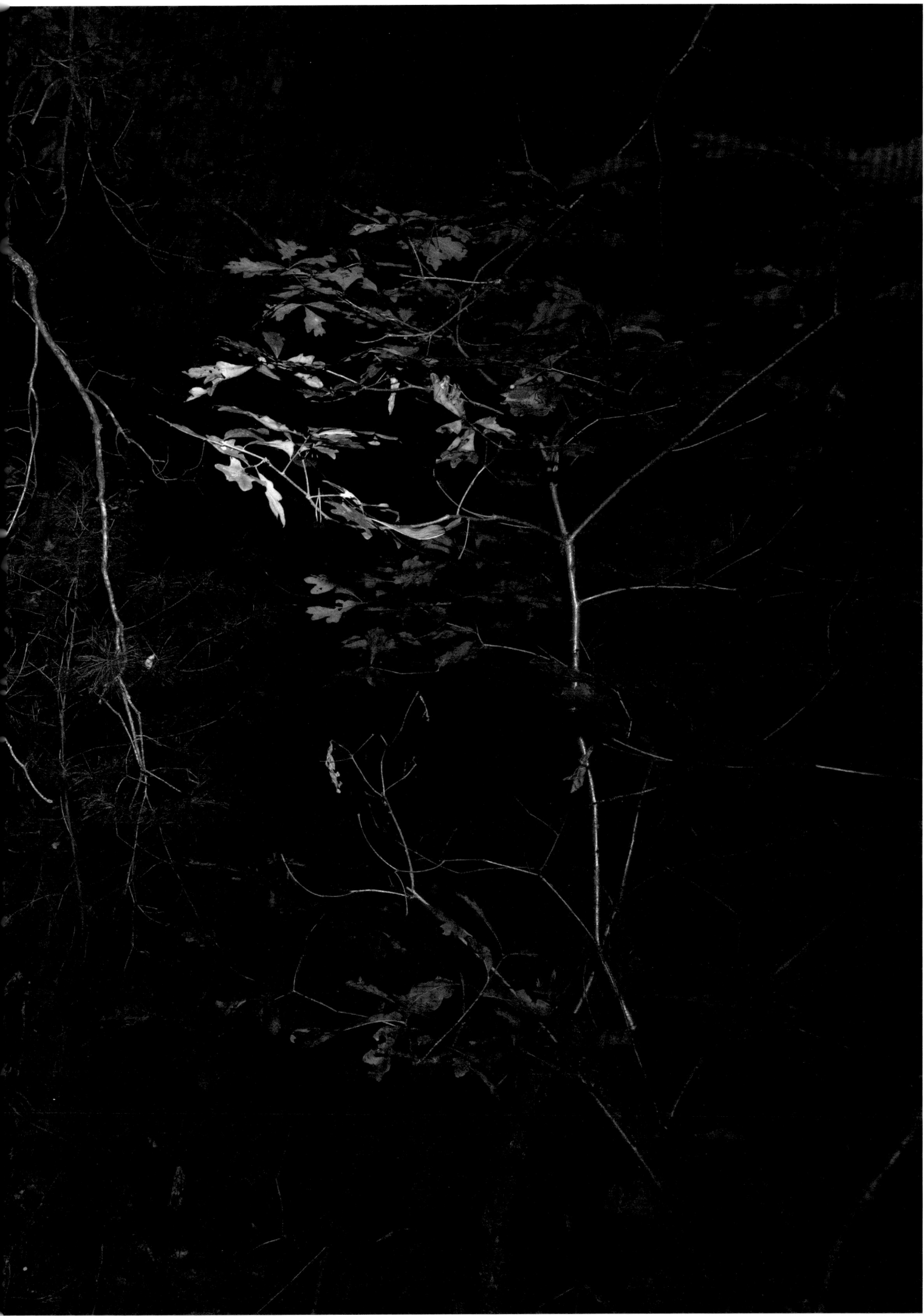

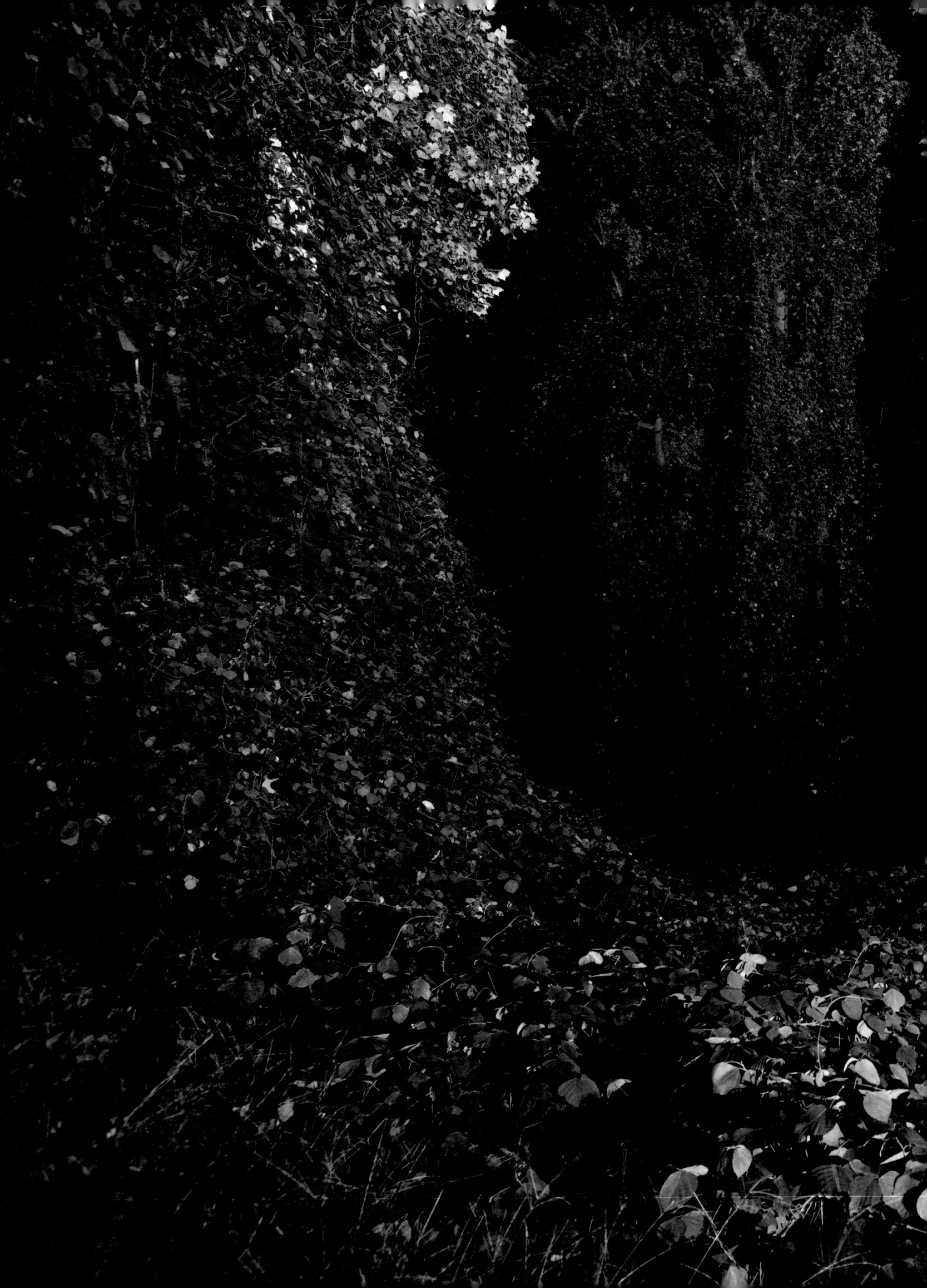

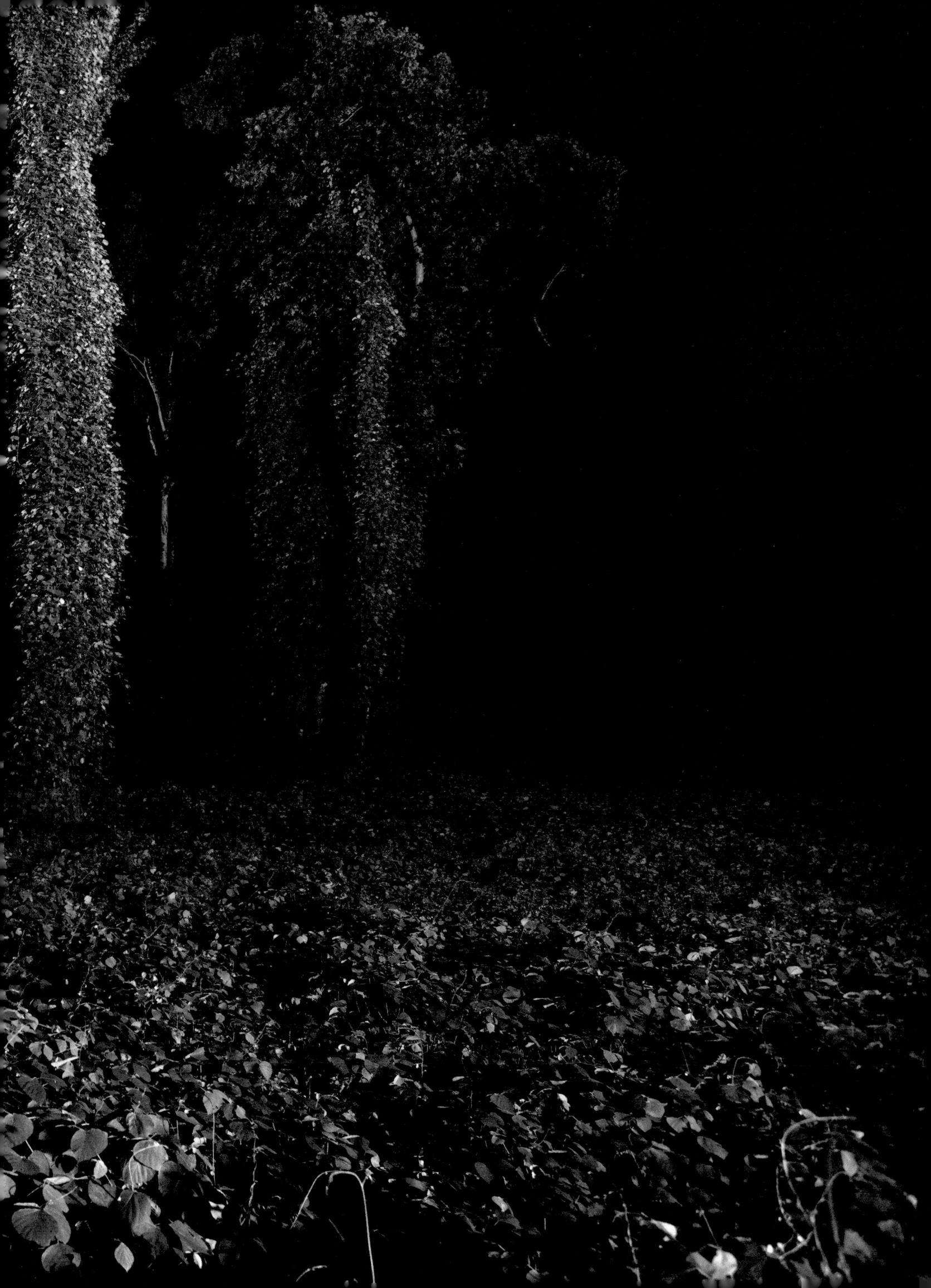

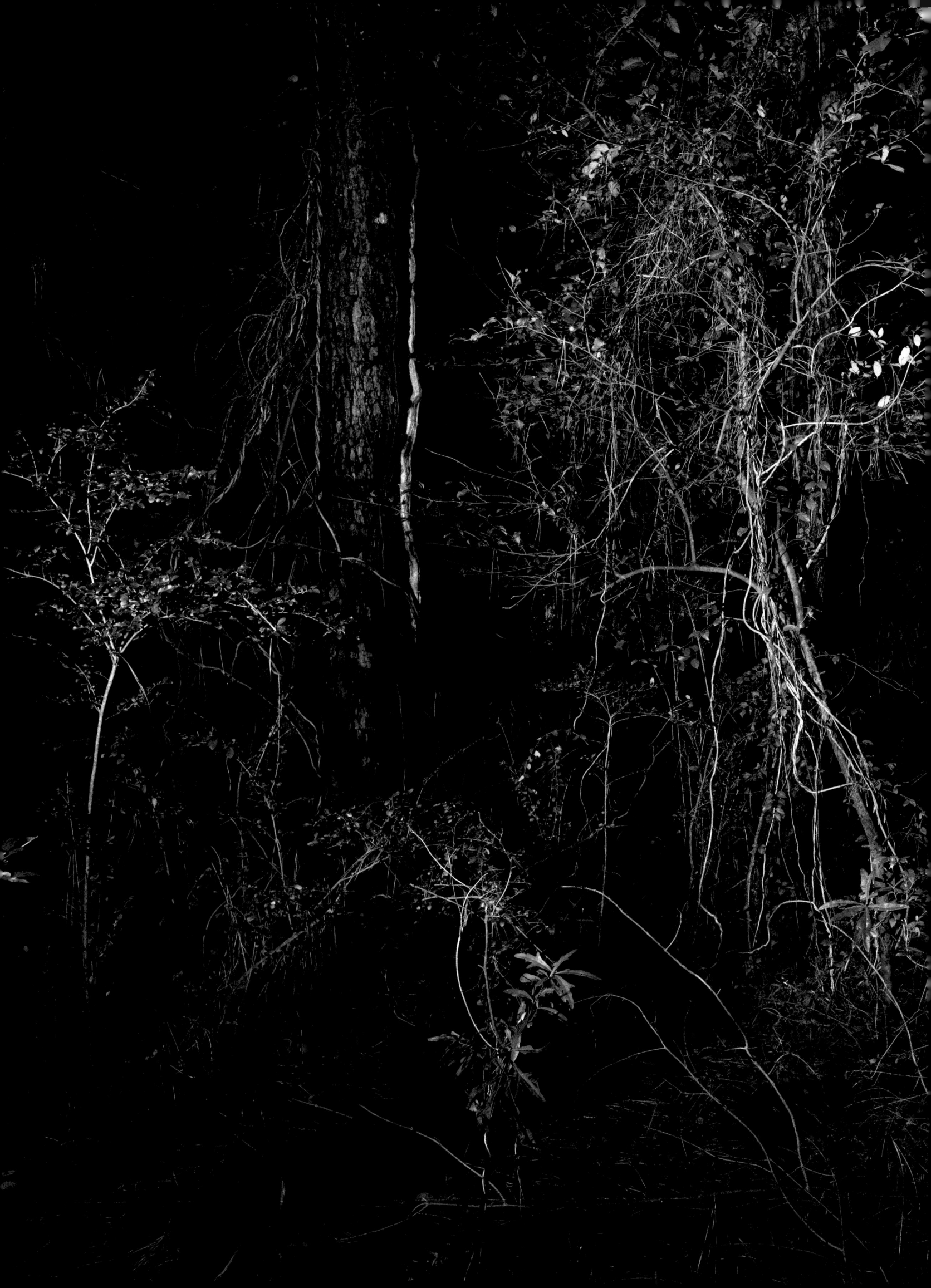

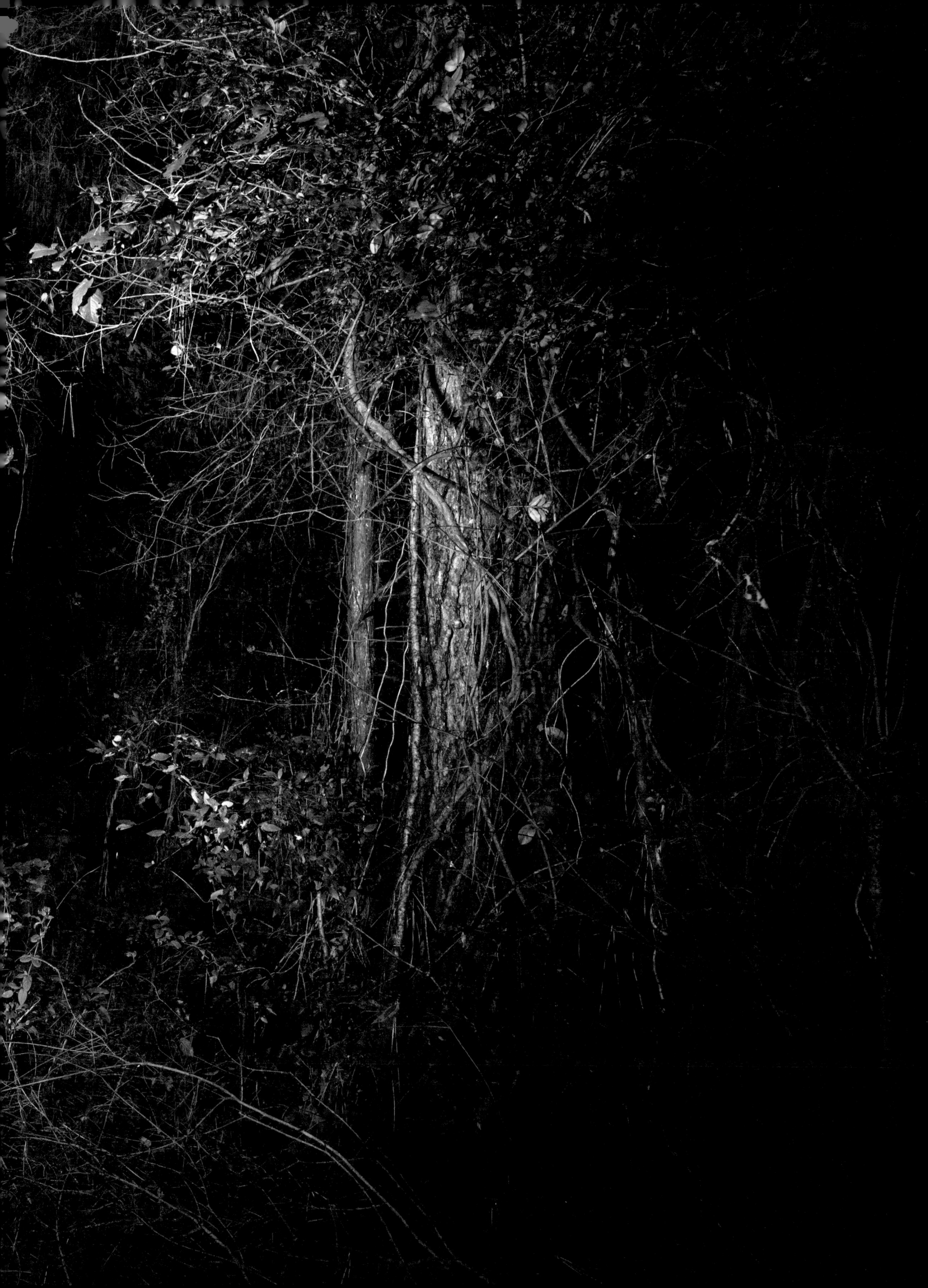

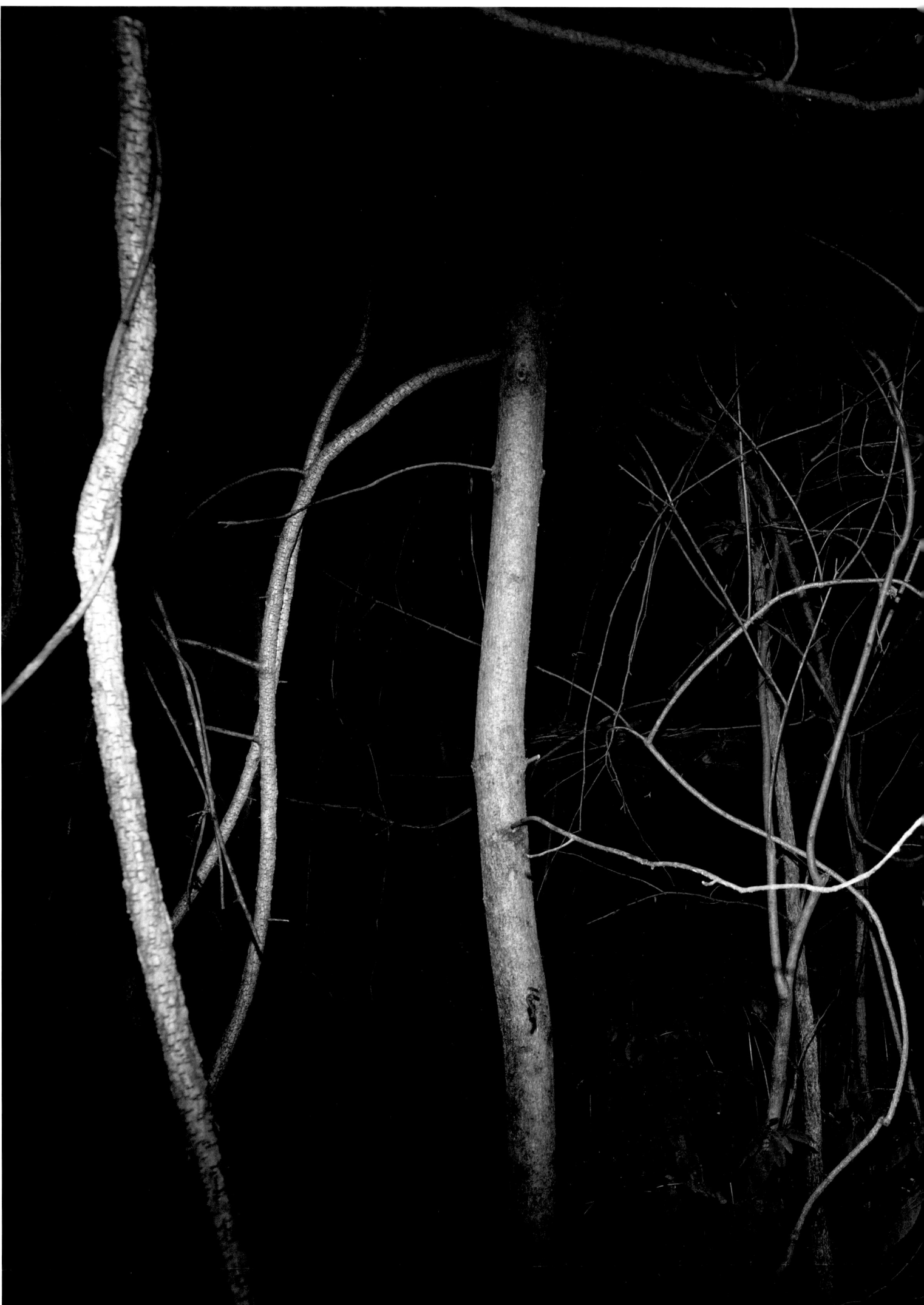

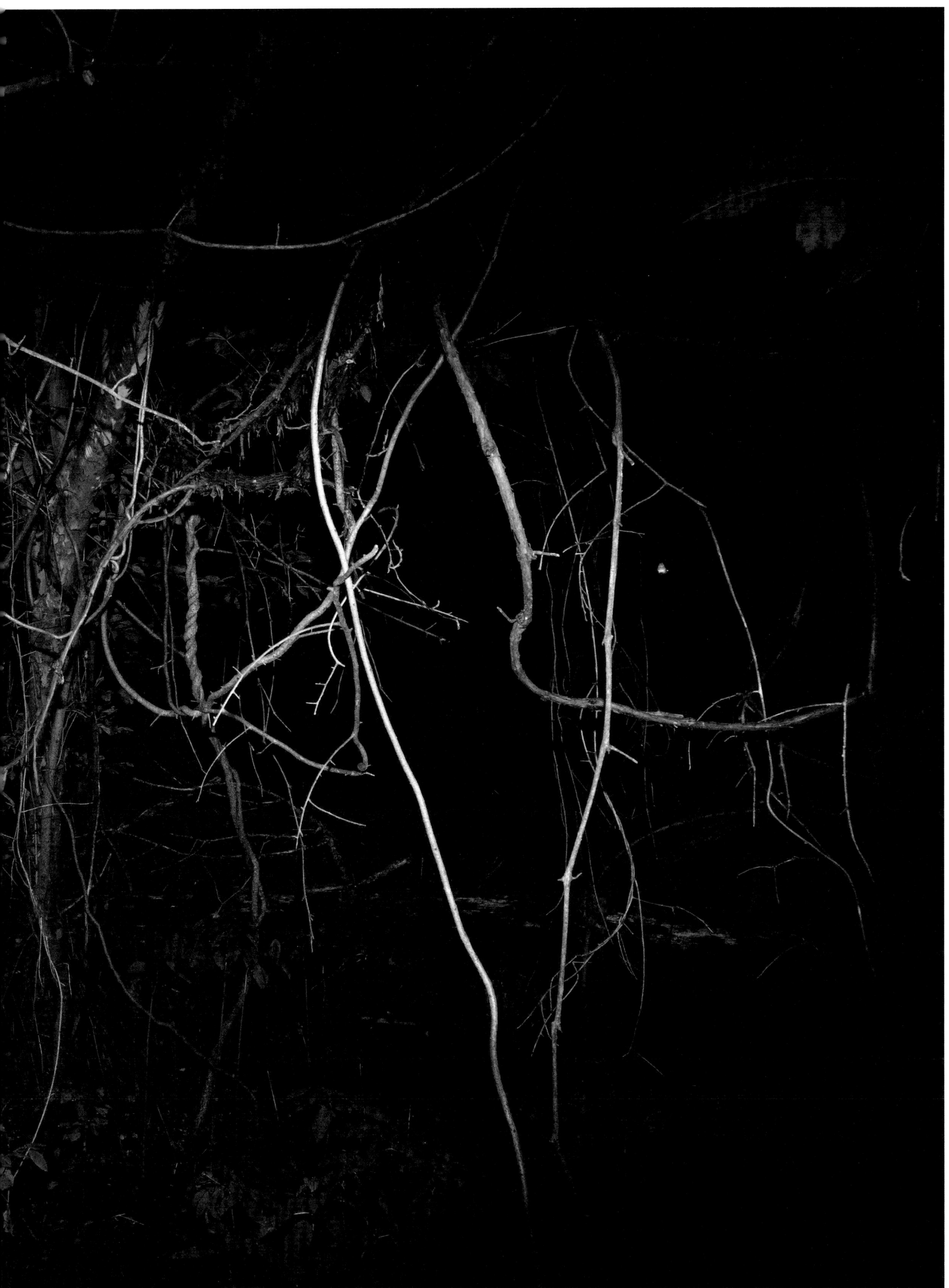

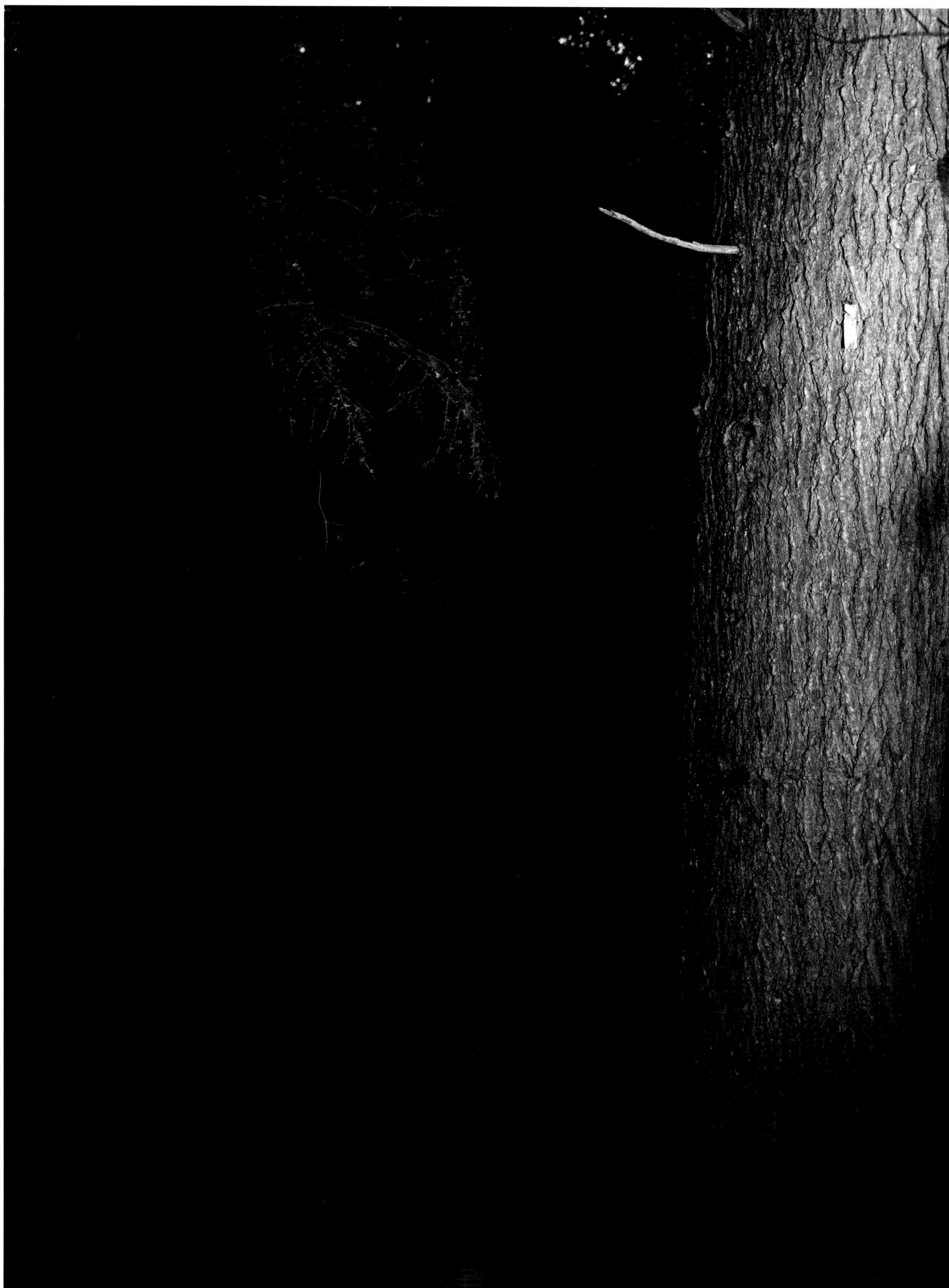

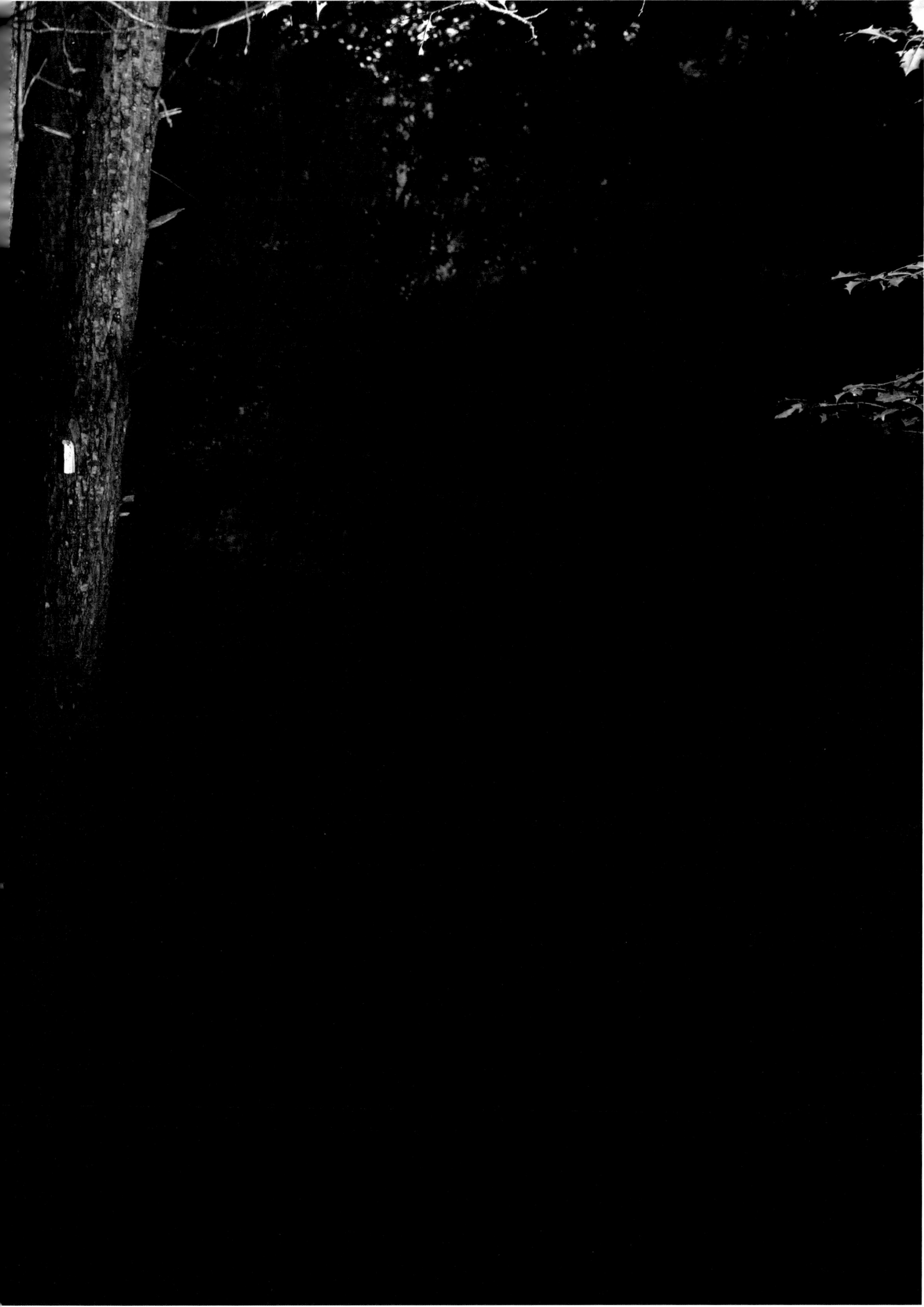

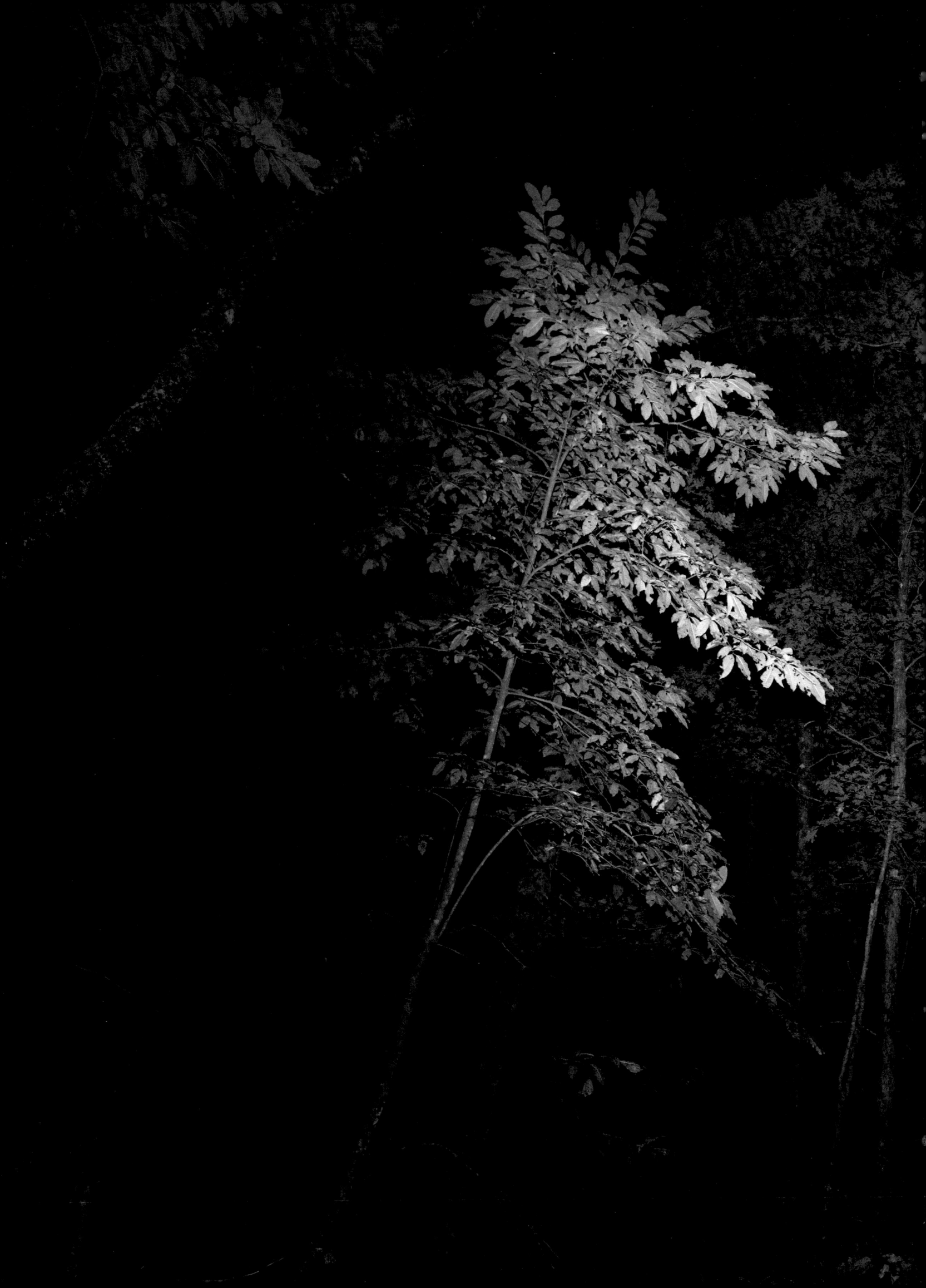

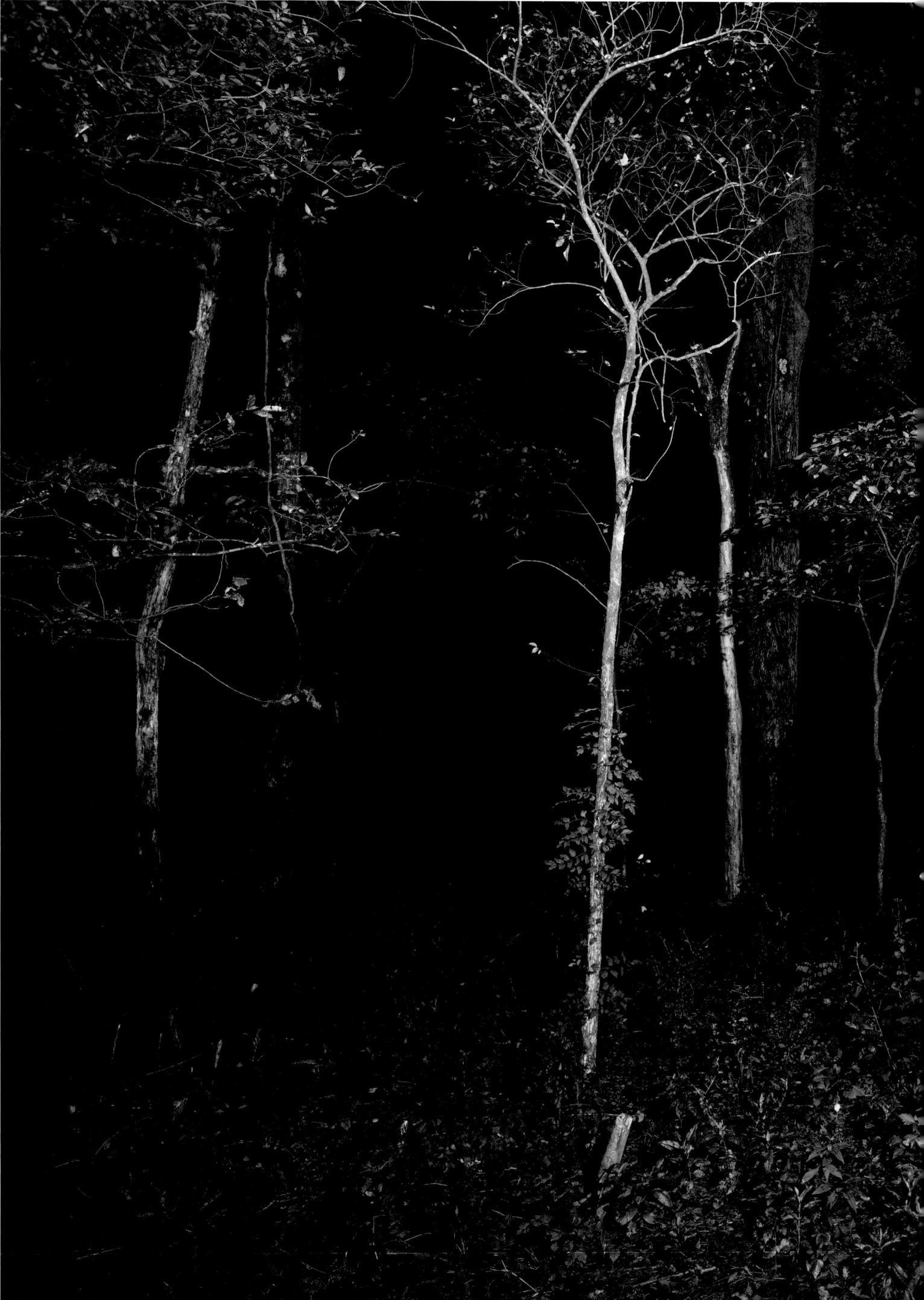

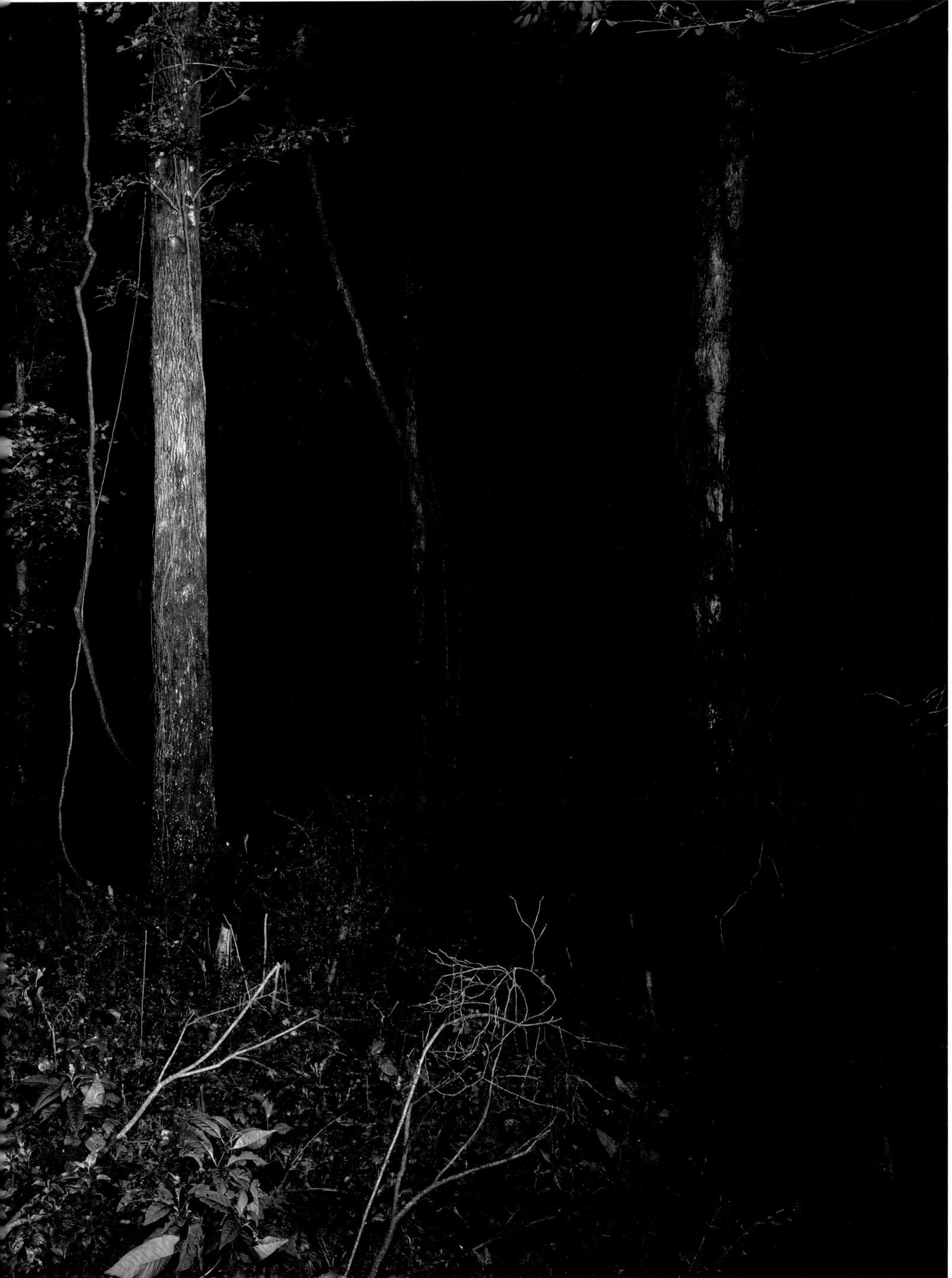

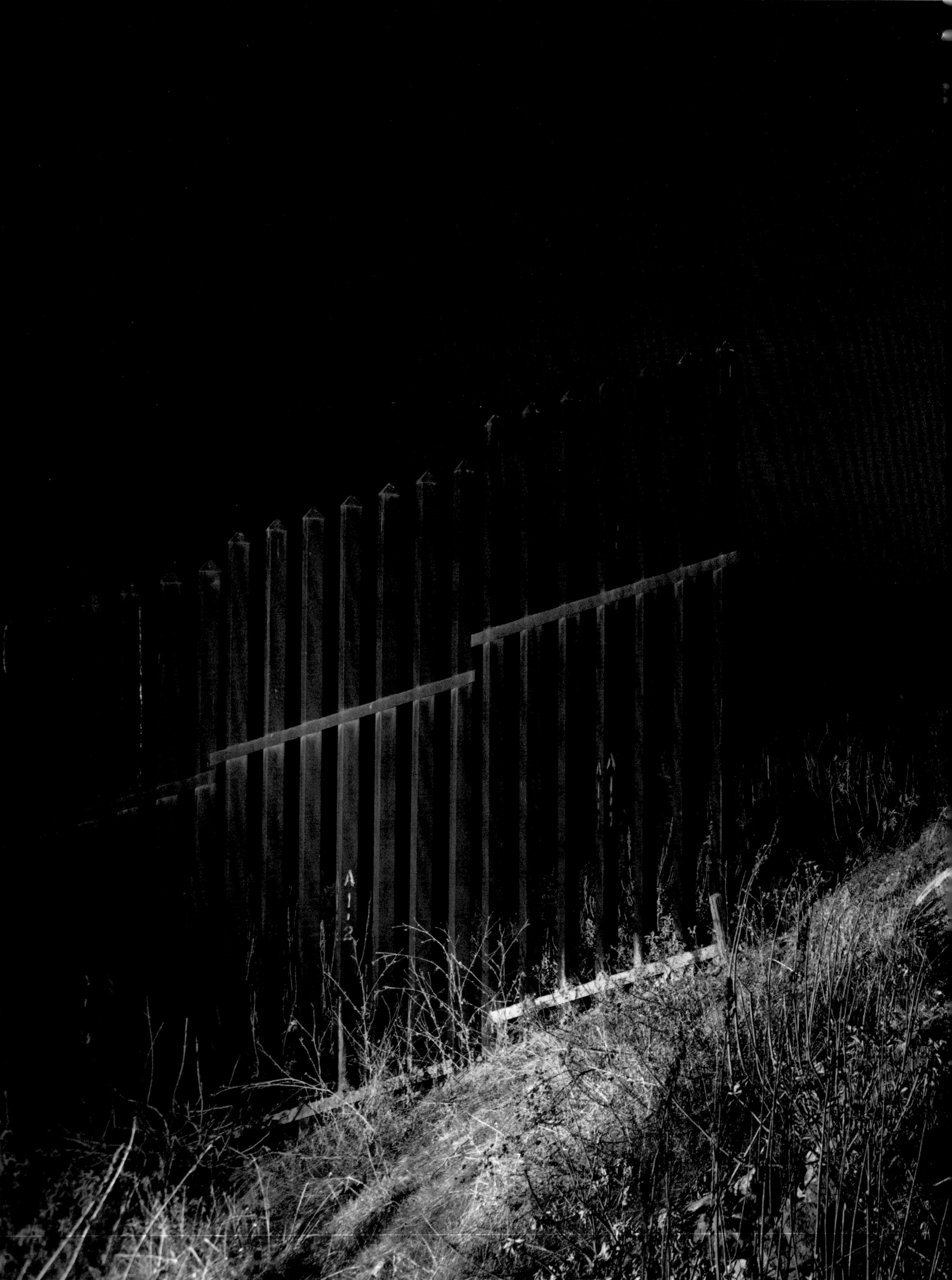

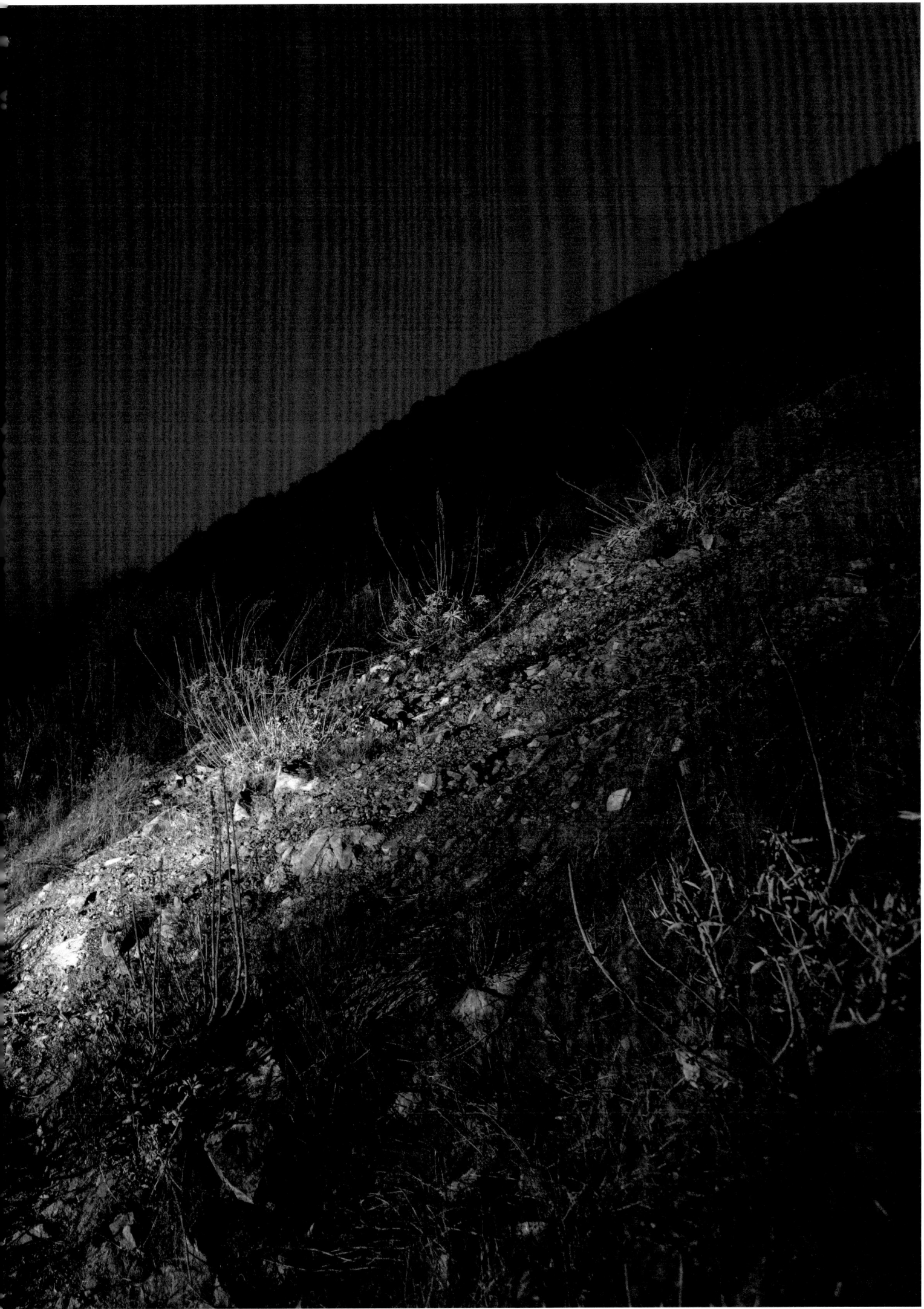

Invasive Oriental Bittersweet, North Carolina, 2018

Kudzu Shading Out Trees, Mississippi Delta, 2018

Invasive Privet, Tennessee Woods, 2018

Oriental Bittersweet, Hudson River, 2018

Treated Hemlocks, Natahuala Forest, North Carolina, 2018

Hemlock Killed by Asian Woolly Adelgid, North Carolina, 2018

"Restored Forest," Memphis, 2018

Edge of Mexico–United States Barrier, 2018

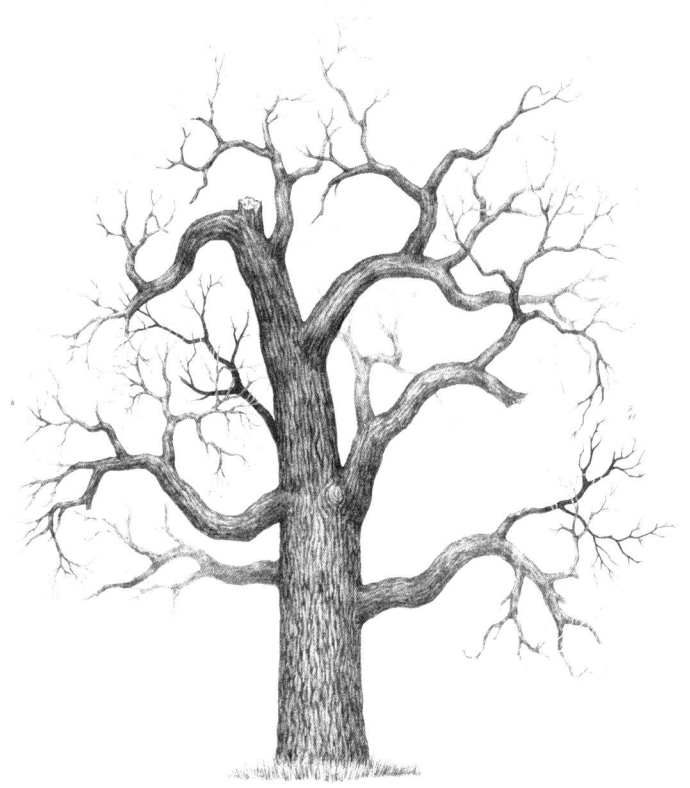

We begin and end this book with illustrations of the American chestnut tree.
They were enormous trees, towering up to 100 feet high with trunks ten feet in diameter,
producing immeasurable amounts of nuts that deer, black bear, turkeys, and other
animals could reliably count on before winter arrived. They comprised a quarter of all trees
in their Eastern range and numbered over three billion strong.

I wanted to photograph a healthy tree but couldn't find one, as only a handful remain
in their natural range and the locations of those are mostly kept secret. Chestnut blight, an Asian
bark fungus, was unwittingly introduced near what is now the Bronx Zoo in 1904 and quickly
spread, annihilating the species in a span of less than forty years. The USDA classifies them
as "functionally extinct" because the few remaining throw up new shoots from their root
systems each spring, but those too fall ill and die year after year.

And while we are roasting chestnuts in December that are mostly imported
from Europe and China, hundreds of millions of animals are instinctively foraging for
the native ones that can no longer be found.

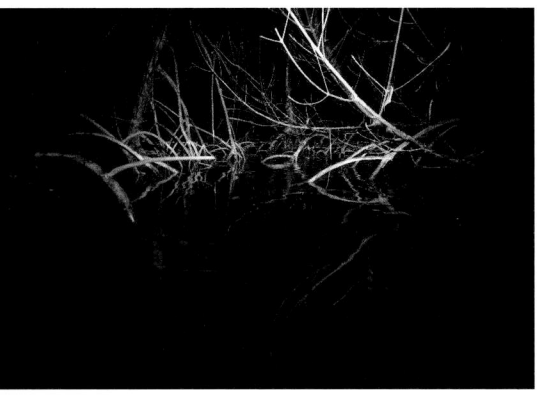

I lead this book with stories about the Everglades in South Florida as it is North America's battlefront against invasive species and myriad anthropogenic issues (human-caused problems). Because of its unique, sensitive environmental features, the Everglades is often cited as the bellwether of how the massive transformations to our natural world will play out. And its fight against sea level rise will be watched by all.

Often called the "River of Grass," the Everglades is essentially a slow-moving, fifty-mile-wide river flowing south, which keeps the saltwater of the ocean out by the pressure of freshwater moving in. It's such an incredibly diverse and precisely balanced ecosystem that I found myself making three trips to document it.

The low-lying peninsula we call Florida has been oscillating between being above and below sea level for 180 million years, when it fractured off from what is now Africa. In its time under the ocean, a low-lying marine environment deposited the porous rock we can now stand on, and it's the unique composition of this rock that keeps the hydrology in check.

Although mostly comprised of the sawgrass marshes we're all familiar with, the Everglades includes many interdependent ecosystems, from tropical hardwoods like mahogany to open savannahs, mangrove forests, and even pine rockland. It's the largest subtropical wilderness in North America, and a rare ecological community where temperate animals such as white-tailed deer, black bears, and jaguars live alongside tropical species such as alligators and what remain of the American flamingo. *And in this century all of it may soon be nothing more than open ocean due to saltwater intrusion and sea level rise.*

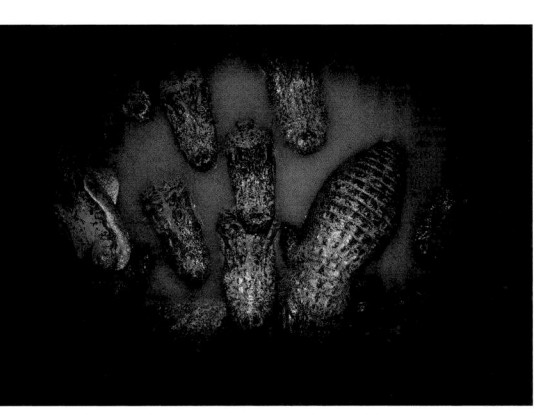

The American alligator has remained mostly unchanged for 150 million years, managed to survive the mass extinction that killed off the dinosaurs, and has lived and bred in North America for at least eight million years.

Dreadfully, it was hunted almost to extinction by the 1970s for shoes and accessories. The American alligator was fortunately placed on the federal endangered species list in 1973, and due to successful propagation was removed from the list in 1987. One of the endangered species list's greatest accomplishments.

Less than half of one percent of species listed as endangered have ever reestablished or been removed from the list.

The Everglades has been absolutely ravaged by human-introduced species, and what we can now experience and observe hardly resembles what once was there.

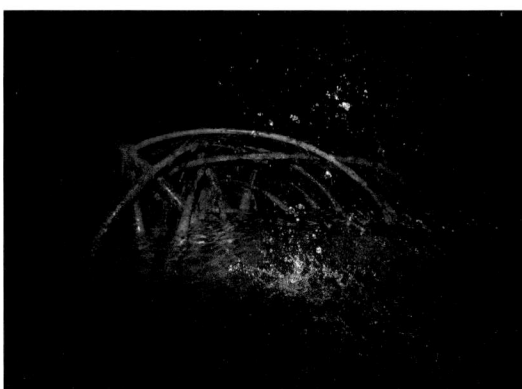

Entire ecosystems that formed over tens of millions of years are now confronted with a potpourri of alien species from around the world. The invasive creatures and plants often extract much from the ecology yet give little back. They provide scant food value, meager habitat value, and unbalanced predator-prey relationships.

Additionally, invasives can out-compete native species for resources, inhibit reproduction, and sometimes completely alter biodiversity.

Examples:

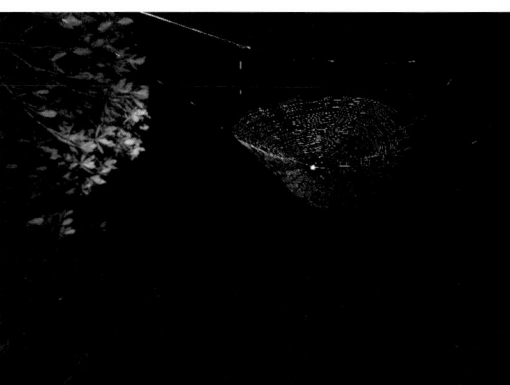

· In extreme cases, many plants use a form of chemical warfare called allelopathy to alter the soil. More than 800,000 acres of invasive Brazilian peppertree forests have altered the soil to prevent other plants from germinating, and thus have created enormous monoculture forests where these nonnative species have become the primary plant.
· More than one thousand nonnative insect species are present, including many that were introduced specifically for agricultural pest control. In only one example of great harm caused by small invasives — apple snails (a mollusk which grows to the size of a tennis ball) cause algae blooms by feeding on aquatic plants that keep the algae in check.
· Almost half the reptiles, such as the famed green iguana, and at least twenty two invasive mammals, including the highly destructive European hog, have been introduced into the Everglades.

· Scores of alien freshwater invertebrates now call the Everglades home, most being unintentionally deposited in the region by contaminated boats. These include mollusks, which filter the water and alter the lower dynamics of the food chain, degrading it all the way to the top. All the way to the alligator, the manatee, the raccoon, and the bobcat.
· On the vegetation front, one fifth of all the acreage of South Florida is covered by alien plants, with about 1,000 out of 4,200 plants having been introduced by humans.
· At least 100,000 acres of watershed are choked by hydrillia, which was dumped out from residents' fish tanks, and another 120,000 acres have been overtaken by water hyacinth, which was introduced to homeowners in 1884 as an ornamental. Add to it another half a million acres of Australian paperbark, a foreign tree that was actually planted in the early 1900s to drain the swamp. The swamp we now wish we could fill with fresh water again.

I'll stop there but things in the Everglades are very different now.

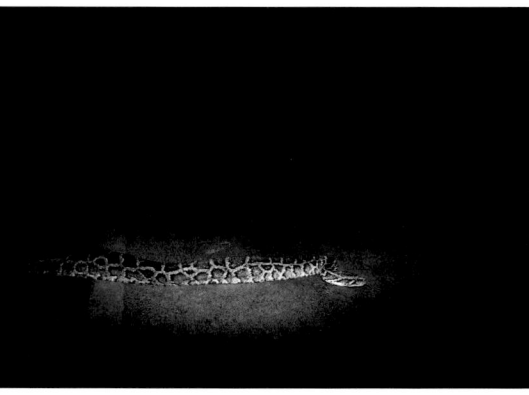

Rightfully, due to its twenty-foot size and voracious appetite, the poster child for all of this mayhem is the Burmese python. Originally from Southeast Asia and having been introduced through the pet trade, it has established a strong breeding population in the sawgrass marshes and has devastated mammal and bird populations.

In this area, threats to biodiversity and balance of the ecosystem have caused the loss of 98.9 percent of opossums, 99.3 percent of raccoons, and 90 percent of bobcats. A recent study of the marshes concluded that cottontail rabbits and foxes are locally extinct while dozens of other species are quickly becoming what is called "functionally extinct." Their populations are now too small to sustain or maintain a healthy genetic diversity and local extinction is inevitable.

While the National Park Service has removed more than two thousand Burmese pythons from the Everglades since the early 2000s, it estimates that over 150,000 are actively breeding.

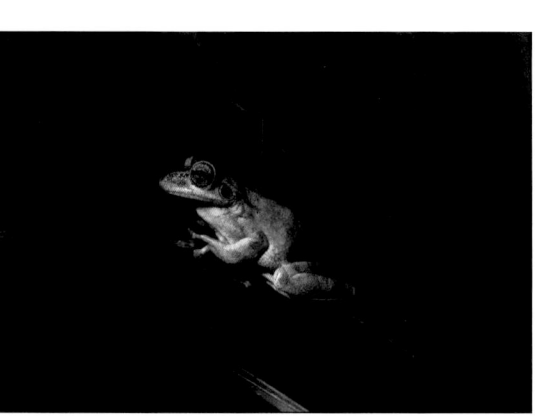

The invasive Cuban tree frog was introduced to the Everglades from the Bahamas in the 1920s and is now North America's largest tree frog. As this species rapidly established itself in its new environment, scientists observed the disappearance of other native tree frogs, toads, and lizards, which were predator-naïve to the Cuban that feeds on them. By evolving within their own local ecosystem, these species never had to avoid this hunter, just as rabbits and foxes never needed to be prepared for giant Asian constrictor snakes.

These frogs are literally everywhere on the peninsula and I could easily have grabbed one in the parking lot after a rainstorm. However, to prove a point, I shipped this one into the Everglades from the pet trade, photographed it, then sent it back. It's illegal to let an invasive species loose in the wild and while public service announcements instruct locals on how to kill the Cuban tree frog in their freezers, I could legally ship one to my hotel in the heart of the crisis.

But none of this may matter soon.

The mangrove forests in these photos (many of which were completely destroyed by unusually strong hurricanes in 2018) are sanctuaries for hundreds of species and some of the most carbon-rich environments in the world. They live in the brackish water where the ocean and fresh water meet. But despairingly, they're retreating from the Everglades on a death march inland.

Sea level rise and draining (by eight million humans) of the major source of fresh water for the Everglades, the Biscayne Aquifer, is forcing the mangroves of the coast inland at a rate of about one hundred feet per year—where they are backed up against a man-made levee (L-31E to be exact) and are making their final stand. According to Florida International University, they are likely to be submerged inside of this century.

The mangroves move inland. The sawgrass marshes are transforming into open ocean. Over half of the Everglades has been lost in the past century alone, and there is no other Everglades.

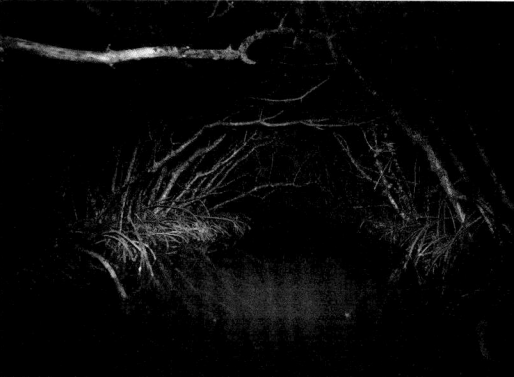

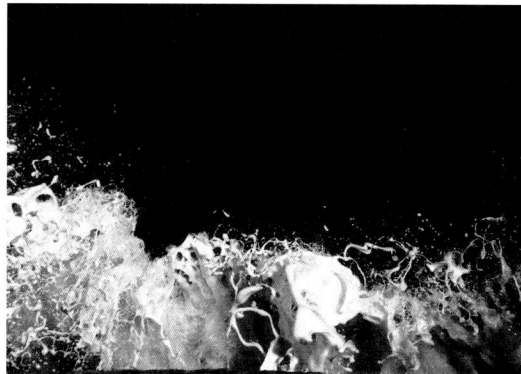

33.069632, 117.303387

Tree-ring studies (and other data) have shown that periods of drought in the Southwest states have commonly lasted ten to twenty years, although there have been extreme cases, such as a massive 240-year drought that started in 850 AD.

These same studies confirm the twentieth century was one of the wettest the Southwestern United States has experienced in 7,000 years, and that these observations set inaccurate rainfall expectations for the future. In the same unusually wet century, fifty million people flocked to the region, built damns, rerouted entire river systems, and built a $60 billion a year agriculture center in what was historically a desert.

In the end, what many refer to as "the drought" is more likely the West returning to its natural arid state.

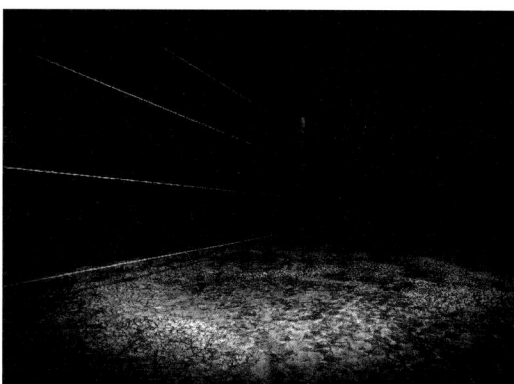

33.33846, 116.29889

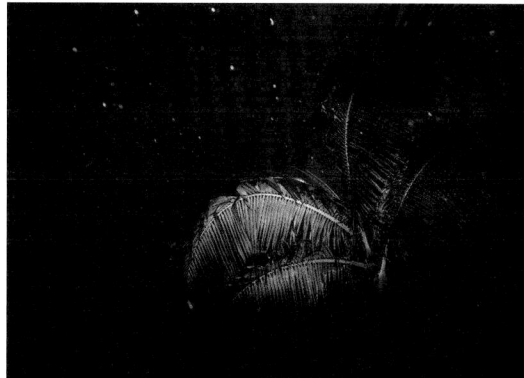

33.075570, 117.303034

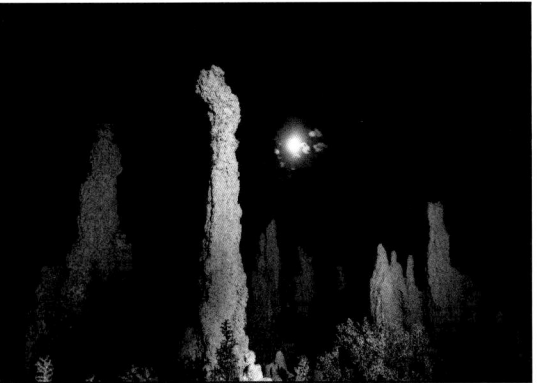

37.978430, -119.125254

Believed to be at least 760,000 years old, Mono Lake in California is one of the oldest and most unique freshwater ecosystems in North America. This desert lake is fishless but provided brine shrimp critical for feeding millions of migratory birds each year when their instincts steered the flocks to it mid journey.

In 1941 the Los Angeles Department of Water and Power extended its aqueduct system 345 miles northward into the Mono Basin, draining its tributaries, cutting its volume by half and dropping its surface 46 vertical feet (so far).

In 1948 nearly a million migrating ducks shared Mono Lake's surface while a census in the mid 1980s counted a stopover of only 14,000. These numbers say nothing of declines of more than three hundred other bird species that seek refuge there.

The rare and extraordinary tufa towers you see here were created over thousands of years as calcium-rich water flowed up through springs creating these immense, hollow limestone formations. Formations that should be forty feet below water.

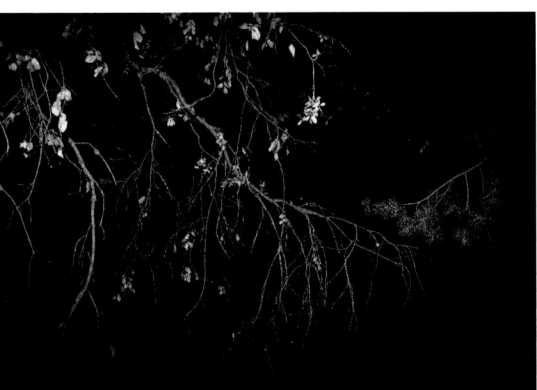

33.79114, -116.74070

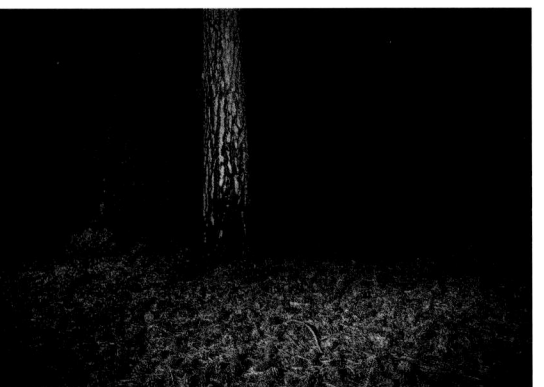

37.83743, -118.96780

North America is home to numerous forest ecosystems, from the predominantly broad-leaved trees of the East to the mostly coniferous forests in the West, and fire has been cleansing them all for tens of millions of years. Ignited by lightning every decade or so, small ground fires cleared the forests of grasses and deadwood, returned nutrients to the soil, thinned them by killing off excess saplings and made room for healthy growth.

Fifteen thousand years ago, the first humans were well established on the American continent and over time increased the frequency of fires, purposefully burning large areas for agriculture and to improve hunting habitat for elk, deer, bison, and other game and to make way for planting crops. By the 1800s, Europeans had entered the already-changed landscape and cleared and cut two thirds of the forests to satisfy an insatiable thirst for fences, buildings, and firewood. Many of the forests grew back and were clear-cut a second time.

In the hot and arid year of 1910, the Great Fire burned over three million acres in the West (the fire was started by embers from coal burning locomotives) and its losses were the catalyst for the current Forestry Service's policy of extinguishing every wildfire. This unnatural fire suppression has altered the landscape as much as clearing and cutting and directly produced the overly crowded and highly stressed forests we see across North America today.

Historically, relatively cool-burning fires crept along the understory and stayed out of the canopies, leaving the mature trees unharmed. But now, immeasurable amounts of uncleared deadfall and trees of all ages and heights act as ladder fuels that lift flames into the canopies where they don't belong. Fires, which were once essential, have now become enormous and lethal to the trees that formerly relied on them.

An example: Old-growth ponderosa forests in the West used to grow an average of 25–50 trees per acre with routine and natural thinning by fires. Many accounts report the forests were open enough to drive a horse-drawn wagon through without a road. After a century of modern wildfire suppression the forests now grow as many as 500–1,000 trees in the same acre.

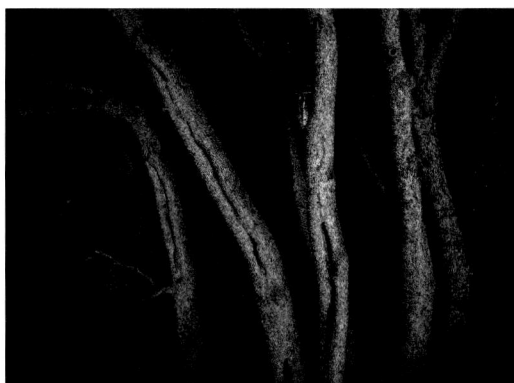

33.79846, 116.75861

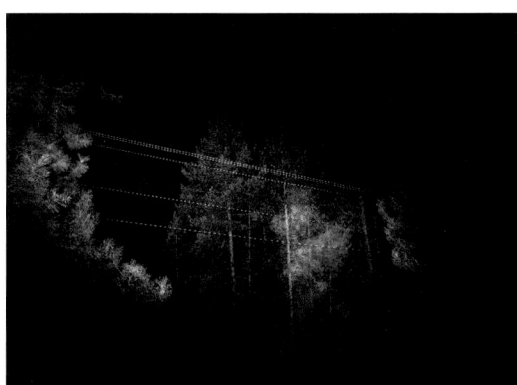

49.43917, 119.73373

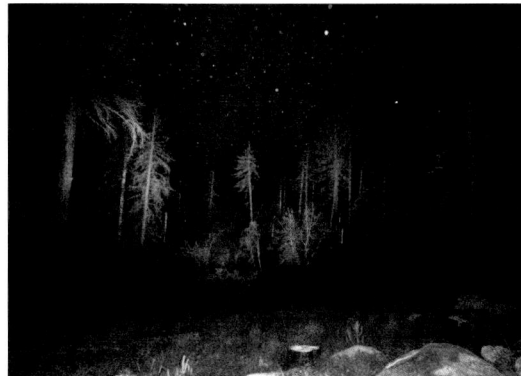

33.70962, 116.71901

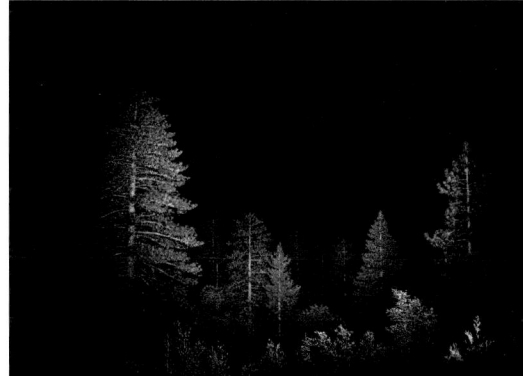

33.81121, 116.73630

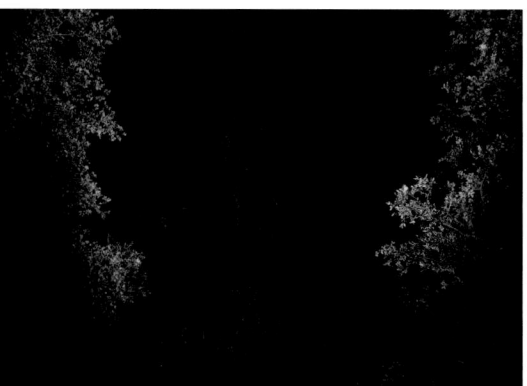

33.81419, 116.75182

Enormous outbreaks of the mountain pine beetle have killed millions of acres of Western forest in the past decade—far more than have succumbed to forest fires. The culprit beetles are native and include only five of about six hundred bark beetle species in North America, but newly warmer winters have stopped the normal larvae die-off that historically kept their population in check.

In parts of the southern Sierra Nevada, beetles have killed every low-level ponderosa, and many conservationists anticipate a transition from conifer forests to oak woodlands as a direct result.

Normally, robust trees can "pitch out" enough of the rice-grain sized beetles by drowning them in a defensive, resinous sap, but drought and water scarcity due to increased tree populations have stressed and hindered this mechanism.

32.91329, 116.5734

Since its detection in the Cleveland National Forest in 2004, the invasive goldspotted oak borer (GSOB) populations have exploded, killing more than 80,000 oak trees.

The beetles' larvae bore tunnels under the bark as they feed and grow in the trees' cambium—the circulatory system of the tree, which moves nutrients and water from its roots to its leaves. Eventually, the entire circumference is damaged and the tree quickly dies.

The GSOB is native to Arizona and New Mexico but was likely carried to Southern California in firewood. (What we know for certain is that it did not cross the desert on its own.)

Oak woodlands provide one of the most resource-rich habitats of any in Southern California, and if the oaks lose this battle, the woodlands will likely convert to open scrub and grasslands.

Eighty percent of the terrain of the continental United States is located within one half mile of a roadway and noise produced by vehicles. Combined with the inescapable sounds of commercial aircraft, noise distresses wildlife populations everywhere in America.

Sound levels in critical habitats of our national parks routinely measure two to ten times natural levels *and these are the quiet places*. Levels this loud are deadening perception of 50 to 90 percent of sounds and damaging the well-tuned balance between predator and prey, species communication, navigation, and mating vocalizations at a minimum.

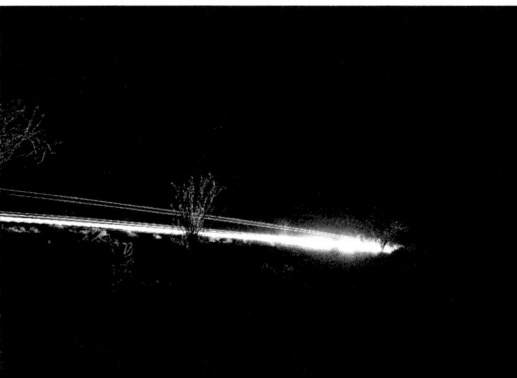

32.96900, 116.33037

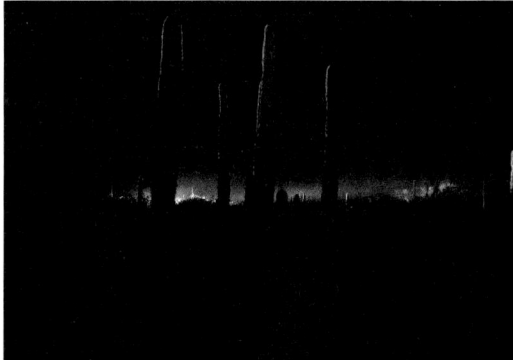

31.99448, 112.74705

There are over 4,000 native bee species in North America, most of which are solitary and ground-dwelling. In 1622, colonists imported the European honey bee to Jamestown, Virginia, where it quickly ran feral and spread west.

Despite the rallying cries of a thousand bumper stickers, *this is the last insect that needs to be saved*. Domesticated for thousands of years, it's found on every continent but Antarctica and is endlessly pampered. The angiosperms (flowering plants, including most trees) owe most of their offspring to bees, but the flora of North America was successfully pollinated since its beginnings without the help of this species. Currently, the honey bee spreads pathogens and agricultural pesticides harming native bee populations and competes with them for resources.

Alas, the "Save the Bees" movement is really an issue of human agriculture and not a true environmental one.

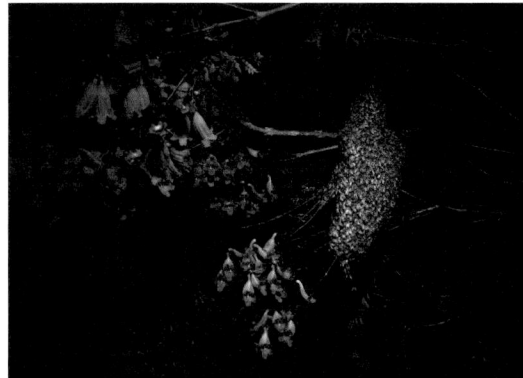

32.74480, 117.18588

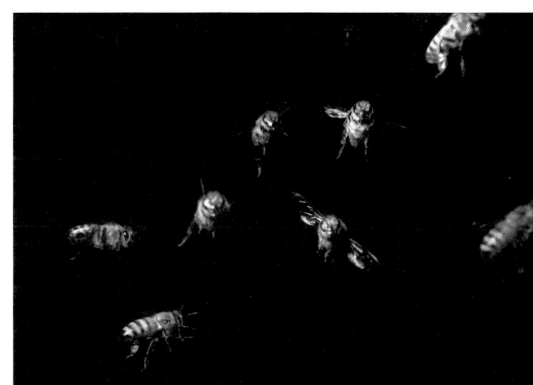

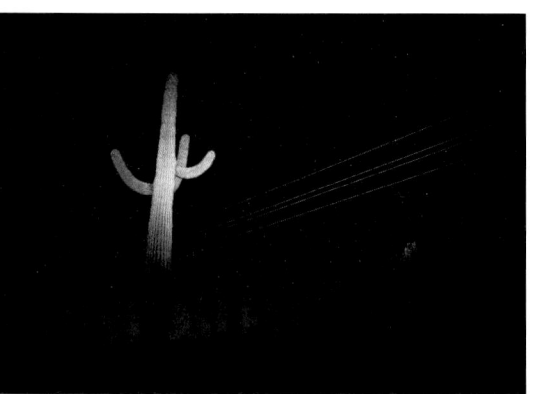

31.99448, -112.74705

We've long known that many animals avoid power lines and only recently partially concluded why: To many animals, power lines emit terrifying and distressing bursts of light known as corona discharges. They crackle audibly and shoot enormous sparks from electrical transmissions that aren't well shielded (you can easily view footage of this online, posted by power providers inspecting cables with UV cameras).

Humans can't see corona discharges because the ultraviolet spectrum isn't visible to us, but thousands of species can— birds, some reptiles and amphibians, reindeer, and both your dog and cat can perceive the spectrum.

It has yet to be studied fully, but it is very plausible that power lines affect certain mammal migrations and thus divide gene pools at least to some degree.

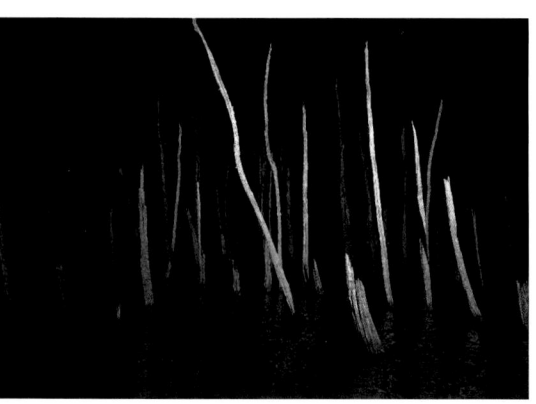

34.705513, -90.481130

The Mississippi River has been so heavily modified that it no longer fits the definition of a river: "a natural watercourse flowing toward an ocean, lake, or sea." Historically flooding its banks year after year, the river changed course often and deposited much of the nutrients that make the Mississippi Delta so rich and fertile. After three centuries of tampering, the river has been pounded into its current shape with more than 3,500 miles of levees averaging twenty-five feet high and more than 190 bendway weirs that redirect its flow.

The changes date back to 1724 and the founding of New Orleans, where a decree to build levees was put into effect to hold the river's shape as new towns and industry were built along its banks. Over the years, the U.S. Army Corps of Engineers built hundreds of dams, straightening the river to make shipping more efficient, cutting off bends in the process and isolating hundreds of "oxbow lakes" where the curves used to be.

Areas such as the one in this photo have been cut off and drowned out; the river no longer floods, the delta is thusly no longer nourished, and manufactured fertilizers are sprayed on the land instead.

North America has the most diverse freshwater fish fauna in the world and historically a fish species went extinct only once every three million years or so. Now, with over half of the planet's sizable rivers heavily modified, forcibly altered migration patterns, pollution, and invasive species, our freshwater fish are going extinct at astronomical rates. *At least fifty-seven species disappeared in North America in the past century alone* and that rate is rapidly accelerating.

Four species of invasive Asian carp plague the watersheds of the Mississippi, Missouri, and Illinois rivers.

The invasion is so rampant that carp constitute 82 percent of commercial catch in the Illinois River. Moreover, the Missouri Department of Conservation believes the fish make up 95 percent of the biomass in all the state's waters.

Voracious feeders and equally fecundate, they aggressively crowd out and starve native fish by stripping freshwater ecologies of zooplankton—a food source all fish need in their larval stage. Ironically, they were introduced to North America to filter commercial aquaculture ponds of the very same microorganisms before they escaped into the open waterways during flooding.

In 2002, in an effort to mitigate the crisis, the U.S. Army Corps of Engineers erected enormous underwater electric barriers just south of Chicago to block the carp from gaining access to the Great Lakes and, thus, most of the waterways of North America.

When they pass the electric barrier and gain access to the second largest freshwater system on Earth—*and they will*—Asian carp populations and their territory will likely expand until they're the predominant North American fish, just as they have in the Mississippi, Missouri, and Illinois river basins.

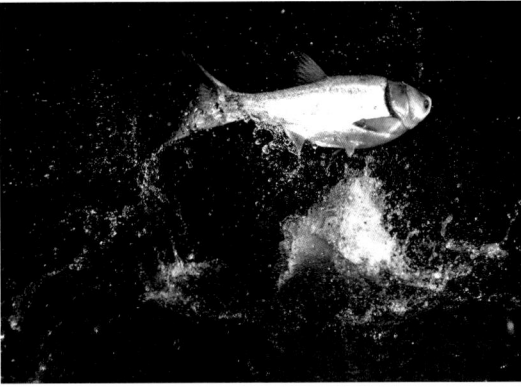

34.693174, 90.469449

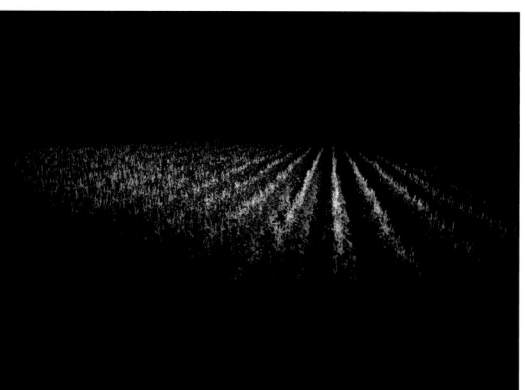

32.90930, 115.59490

33.011307, 116.563300

It's difficult to photograph a mass extinction, but if I had to reduce these images to a singular concern, it would have to be this one: Agriculture.

Land transformation due to agriculture, its ensuing habitat loss, and run-off pollution are the leading drivers of the current Holocene Extinction. With extinction rates approximately one thousand times prehuman levels, *The Proceedings of the National Academy of Sciences* has labeled the present crisis a "biological annihilation."

The conclusions in the scientific studies below are so alarming that I'll cite references should anyone question the extremities of the numbers. Consistent and overlapping findings by numerous organizations confirm the severity of it all.

· Forty percent of Earth's land surface has been transformed for agriculture, with 30 percent of all existing terrain purposed solely for livestock. (United Nations Food and Agricultural Organization)

· In a study of 3,700 species, the number of wild animals worldwide has been found to have been cut by half in the past forty years alone. In that same time, amphibians were reduced by 80 percent and freshwater fish by 65 percent. (Zoological Society of London)

· In an extensive study of 27,600 vertebrate species (comprising half of all known fish, amphibians, mammals, and birds), 32 percent are decreasing, with over 40 percent of mammals experiencing severe population declines. (Proceedings of The National Academy of Sciences)

· "Rivers and lakes are the hardest hit habitats, with animal populations down by 81 percent since 1970 due to water extraction, pollution, and dams." (World Wildlife Fund)

The rates of myriad extinction drivers are accelerating far faster than we can debate them or attempt intervention with a species by species approach. Famed biologist E. O. Wilson estimates that if current rates of human destruction of the biosphere continue, one half of all animal and plant species will be extinct in one hundred years.

Relics of the last ice age, this is the only natural grove of native palm trees in Arizona — *Washingtonia filifera*, the California fan palm. *Every other palm you see in the state was imported or planted.*

High in a narrow ravine atop the Kofa Mountains, which rise suddenly from the flat desert, these trees retreated to this cool refuge as the area dried and converted to desert. Hidden from the sun for all but a brief period when it passes across the crevice each afternoon, the grove has survived with scant water for thousands of years.

If our atmosphere warms at the rate scientists have predicted, narrowly surviving niches like this one may not have the time necessary to adapt.

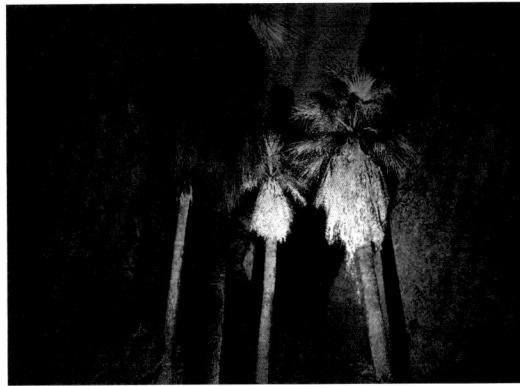

33.363438, 114.098421

Estimated to be over one thousand years old, this enormous Douglas fir stands twenty-three stories tall, and is on record as the second largest Douglas fir in all of Canada. With a base larger than the average living room, it stands in the mangle of a clear cut forest with fully mature pines in the distance and was spared by a sympathetic logger who tagged it with the words "Do Not Cut."

Deforestation driven by the demands of agriculture and lumber has spared less than one percent of old-growth Douglas fir trees in British Columbia. Giants like these were once common across many species, but almost all were destoyed before modern times.

And for broader perspective, in the lower forty-eight states, 90 percent of the virgin forests have been cleared since the 1600s. Much of them twice.

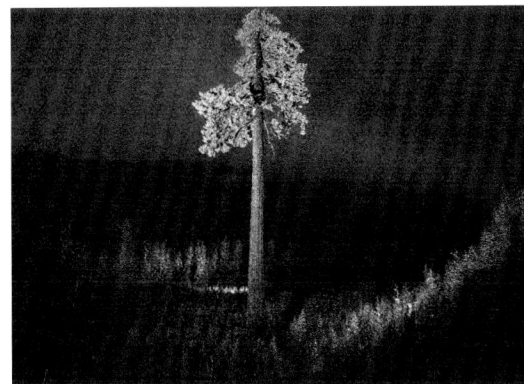

48.64640, 124.45000

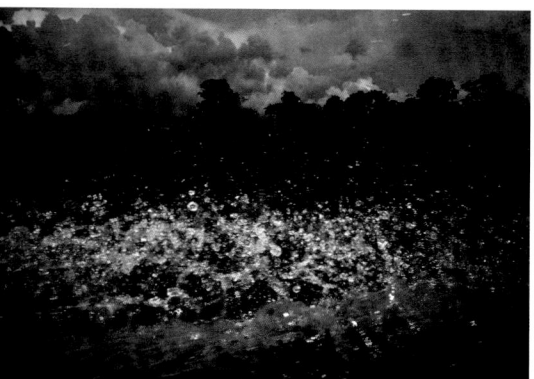

4.112093, -73.321953

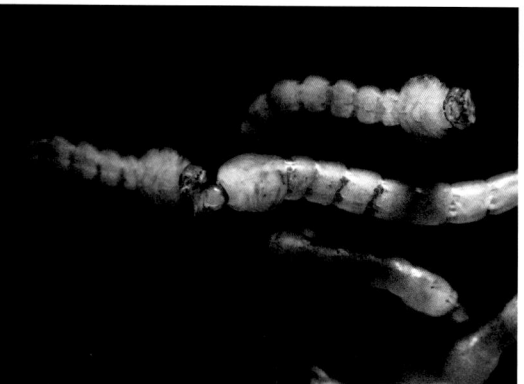

33.645152, -117.846474

Mosquitoes are the deadliest animals in the world and spread diseases that kill more than 700,000 humans annually, but that's not all they hurt. Transported by hull water in ships, dozens of mosquito species have become invasive around the globe where they adversely affect wildlife as well.

On the remote islands of Hawaii (the extinction capital of the world), invasive mosquitoes have transmitted avian malaria and avian pox to the endemic bird populations and absolutely decimated them. Between habitat loss and the introduction of invasive animals, 95 out of 142 birds found nowhere else in the world are now extinct in the Hawaiian Islands. Out of the 47 remaining endemic birds 33 are listed as endangered.

To do the math: Only 14 out of 142 Hawaiian birds remain neither extinct nor endangered.

Pictured are genetically modified mosquito larvae, *Aedes aegypti* (the yellow fever mosquito), which originated in Africa but is now invasive to North America and much of the world. In the fight to combat these issues, these particular larvae were modified to resist malarial transmission. Other laboratories have genetically engineered mosquitoes to have sterile offspring and diminish populations in the wild. And without our knowing how they may alter the environment, they've already been released in three countries.

We say human-introduced species are "nonnative" or "alien," but occasionally one of these populations balloons out of control, distresses an ecosystem, and becomes "invasive." Next to habitat destruction, invasive species are the leading drivers of biodiversity loss and extinctions in North America and much of the planet, and every wildland director I spoke with led our conversation with the issue.

These invasive organisms left their natural predators behind when they arrived. Grazing animals don't like the way the new grasses taste, invasive insects aren't recognized by local birds as food, and so on, so there's little to keep them in check. Without having to expend vital resources on survival, these species reproduce rapidly and can overwhelm their new spaces, often creating large monocultures and diminishing biodiversity.

The rates at which new species cross what were once natural barriers is ever accelerating through the global transfer of goods and the ease of modern travel. The emerald ash borer arrived in wood pallets from China, the zebra mussel in ballast water from the Caspian Sea, *and I plucked four species of plant seeds from my boots when boarding a return flight from Panama just last week.* It happens that fast.

Tumbleweed, or Russian thistle, remains the iconic metaphor for desolation in the western film genre, but is actually invasive to North America. Immigrants from Europe transported the species in tainted flaxseed to their homesteads in South Dakota around 1873. Once in the soil, the seeds rapidly grow into a bush that dies after one year, breaks off and rolls in the wind dropping more seeds.

Thriving on dry and disturbed land from overgrazing, the plant is now widespread across all arid areas in North America and infests around 100 million acres of land.

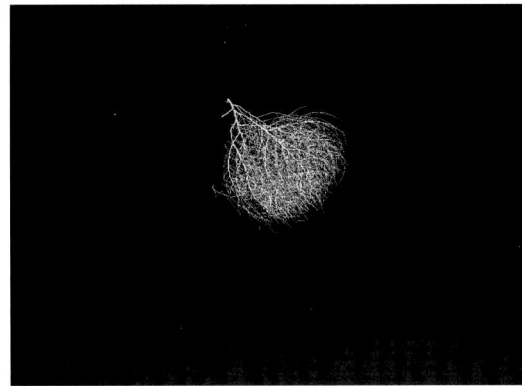

34.55634, 117.19957

Oriental bittersweet is native to China, Korea, and Japan and was sold in North America as an ornamental plant in seed catalogs by 1886. Planted in gardens for its dramatically colored berries, mammals and birds soon took to them and dispersed the seeds widely. Aggressive and hardy, the vines quickly grow over native trees and vegetation, shading them out and girdling (strangling) the trunks and limbs.

The vines reach forest canopies and become so heavy they can pull down enormous native trees.

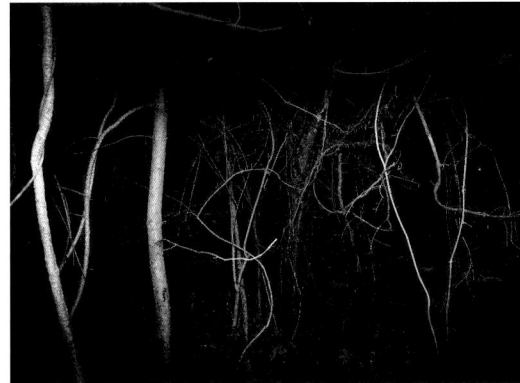

42.57396, 73.74718

Kudzu, dubbed "the vine that ate the South," was introduced from Japan at the Centennial Exposition in Philadelphia in 1876 as an ornamental to shade porches.

In the first half of the twentieth century it was planted along roadsides to abate soil erosion during the Dust Bowl, and government programs paid Southern farmers to grow it as a high-protein ingredient in cattle feed. Unfortunately, it can grow up to sixty feet per season and smothers and "shades out" other plants and trees as well.

As the story goes, when invasive boll-weevil infestations killed off cotton crops, bankrupt farmers abandoned their kudzu as well and it's grown unimpeded ever since.

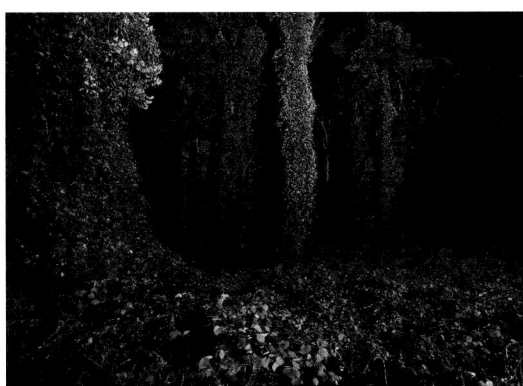

35.05357, 89.82294

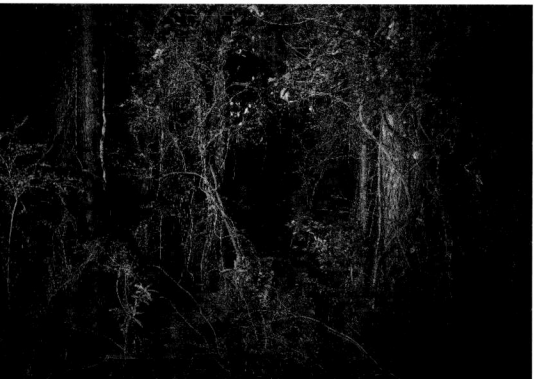

35.61755, 82.59282

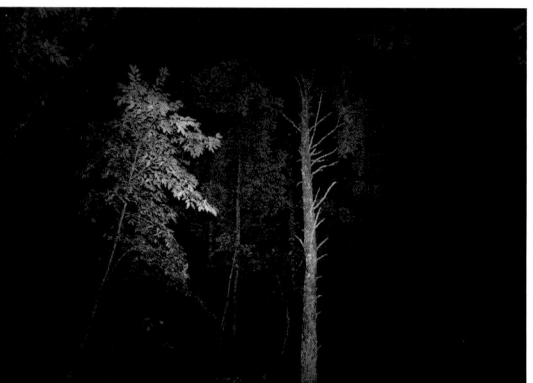

35.28520, 82.79564

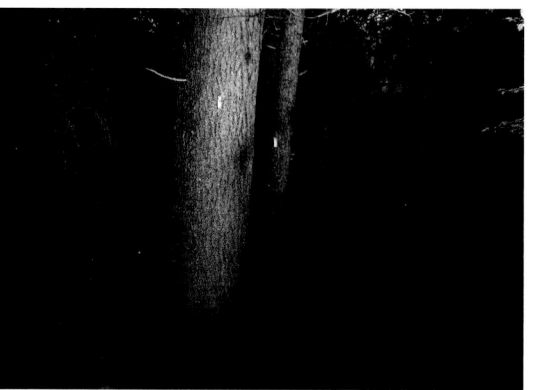

35.28178, 82.72056

"Privet" refers to more than fifty species of shrubs and small trees in the genus *Ligustrum* native to the Old World, and all nine growing in the United States are considered invasive. In the Northeast, European privet is the main invader, while farther south, the Chinese variant dominates.

Just as many infestations begin, these were brought to America purposefully for use as hedges and boundary lines for gardens. Both crowd out other plants and alter ecosystems by changing the understory of the forest, but the Chinese privet is now naturalized thoroughly in the South and causing large-scale transformations near many cities.

Called "the redwood of the East," Eastern hemlocks can grow 150 feet tall, five feet wide, and live over five hundred years. Not only is it one of the largest trees on the East Coast, but it's also the most shade tolerant, forming cool, dense canopies that provide unique habitats underneath. They're also one of the most common trees in the Smoky Mountains.

Most mature trees were cut by the 1800s but the hemlock woolly adelgid may be their worst aggressor yet. These tiny sap-sucking insects were introduced from Japan around 1950 and currently occupy 90 percent of the geographic range of the trees. In many areas, as much as 80 percent of the Eastern hemlocks have already weakened and died.

Pesticide treatments at the base of each individual tree, along with the introduction of several nonnative beetles that prey on them, appear to be slowing the insects' progress in some areas.

Acknowledgments

Thank you dearly Sherpa Robert Blackwell for your friendship, dedication, and taking that treble hook deep into your leg while pulling zebra mussels from the Arkansas River. And to my wife, Megan, for letting me bring this dark conversation into our home for the past three years. E. O. Wilson for your wisdom and words. Josette lAta for sharing the Everglades; the National Park Service; Florida Fish and Wildlife; Zoological Society of London; Harvard Museum of Comparative Zoology; Florida Department of Enviornmental Protection; Hank Johns; Okanagan Nation Alliance; Barbara Wilson; U.S. Fish and Wildlife Service; Angela Harkin for your persistence and midnight oil; Albert Thurman; Garrett Priddy; Brad Smith; Bruce Gartrell; Captain Joe Williams; Muyuna Lodge; Bob Gale; Mountain True; Shelby Farms; Linda Brashear; Wolf River Conservancy; Dr. Anthony James and the University of California, Irvine; Catherine Justis; Neptunic Sharksuits; Nathan Cooper; Bo Cross; Ursula Damm; Barbara Richard; The Museum of Photographic Arts; *Mother Jones*; *The Smithsonian*; American Photographic Artists; Wendy Fiskhand; Scott Davis; Jonathan Blaustein; Mark Hoddle; Ann Wycoff; John Durant; Carrie Gordh; Adala Zelman; Zoe Keller for the incredible illustrations; and thousands of scientists, naturalists, and conservationists who anonymously dedicate their lives so we might understand this place.

The current U.S.–Mexico border is home to numerous wide-ranging animals, including bighorn and pronghorn sheep, the Mexican gray wolf, ocelots, and the elusive North American jaguar, along with dozens of others that migrate North and South each year. Also in range are 1,500 other native animals; 62 of which are listed as critically endangered.

As the planet's temperature increases, animals (and plants) are currently migrating up slopes and toward the poles, *both of which are cooler*.

The consequences of building a 1,500-mile long permanent barrier across one of the most sensitive landscapes in America is unimaginable and could literally split breeding animal populations in half. It could also leave the southern creatures trapped while the other half slowly migrates to the cooler north.

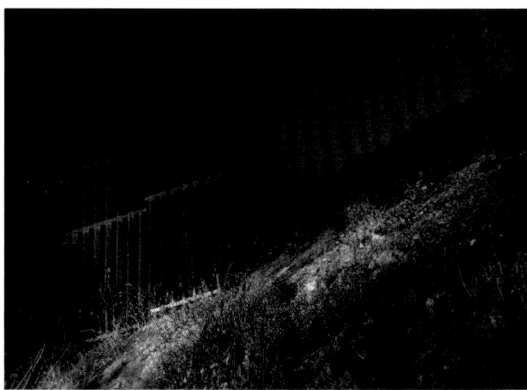

32.56270, 116.79945

PREFACE

My passion for this book started three years ago when my wife and I were hiking a mountain range I recalled as being more open and spacious—but the forest was now impossible to navigate without a machete and chainsaw. My memories were foggy and nebulous. *Is it me? Is it possible the forest changed?*

Humans are remarkably adaptable animals. There's a process termed "shifting baseline syndrome" whereby we establish norms with our recent memory as opposed to giving them an accurate historical value. Entomologists, with little historical data to point to, dubbed their notion that global insect populations are declining the "windshield phenomenon." This is in reference to the goop we once routinely cleaned from our cars after evening drives but don't anymore. We wave our arms in the air and think to ourselves, *Weren't there more bugs when I was a child?* But they're just feelings. Anecdotes.

The fantasy that nature television programming creates with all of its florid colors and incongruent soundscapes is made, in reality, with a caravan of film trucks complete with catering crews and satellite-dish internet. Advancing increasingly deeper into our shrinking wildlife areas, they find themselves hard pressed to find angles that exclude human effect. They produce illusions.

Regardless of how natural our personal setting *feels*, this planet is already so radically changed that anyone stepping into it from the recent past would balk at the notion it could be "saved." Or that there's an impending "carbon tipping point." Or that the separated lands of our experimental wildlife parks function as much more than open-air zoos. African rhinos are assigned private militia to combat poachers. Jaguars roam the Sonoran Desert wearing GPS collars. We have enormous underwater electric fences to keep invasive Asian carp from swimming into the Great Lakes, which would allow them to gain access to most major North American waterways and kill nearly all of the other fish. And soon they will. Things are different now.

To assist us in stepping back for a clearer view we can modify a page from scholar Max Roser's thought experiment *What if we were on a hundred year news cycle?* The headline would have no vehement politicians and no singular examples of how the "pretty" monarch butterfly populations are down by 90 percent. It would read "*Humans release carbon, warm planet, acidify ocean, plow 40 percent of all land, cut wild mammal populations by 83 percent, kill half of all plants, kill 58 percent of all vertebrates, melt ice sheets, and punch hole in ozone layer while arguing policy.*" And I'm being conservative.

And all mostly in my lifetime.

The stories in this book take place in North America, mostly because I live there and it was convenient for me, but it could have been written anywhere. Ravaged by invasive species and overconsumption since the start of the Columbian exchange, we can look at the enormous environmental changes in brushstrokes large or small or one coast at a time.

Stick with me here.

Two hundred and fifty years ago on the left coast, Spanish speaking Europeans brought horses and blankets and feed tainted with tiny European grass seeds that swiftly out-competed the native grasses—*commencing the largest grassland conversion ever seen on the planet.* California's coastal prairies quickly transformed from longer-lived perennials to seasonal (annually dying) Mediterranean grasses. Today what we identify as "the Golden Hills of California" were once much, much greener.

One hundred years later, on the opposite coast, delicate marshlands hugged the shoreline from New York up past the Canadian border. That is until we introduced the dime-sized periwinkle in Nova Scotia in the early 1800s. This small European snail, probably carried in ballast water or let loose for food, consumed the roots, algae, and flora of the Northeastern coastline so thoroughly that the ocean waves carried away every last bit of sand, leaving the current rocky coastline we see on postcards of Maine. An entire ecosystem with thousands of species displaced, starving, stressed, and killed. A coastline converted from marshland to rock in one hundred years. All by a snail.

Swim past either coastline and we've killed off one fifth of the coral and 70 percent of predatory fish. Ride between these coasts and we've displaced most everything, plowed just over 40 percent of the land for agriculture, depleted the soil, and pounded it into symmetrical, pesticide-filled rows.

Before that, we cut down the trees because we were afraid of the dark and burned them because we were cold. Just as in Europe, where the great forests are no more, there are fewer than ten percent of old-growth forests left in the United States.

Mass extinctions are exceptionally rare events and during our brief lifetimes, *we have entered the sixth*. The most recent other mass extinction is the one we all learned of in grade school when sixty-six million years ago a big rock hit our planet and the dinosaurs died off, and the pathway to mammals and modern-day birds and humans was forged. There were four other extinction events we know of, but this brings it to only five times in 3.7 billion years. And the beginning of the sixth is now.

With extinctions of species occurring at a rate as much as one thousand times prehuman levels, there is much suffering on this planet. Death seldom comes with warm hands. Individual animals starve when agriculture consumes their habitat, temperatures are fluctuating beyond abilities to endure and impossible to predict calamities abound when we rearrange the locations of the planet's biota. (Worldwide, the class of creatures known as amphibians are dying of heart attacks because of a simple fungus we unwittingly spread during the Korean War.) For most, the world is no longer a very nice place to be.

And here we are.

I present this work as evidence. Light and sound pollution, fences, roadways, water diversions, terraforming, agriculture, temperature rise, deforestation, globalization vectors in the movement of goods, newly introduced resource competition by invasive species, and innumerable other recent changes have made much of our planet unrecognizable to the existing instincts and genetic memory of countless species.

Many of these creatures are threat naive and unaware. This is why I shoot in the dark and why so many of my photographs might be reminiscent of Weegee's black and white, hard-flash murder scenes. Because they are just that.

Werner Herzog once said, "Civilization is like a thin layer of ice upon a deep ocean of chaos and darkness." The more I pay attention, the more I agree.

—Bil Zelman

What is man?

Storyteller, mythmaker, and destroyer of the living world. Thinking with a gabble of reason, emotion, and religion. Lucky accident of primate evolution during the late Pleistocene. Mind of the biosphere. Magnificent in imaginative power and exploratory drive, yet yearning to be more master than steward of a declining planet. Born with the capacity to survive and evolve forever, able to render the biosphere eternal also. Yet arrogant, reckless, lethally predisposed to favor self, tribe, and short-term futures. Obsequious to imagined higher beings, contemptuous toward lower forms of life.

—E. O. Wilson

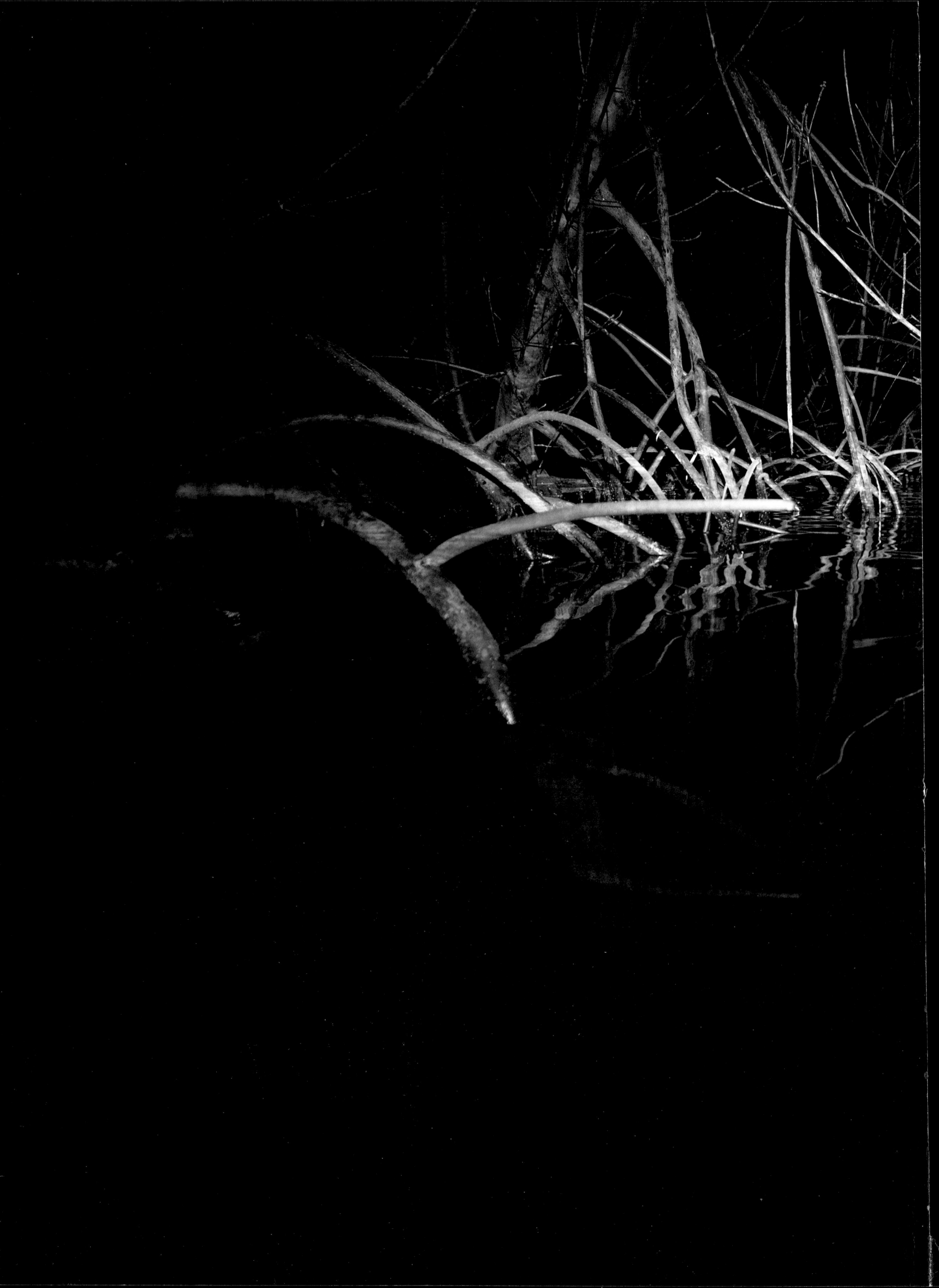